MARCOS CARS 1960-1988

Compiled by
R.M. Clarke

ISBN 1 870642 643

Distributed by
Brooklands Book Distribution Ltd.
'Holmerise', Seven Hills Road,
Cobham, Surrey, England
Printed in Hong Kong

BROOKLANDS BOOKS

BROOKLANDS BOOKS SERIES
AC Ace & Aceca 1953-1983
AC Cobra 1962-1969
Alfa Romeo Alfasud 1972-1984
Alfa Romeo Alfetta Coupes GT.GTV.GTV6 1974-1987
Alfa Romeo Guilias Berlinettas
Alfa Romeo Giulia Berlinas 1962-1976
Alfa Romeo Giulia Coupés 1963-1976
Alfa Romeo Spider 1966-1987
Allard Gold Portfolio 1937-1958
Aston Martin Gold Portfolio 1972-1985
Austin Seven 1922-1982
Austin A30 & A35 1951-1962
Austin Healey 100 1952-1959
Austin Healey 3000 1959-1967
Austin Healey 100 & 3000 Collection No. 1
Austin Healey 'Frogeye' Sprite Collection No. 1
Austin Healey Sprite 1958-1971
Avanti 1962-1983
BMW Six Cylinder Coupés 1969-1975
BMW 1600 Collection No. 1
BMW 2002 1968-1976
Bristol Cars Gold Portfolio 1946-1985
Buick Automobiles 1947-1960
Buick Riviera 1963-1978
Cadillac Automobiles 1949-1959
Cadillac Automobiles 1960-1969
Cadillac Eldorado 1967-1978
Camaro 1966-1970
Chevrolet Camaro & Z-28 1973-1981
High Performance Camaros 1982-1988
Chevrolet Camaro Collection No. 1
Chevrolet 1955-1957
Chevrolet Impala & SS 1958-1971
Chevelle & SS 1964-1972
Chevy II Nova & SS 1962-1973
Chrysler 300 1955-1970
Citroen Traction Avant 1934-1957
Citroen DS & ID 1955-1875
Citroen 2CV 1948-1988
Cobras & Replicas 1962-1983
Cortina 1600E & GT 1967-1970
Corvair 1959-1968
Daimler Dart & V-8 250 1959-1969
Datsun 240z 1970-1973
Datsun 280Z & ZX 1975-1983
De Tomaso Collection No. 1
Dodge Charger 1966-1974
Excalibur Collection No. 1
Ferrari Cars 1946-1956
Ferrari Cars 1962-1966
Ferrari Cars 1969-1973
Ferrari Dino 1965-1974
Ferrari Dino 308 1974-1979
Ferrari 308 & Mondial 1980-1984
Ferrari Collection No. 1
Fiat-Bertone X1/9 1973-1988
Fiat Pininfarina 124+2000 Spider 1968-1985
Ford Falcon 1960-1970
Ford Mustang 1964-1967
Ford Mustang 1967-1973
High Performance Mustangs 1982-1988
Ford RS Escort 1968-1980
Honda CRX 1983-1987
High Performance Escorts MkI 1968-1974
High Performance Escorts MkII 1975-1980
Hudson & Railton Cars 1936-1940
Jaguar XK120 XK140 XK150 Gold Portfolio 1948-1960
Jaguar Cars 1957-1961
Jaguar Cars 1961-1964
Jaguar MK2 1959-1969
Jaguar E-Type 1961-1966
Jaguar E-Type 1966-1971
Jaguar E-Type V12 1971-1975
Jaguar XKE Collection No. 1
Jaguar XJ6 1968-1972
Jaguar XJ6 Series II 1973-1979
Jaguar XJ6 & XJ12 Series III 1979-1985
Jaguar XJ12 1972-1980
Jaguar XJS Gold Portfolio 1975-1988
Jensen Cars 1946-1967
Jensen Cars 1967-1979
Jensen Interceptor Gold Portfolio 1966-1986
Lamborghini Cars 1964-1970
Lamborghini Cars 1970-1975
Lamborghini Countach Collection No. 1
Lamborghini Countach & Urraco 1974-1980
Lamborghini Countach & Jalpa 1980-1985
Lancia Stratos 1972-1985
Land Rover 1948-1973
Land Rover Series II & IIa 1958-1971
Land Rover Series III 1971-1985
Land Rover 90 & 110 1983-1989
Lotus Cortina 1963-1970
Lotur Elan Gold Portfolio 1962-1974
Lotus Elan Collection No. 2
Lotus Elite 1957-1964
Lotus Elite & Eclat 1974-1981
Lotus Turbo Esprit 1980-1986
Lotus Europa 1966-1975
Lotus Europa Collection No. 1
Lotus Seven 1957-1980
Lotus Seven Collection No. 1
Maserati 1965-1970
Maserati 1970-1975
Marcos Cars 1960-1988
Mazda RX-7 Collection No. 1
Mercedes 190 & 300SL 1954-1963
Mercedes 230/250/280SL 1963-1971
Mercedes 350/450SL & SLC 1971-1980
Mercedes Benz Cars 1949-1954
Mercedes Benz Cars 1954-1957
Mercedes Benz Cars 1957-1961
Mercedes Benz Competition Cars 1950-1957

Metropolitan 1954-1962
MG Cars 1929-1934
MG TC 1945-1949
MG TD 1949-1953
MG TF 1953-1955
MG Cars 1957-1959
MG Cars 1959-1962
MG Midget 1961-1980
MGA Collection No. 1
MGA Roadsters 1955-1962
MGB Roadsters 1962-1980
MGB GT 1965-1980
Mini Cooper 1961-1971
Morgan Cars 1960-1970
Morgan Cars 1969-1979
Morris Minor Collection No. 1
Old's Cutlass & 4-4-2 1964-1972
Oldsmobile Toronado 1966-1978
Opel GT 1968-1973
Packard Gold Portfolio 1946-1958
Pantera 1970-1973
Pantera & Mangusta 1969-1974
Plymouth Barracuda 1964-1974
Pontiac Fiero 1984-1988
Pontiac GTO 1960-1970
Pontiac Firebird 1967-1973
Pontiac Firebird and Trans-Am 1973-1981
High Performance Firebirds 1982-1988
Pontiac Tempest & GTO 1961-1965
Porsche Cars 1960-1964
Porsche Cars 1964-1968
Porsche Cars 1968-1972
Porsche Cars in the Sixties
Porsche Cars 1972-1975
Porsche 356 1952-1965
Porsche 911 Collection No. 1
Porsche 911 Collection No. 2
Porsche 911 1965-1969
Porsche 911 1970-1972
Porsche 911 1973-1977
Porsche 911 Carrera 1973-1977
Porsche 911 SC 1978-1983
Porsche 911 Turbo 1975-1984
Porsche 914 Gold Portfolio 1969-1988
Porsche 914 Collection No. 1
Porsche 924 1975-1981
Porsche 928 Collection No. 1
Porsche 944 1981-1985
Porsche Turbo Collection No. 1
Reliant Scimitar 1964-1986
Riley 1½ & 2½ Litre Gold Portfolio 1945-1955
Rolls Royce Silver Cloud 1955-1965
Rolls Royce Silver Shadow 1965-1980
Range Rover Gold Portfolio 1970-1988
Rover 3 & 3.5 Litre 1958-1973
Rover P4 1949-1959
Rover P5 1955-1964
Rover 2000 + 2200 1963-1977
Rover 3500 1968-1977
Rover 3500 & Vitesse 1976-1986
Saab Sonett Collection No. 1
Saab Turbo 1976-1983
Studebaker Hawks & Larks 1956-1963
Sunbeam Tiger And Alpine Gold Portfolio 1959-1967
Thunderbird 1955-1957
Thunderbird 1958-1963
Thunderbird 1964-1976
Toyota MR2 1984-1988
Triumph 2000-2.5-2500 1963-1977
Triumph Spitfire 1962-1980
Triumph Spitfire Collection No. 1
Triumph Stag 1970-1980
Triumph Stag Collection No. 1
Triumph TR2 & TR3 1952-1960
Triumph TR4.TR5.TR250 1961-1968
Triumph TR6 1968-1976
Triumph TR6 Collection No. 1
Triumph TR7 & TR8 1975-1982
Triumph GT6 1966-1974
Triumph Vitesse & Herald 1959-1971
TVR Gold Portfolio 1959-1988
Volkswagen Cars 1936-1956
VW Beetle 1956-1977
VW Beetle Collection No. 1
VW Golf GTi 1976-1986
VW Karmann Ghia 1955-1982
VW Scirocco 1974-1981
VW Bus-Camper-Van 1954-1967
VW Bus-Camper-Van 1968-1979
Volvo 1800 1960-1973
Volvo 120 Series 1956-1970

BROOKLANDS MUSCLE CARS SERIES
American Motors Muscle Cars 1966-1970
Buick Muscle Cars 1965-1970
Camaro Muscle Cars 1966-1972
Capri Muscle Cars 1969-1983
Chevrolet Muscle Cars 1966-1972
Dodge Muscle Cars 1967-1970
Mercury Muscle Cars 1966-1971
Mini Muscle Cars 1961-1979
Mopar Muscle Cars 1964-1967
Mopar Muscle Cars 1968-1971
Mustang Muscle Cars 1967-1971
Shelby Mustang Muscle Cars 1965-1970
Oldsmobile Muscle Cars 1964-1970
Plymouth Muscle Cars 1966-1971
Pontiac Muscle Cars 1966-1972
Muscle Cars Compared 1966-1971
Muscle Cars Compared Book 2 1965-1971

BROOKLANDS ROAD & TRACK SERIES
Road & Track on Alfa Romeo 1949-1963
Road & Track on Alfa Romeo 1964-1970
Road & Track on Alfa Romeo 1971-1976

Road & Track on Alfa Romeo 1977-1984
Road & Track on Aston Martin 1962-1984
Road & Track on Auburn Cord & Duesenberg 1952-1984
Road & Track on Audi 1952-1980
Road & Track on Audi 1980-1986
Road & Track on Austin Healey 1953-1970
Road & Track on BMW Cars 1966-1974
Road & Track on BMW Cars 1975-1978
Road & Track on BMW Cars 1979-1983
Road & Track on Cobra, Shelby &
  Ford GT40 1962-1983
Road & Track on Corvette 1953-1967
Road & Track on Corvette 1968-1982
Road & Track on Corvette 1982-1986
Road & Track on Datsun Z 1970-1983
Road & Track on Ferrari 1950-1968
Road & Track on Ferrari 1968-1974
Road & Track on Ferrari 1975-1981
Road & Track on Ferrari 1981-1984
Road & Track on Fiat Sports Cars 1968-1987
Road & Track on Jaguar 1950-1960
Road & Track on Jaguar 1961-1968
Road & Track on Jaguar 1968-1974
Road & Track on Jaguar 1974-1982
Road & Track on Jaguar 1983-1989
Road & Track on Lamborghini 1964-1985
Road & Track on Lotus 1972-1981
Road & Track on Maserati 1952-1974
Road & Track on Maserati 1975-1983
Road & Track on Mazda RX7 1978-1986
Road & Track on Mercedes 1952-1962
Road & Track on Mercedes 1963-1970
Road & Track on Mercedes 1971-1979
Road & Track on Mercedes 1980-1987
Road & Track on MG Sports Cars 1949-1961
Road & Track on MG Sports Cars 1962-1980
Road & Track on Mustang 1964-1977
Road & Track on Peugeot 1955-1986
Road & Track on Pontiac 1960-1983
Road & Track on Porsche 1951-1967
Road & Track on Porsche 1968-1971
Road & Track on Porsche 1972-1975
Road & Track on Porsche 1975-1978
Road & Track on Porsche 1979-1982
Road & Track on Porsche 1982-1985
Road & Track on Rolls Royce & Bentley 1950-1965
Road & Track on Rolls Royce & Bentley 1966-1984
Road & Track on Saab 1955-1985
Road & Track on Toyota Sports & G T Cars 1966-1986
Road & Track on Triumph Sports Cars 1953-1967
Road & Track on Triumph Sports Cars 1967-1974
Road & Track on Triumph Sports Cars 1974-1982
Road & Track on Volkswagen 1951-1968
Road & Track on Volkswagen 1968-1978
Road & Track on Volkswagen 1978-1985
Road & Track on Volvo 1957-1974
Road & Track on Volvo 1975-1985
Road & Track Henry Manney At Large & Abroad

BROOKLANDS CAR AND DRIVER SERIES
Car and Driver on BMW 1955-1977
Car and Driver on BMW 1977-1985
Car and Driver on Cobra, Shelby & Ford GT40
  1963-1984
Car and Driver on Datsun Z 1600 & 2000
  1966-1984
Car and Driver on Corvette 1956-1967
Car and Driver on Corvette 1968-1977
Car and Driver on Corvette 1978-1982
Car and Driver on Corvette 1983-1988
Car and Driver on Ferrari 1955-1962
Car and Driver on Ferrari 1963-1975
Car and Driver on Ferrari 1976-1983
Car and Driver on Mopar 1956-1967
Car and Driver on Mopar 1968-1975
Car and Driver on Mustang 1964-1972
Car and Driver on Pontiac 1961-1975
Car and Driver on Porsche 1955-1962
Car and Driver on Porsche 1963-1970
Car and Driver on Porsche 1970-1976
Car and Driver on Porsche 1977-1981
Car and Driver on Porsche 1982-1986
Car and Driver on Saab 1956-1985
Car and Driver on Volvo 1955-1986

BROOKLANDS MOTOR & THOROUGHBRED & CLASSIC CAR SERIES
Motor & T & CC on Ferrari 1966-1976
Motor & T & CC on Ferrari 1976-1984
Motor & T & CC on Lotus 1979-1983
Motor & T & CC on Morris Minor 1948-1983

BROOKLANDS PRACTICAL CLASSICS SERIES
Practical Classics on Austin A 40 Restoration
Practical Classics on Land Rover Restoration
Practical Classics on Metalworking in Restoration
Practical Classics on Midget/Sprite Restoration
Practical Classics on Mini Cooper Restoration
Practical Classics on MGB Restoration
Practical Classics on Morris Minor Restoration
Practical Classics on Triumph Herald/Vitesse
Practical Classics on Triumph Spitfire Restoration
Practical Classics on VW Beetle Restoration
Practical Classics on 1930S Car Restoration

BROOKLANDS MILITARY VEHICLES SERIES
Allied Military Vehicles Collection No. 1
Allied Military Vehicles Collection No. 2
Dodge Military Vehicles Collection No. 1
Military Jeeps 1941-1945
Off Road Jeeps 1944-1971
V W Kubelwagen 1940-1975

BROOKLANDS BOOKS

CONTENTS

BROOKLANDS
BOOKS

ACKNOWLEDGEMENTS

As this is our first title on Marcos cars it might be reasonable to assume that it could be your first encounter with one of our books. A few words therefore might not be out of place explaining our objectives and where we fit into the spectrum of motoring literature.

Brooklands are a small company that specialises in the reissuing of lost automotive information, nothing we produce is original. Our aim is to put at the disposal of motoring enthusiasts an affordable and accessible archive. It is our hope that we will eventually cover not only the prolific marques but also the smaller manufactures who add variety and spice to our driving.

For those readers who had hoped to find here a lengthy introduction to the Marcos range and who now feel let down, may I suggest you turn to Thoroughbred & Classic Cars' excellent article on page 92. This piece by Jeremy Coulter covers not only the historical facts, but leads us expertly through the variety of engines that have at one time or another powered these graceful machines.

Our reference series, which now runs to over 300 titles, is fortunate in having the support of the world's leading publishing houses. They have, for over 30 years, generously allowed us to include copyright stories from their magazines for the benefit of owners, restorers and others that indulge in the hobby. Our thanks in this instance go to the management of Australian Motor Manual, Australian Motor Sports, Autocar, Autosport, Car and Car Conversions, Car and Driver, Cars Illustrated, Fast Lane, Modern Motor, Motor, Motor Racing, Motor Sport, Motor Trend, Practical Classics, Road & Track, Road Test, Sports Car Mechanics, Sports Car World, Thoroughbred & Classic Cars and the World Car Catalogue for their co-operation and understanding.

R.M. Clarke

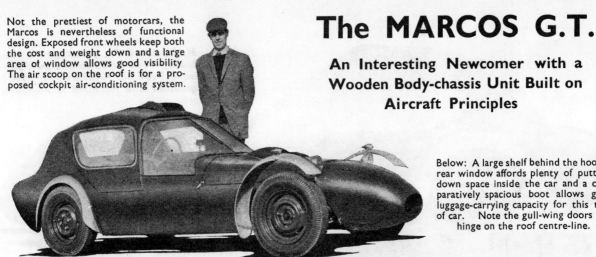

Not the prettiest of motorcars, the Marcos is nevertheless of functional design. Exposed front wheels keep both the cost and weight down and a large area of window allows good visibility The air scoop on the roof is for a proposed cockpit air-conditioning system.

The MARCOS G.T.

An Interesting Newcomer with a Wooden Body-chassis Unit Built on Aircraft Principles

Below: A large shelf behind the hooded rear window affords plenty of putting-down space inside the car and a comparatively spacious boot allows good luggage-carrying capacity for this type of car. Note the gull-wing doors that hinge on the roof centre-line.

IT is perhaps surprising that while the aircraft industry has been using wood to build aeroplanes since the Wright brother's first flight in 1903, the motor industry has virtually neglected the possibilities of wooden construction for cars in favour of a metal, and more recently, a glass-fibre basis.

Wood, properly used, is strong, light in weight, abundant and relatively cheap. It was with these considerations in mind that the interesting new Marcos G.T., revealed recently by Speedex Castings and Accessories, Ltd., has been made. Designed by Frank Costin (who was responsible for the aerodynamics of both Vanwall and Lotus as well as a number of successful gliders and light aircraft) the Marcos is of wooden monocoque construction built entirely on aircraft principles.

Spruce and marine plywood, impregnated with fireproof material, have been used to form the main body-chassis unit, two large-section "boxes" running down either side of the car, joined by a number of cross members and bulkheads, giving exceptional torsional rigidity. No rivets, screws or bolts have been used in the construction, all joints being spliced and glued. Although the car has been designed specifically as a closed coupé two-seater, the hard top is no way part of the main structural unit, all torsional rigidity coming from below the waistline. Gull-wing doors allow easy access to the aircraft-like cockpit, the seats of which form part of the basic chassis unit. Hence optional seating positions can only be obtained with extra (or less) cushioning. Further stiffness is also obtained from the slightly offset propeller-shaft housing that divides the interior.

MARCOS SPECIFICATION

Engine : Ford 100E with Speedex modifications. Alternatively Ford 105E or B.M.C. "A" series. Tuned versions by Wilen Engineering and Speedwell respectively.

Transmission : Ford 100E three-speed gearbox and shortened 100E propeller shaft. Girling hydraulic clutch assembly (corresponding gearbox with other power units), Nash Metropolitan rear axle.

Chassis/body : Pure monocoque construction using fireproof impregnated spruce and marine ply.

Brakes : Girling hydraulic drum brakes front and rear.

Suspension : Front : Modified Triumph Herald independent by coil springs and wishbones and telescopic shock absorbers.

Rear : Nash Metropolitan solid axle located by panhard rod and parallel radius rods. Suspension by coil springs and enclosed spring shock absorber units.

Steering : Rack and pinion. 2.6 turns from lock to lock. 15 in. diameter wheel.

Dimensions : Wheelbase, 7 ft. 3 in.; Track (front) 4 ft. track (rear), 3 ft. 9 in.; Overall length, 12 ft. 1 in.; overall width, 4 ft. 7 in.; turning circle, 36 ft.; weight (dry) 7¾ cwt.

Manufacturers : Speedex Castings and Accessories, Ltd., 17a Windsor St., Luton, Bedfordshire.

Pick-up points for the front and rear suspension and engine mountings are steel fittings bolted to specially reinforced areas of the wooden chassis. Front suspension is by modified Triumph Herald coil and wishbone and at the rear, because of its light weight, a Nash Metropolitan axle has been used in conjunction with coil springs and telescopic dampers. This rear axle also allows a choice of five alternative gear ratios.

The sparsely furnished interior of the Marcos G.T. Later production models will have increased leg room for the driver and a choice of interior trim.

The power unit is offset and laid over to the right, thus allowing a low frontal area and more room for the driver's feet. At the moment a Speedex-modified Ford 100E engine is installed, but the car has been designed to take both Ford 105E and B.M.C. "A" series units. And minor modifications will permit the installation of a 1,100 c.c. Coventry Climax engine. Even with moderately tuned production engines of around one litre, however, the car's weight of a little over 8 cwt. should allow excellent b.h.p. per ton figures and a consequent high performance.

It is interesting to note that the entire body-chassis-hard top unit, complete with various mountings, seats, windscreen and doors weighs a mere 1½ cwt.—less than one-fifth of the car's entire weight.

To keep the cost to an absolute minimum, two-dimensional curves in the bodywork such as the radiator nose cowling, gull-wing doors and boot lid will be made of glass-fibre and it is hoped that production of cars for home assembly will start in the near future at a competitive price.

The prototype, shown on this page, will be seen in selected G.T. races during the coming season, with Jem Marsh, past 750 Formula champion and co-promoter of the Marcos, at the wheel.

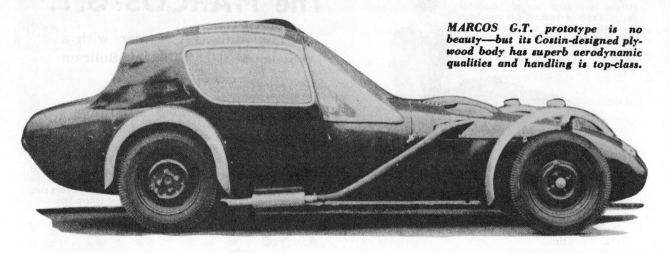

MARCOS G.T. prototype is no beauty—but its Costin-designed plywood body has superb aerodynamic qualities and handling is top-class.

The FLYING SPLINTER

WOODEN cars went out with the handlebar moustache—but the latter returned with World War II, and now it seems that wooden bodywork might also make a comeback.

If it does, the credit (or blame?) will belong to two English speed merchants, Jem Marsh and Frank Costin. They've launched a totally unexpected "back-to-timber" campaign by building a curiously shaped but extremely efficient plywood sports coupe called the Marcos G.T.

I had a run in it the other day and am satisfied that the idea isn't as crazy as it sounds. But readers 10,000 miles away may be harder to convince—so, before discussing the Marcos, let me tell you something about its creators.

No Amateurs

There's nothing amateurish about either of them—both are acknowledged experts in their respective fields, with some spectacular successes to back up their theories of car design and construction.

Jem Marsh runs a thriving automotive parts factory called Speedex Ltd. in Luton (famous for its girls' choir, hats—and Vauxhalls).

He manufactures castings and other "bits" for 750 Formula Specials (basically old-type Austin Sevens), builds and sells go-karts, space frames, light-alloy and plastic bodies, and lashings of the various odds-and-ends that enthusiasts spend their money on.

Jem is also a champion 750 Formula driver, having collared the top award with his beautifully prepared Austin Special in last year's contests, which were staged all over Britain.

Frank Costin has an even greater claim to fame—it was he who first put Lotus cars on the road to high speed with small horsepower when he designed the original wind-cheating Lotus Mark 8 body—a shape that enabled Colin Chapman's offspring to hurtle along at around 130 m.p.h. on a mere 1100c.c. and 70 b.h.p.

Costin (whose brother Mike is still chief development engineer with Lotus) not only designed the body but was game enough to have himself strapped to the prototype's wing so he could study the behaviour of glued-on cotton-wool tufts under the wheel arches at 120 m.p.h.

Success of the Lotus earned Frank a big reputation in the motor-racing world as an aerodynamics expert. He is, in fact, an aircraft engineer with

REAR of roof has a Farina-like overhang, and there's good luggage room in boot. Note outside exhaust.

Amazing moulded-ply coupe may start a "back-to-timber" vogue among sports-car builders, says Douglas Armstrong

NOSE is removed to show Marcos' squat radiator and front suspension. Prototype's skimpy guards will be replaced by mouldings joined to body.

an uncanny knowledge of wind-cheating, gained from his experience at De Havilland's, where he was still working at that time.

Millionaire racing-car builder Tony Vandervell was so impressed by Frank's talents that he asked him to design a new body for the Vanwall G.P. car in 1956; the resulting shape played its part in raising the Van-walls to winning form, which culminated with their winning the Constructors' World Title of 1958.

Meanwhile, Frank Costin had left De Havilland's and joined Brian Lister, to give his cars the clean profile they so badly needed. Maserati approached him for an aerodynamic coupe for their 4.5-litre V8 car, which Moss and Shell drove at Le Mans in 1957; but the job was hurried through Zagato's factory in three weeks—and the less said about the Italian coachbuilders' interpretation of the design the better Frank likes it!

After a spell with Lister, Costin set himself up as design consultant in a remote Welsh village—and now he has formed a new company with Jem Marsh, to produce his latest brainchild.

Why Plywood?

This, of course, is the Marcos G.T. car (Marsh-Costin—get it?), and the No. 1 question, as far as readers are concerned, is why Costin chose plywood construction for it.

The answer lies in Frank's aircraft background. He was with De Havilland's when they developed the famous wartime Mosquito plane—a craft that revolutionised construction methods with its wood-and-glue make-up, giving tremendous torsional strength.

Consequently he was thoroughly familiar with the possibilities of aircraft-type wooden structures, and remembered them when he came to designing a car of his own.

Costin's outlook is that he considers the Lotus Elite to be the most advanced closed motor car in production today, with its pure monocoque fibreglass construction; but he also thinks that fibreglass construction is still in its infancy, and that development time is both lengthy and expensive. What is wanted, he says, is

ENGINE is a modest 1172c.c. Ford side-valve, tilted to allow a low bonnet; yet car can do 96 m.p.h. Climax engine may be used later.

GULL-TYPE doors are simply designed, require no stressing, due to stiffness of body structure. Production models will have neater screen.

MARCOS G.T.

a high-performance vehicle with reasonable comfort and ease of production; moulded plywood should make this possible, and the design formula would also add up to reasonable cost—particularly if the car was a two-seater.

For his design, the Marcos GT, he set to work with a target weight of around 8cwt., and in the prototype vehicle he has achieved 8½cwt. with steel wheels and touring tyres. Later version will be available with light-alloy wheels and racing tyres, which will cut the weight back to the desired 8cwt.

Body Structure

Basis of this interesting (though ugly) duckling is a glued-up wooden structure which employs aircraft methods to gain strength and rigidity, combined with lightness. Materials are mainly spruce and plywood, as used in many modern passenger and military aircraft.

The chassis/body structure can be described as a sort of space frame which employs two main longitudinal box-section members, with a stressed wooden undertray and propshaft tunnel. All timber is fireproofed, and torsional stiffness compares with the very best steel structures, providing a figure of 3000lb./ft. per degree of twist.

Main pick-up points for front and rear suspension are steel fittings bolted directly to the reinforced areas of the structure in typical aircraft fashion, and the generated stresses have been kept very low indeed. The two main side-members are located relative to each other by bulkheads and frames similar to an aereoplane fuselage, and sheer loads are so low that reserve factors of more than 20 occur in many places. The seat forms are integral with the main structure, and suitably shaped cushions enable almost any driving position to be obtained.

To make the car attractive to all types of buyer, Marsh and Costin decided to give it a closed body. Originally it was intended that some part of the torsional loads would be transmitted via the centre of the structure. In fact, initial calculations showed that the required stiffness could be easily achieved by the two large longitudinal torsion boxes.

The cockpit needed careful design, for Jem Marsh (who will race a Marcos) is 6ft. 3in. tall. If he could be made comfortable, most other people would find the accommodation ample for their needs!

The prototype's cockpit is 40in. wide, while the car's overall width is 49¼in. The driver's seat is sensibly made wider than the passenger's, as the latter is usually occupied by the female member of the family; even so, she can be a "big girl" and still enjoy space and comfort. Behind the cockpit there is space for gloves, briefcase, maps, etc.

Access to the cockpit is by "gullwing" doors resembling those of a Mercedes 300 SL, and the simplicity of these is made possible by the immensely stiff chassis structure. Marsh demonstrated to me that door movement relative to door frame is virtually nil.

The wooden-lidded boot contains the 6¾-gallon fuel tank, 12-volt battery, and spare wheel, but still has room for two large suitcases and a shopping basket. The fuel tank is completely isolated in a waterproof bay and isolated from the passenger compartment.

Car's Mechanics

There is nothing startlingly new about the Marcos' mechanical specifications.

Front suspension on the prototype is by Triumph Herald wishbones and coil spring/damper units; production models will have cast wishbones. Rear suspension is by a normal Austin/Nash Metropolitan live axle, chosen because of its low cost and lightness. It is positively located by reversed tubular radius arms and a Panhard rod. Coil spring/damper units supply the suspension medium.

Prototype's power-unit is a mildly "tweaked" Ford 100E side-valve of 1172c.c. It is inclined to the starboard side to allow a low bonnet line and located by two tiny space-frame engine mountings at the front, and a single point built into the tunnel at the rear. The engine is in unit with a three-speed Ford gearbox fitted with Buckler close-ratios.

Minimum ground clearance of 5¾in. is under the sump, which protrudes through the wooden undertray by ¾in. The sump aperture and a 6in. diameter hole beneath the diff housing are the only breaks in the smooth undertray—a great contribution to aerodynamic efficiency.

Tryout Impresses

Jem Marsh took me for a trial run in the Marcos—and, despite the prototype's modest power unit, its performance was an eye-opener. Acceleration thrust hard in the back, and we were doing 80 m.p.h. before you could say "white-ant."

Marsh has had a timed 96 m.p.h. out of this version, so the aerodynamics are not in doubt. "Super" models may be marketed at a later date, with Coventry Climax engines; these should be able to top 125 m.p.h. without any trouble.

Although the Marcos' speed qualities testified to its good shape, it was the structure efficiency that I was mainly interested in, and Marsh soon showed me how good it was.

We approached a roundabout at impossible speed, and while I tried to still my chattering teeth he threw the car into a slide—but a completely controllable one, I'm glad to say! It kept going round with appropriate wheel movements from Marsh, and although we were going fantastically quickly, at no time did it do anything silly.

One could sense the great stiffness of the structure, and certainly the excellence of steering geometry and weight distribution. Most impressive!

I told Marsh I thought the Marcos had great possibilities but that it was an ugly brute. He thereupon produced a drawing of the production version, which has prettier wings blended into the body sides and side windows that line up with the lower windscreen line. Acetate panels in the tops of the gull doors are to be discontinued and the whole thing is a big improvement on the prototype.

Marsh and Costin plan to market these cars in kit form at about £800 stg., the idea being that a normally gifted handyman could build himself an ultra-high-performance car for touring, shopping, and racing—for less than £1000.

This scheme should create a ready demand for the Marcos among the less-moneyed enthusiasts—and if the car "clicks" with the public it could well start a new vogue for plywood constructions among the small-series manufacturers.

Anyway, I'll keep you posted on future developments. ● ● ●

A WOODEN SPORTS CAR

Since the Marcos GT was introduced a little over a year ago, it has gained a considerable amount of success in British club racing, and a great deal of enthusiasm for its design and performance. The Marcos is a very unusual car — it is built almost entirely of wood — a form of construction that makes for reasonable production costs, and great rigidity.

Designer of the Marcos is none other than Frank Costin, the brilliant aerodynamicist who shaped all the earlier Lotus cars, was responsible for the Vanwall bodywork during its successful years, and also designed the shape of the last Lister cars before Brian Lister decided to retire from racing. Late of De Havilland's, Frank Costin has spent most of his working life applying his knowledge to the speeding-up of ultra-high-speed aircraft, and it looks as though his cars will be just as wind-cheating.

The cars are produced by the Monocoque Chassis and Body Co. Ltd., in, of all places, the mountainous district of Llanberis in North Wales. Directors of the Company are Frank Costin, and Jem Marsh of Speedex Ltd., Luton. Marsh not only acts as sales concessionaire for the marque, in Luton, but also actively races the Marcos in British races. Last year, when the prototype made its first appearance, it caused no end of a stir by taking nine first places in nine consecutive events.

The original Marcos models were produced with cycle-type front wings, semi-exposed rear wheels, and very slim bodies. Now the latest models have integral wings and wider, more commodious bodywork. Luggage capacity is also increased. These modifications emphasise the fact that although the Marcos is an excellent car for competition, it is also a thoroughly practical machine for touring, and all ordinary motoring.

Frank Costin first conceived the idea of a wooden sports car after thinking of the fantastic rigidity of the war-time De Havilland Mosquito fighter/bomber — a highly successful World War 2 aircraft which was entirely built of wood. The body/chassis is extremely stiff and light, and is built of spruce and marine plywood. Two massive box-section "longerons", a rigid scuttle, and a box-shaped gearbox cover contribute largely to the extraordinary stiffness. All joints are bonded with high-duty "marine-type" adhesives. It has been found possible to easily repair damage by scarfing plywood into place with these synthetic resin glues.

The prototype covered more than 40,000 miles on both road and track, and was left out in all weathers with its "gull-type" doors both open and closed. It was used as a general "hack" by all members of the company, but in spite of the treatment no structural maintenance was necessary.

Fibre-glass is used for the rear three-quarter panels, and the nose, and a small space frame of 1 inch steel square tubing carrries the front suspension and steering. The front suspension is by unequal length wishbones and coil spring/damper units, and the rack and pinion steering gear gives a ratio of 2.6 turns from lock to lock. The rear suspension is also by coil spring/damper units, and in spite of the fact that an ordinary "live" rear axle is employed, roadholding and handling is first-class. Secret is that the axle beam is located by two leading links (per side) and a Panhard rod.

Normal power-unit is a Ford 105E (997 c.c.) which, fitted with two double-choke Weber carburettors and a special four-branch exhaust manifold develops 50 b.h.p. Gearbox is the excellent standard Ford 105E, and there is a Hardy Spicer propeller-shaft to the axle, with alternative ratios.

Early models were a little spartan but the production cars have carpeted floors, and Vynide-covered facia panel with thick padding on the top edge. Headlining and body trim are also in Vynide cloth, and the bucket seats are well-shaped to hold the more enthusiastic driver (and passenger) during fast cornering. The steering wheel is wood-rimmed, and the dashboard is well instrumented. As previously mentioned the two doors are of the "gull" type, reminiscent of the Mercedes 300SL, and aircraft-type louvres are used for the interior ventilation. Extras include close ratio gears, magnesium-alloy wheels (weighing 7 lb. each), and an electric rev-counter.

The standard, fully equipped Marcos weighs less than 9 cwt., so with the normal 50 b.h.p. engine this exciting car has a power-weight ratio in the order of 120 h.p. per ton. With a fully modified engine this figure goes up to 198 h.p. per ton, with fantastic acceleration, and a top speed of around 115 m.p.h. With its incredible roadholding the Marcos is a car to watch, and only a few weeks ago a well-driven one split the ranks of the works Lotus Elites at Oulton Park.

Like so many exciting British sports car, the Marcos can only be purchased in construction kit form. It costs £795 Stg. in the UK, and due to the fact that the body and chassis are but one unit, it can be put together complete in 50 man hours. It is supplied fully trimmed, but is painted only in primer. It is a pure two-seater but there is ample space for luggage, and a large parcels shelf behind the occupants of the car. These cars are really catching on with the discerning motorist who likes something different, and who likes to travel fast — in a straight line, **and** around corners. Already a new, larger factory is under construction, and the Monocoque Chassis and Body Co. Ltd. is also expecting a large foreign order. Who wood have believed it ?

SPECIFICATIONS:

Wheelbase :	7 ft. 3 in.
Front Track :	4 ft.
Rear Track :	4 ft.
Length :	12 ft.
Width :	4 ft 11¼ in.
Turning Circle :	36 ft.

THE MARCOS GT

by Jack Fairman

A S long as I care to remember I have been an enthusiastic observer of automobile engineering, and being something of an individualist, the unconventional has always had a particular appeal for me—so long as it works, that is! Looking back through 1961, one of my most pleasing experiences has been testing and racing the revolutionary Ferguson P99, so perhaps it was appropriate that another unconventional car should bring my first year of track testing for MOTOR RACING to an end.

Naturally, I had heard of the Marcos GT, and occasionally I had seen one racing or passed one on the road. It struck me as a distinctly individualistic car, but somehow I never got round to taking a really close look at one. It was with more than usual interest, therefore, that I heard, early in December, that the prototype of the 1962 Marcos had been laid on for a test at Brands Hatch.

Apart from knowing that it was made of wood, I knew little about the car, and I was agreeably surprised when I arrived at the paddock to find a sleek, curvacious little red GT car waiting for me. Gone was that bizarre four-section front screen, and the reverse-angle rear window, and the Marcos nameplate now adorned a much smoother looking machine. I said at the beginning that I like the unconventional, but I don't mind contradicting myself by saying that I think the new line, though less original, is a great improvement on the old. I also understand that it has the practical advantages of better penetration and improved cockpit room.

INGENIOUS CONSTRUCTION

Before I set off on the circuit, I spent quite a long time examining the ingenious construction of the car with Jem Marsh, who, with Dennis Adams, has been responsible for the design of the latest Marcos.

The basic structure is fabricated from Grade A aircraft spruce and resin-bonded marine plywood. A series of transverse bulkheads are joined by four longtitudinal members, two of which form the outer edges of the structure and the others the two sides of the central transmission tunnel. It has been designed on the semi-monocoque principle, and on the new car there is a boxed unit at the front, to which are attached a pair of sub-frames in 16 gauge square tubing, on which the front suspensions are hung. On the earlier Marcos I understand the entire front section was in metal, rather like the sub-frame of the 'E' type Jaguar.

Quite a considerable part of the body, including the front-hinged full-width bonnet section, the boot lid, the two gull-wing doors and the top half of the cockpit, are in glass fibre, and this has been blended neatly into the wood section. Even on this prototype car, quite a good standard of moulding has

been achieved, and Jem Marsh intends to turn out production models to a standard that will rival the Italian Abarths.

The one-piece front end body section makes under-bonnet maintenance pretty straightforward, and I liked the neat stowage compartment for the battery in the centre of the bulkhead. Nestling in the front of the frame was a Ford 109E engine with a special cylinder head and twin SU 1½ inch carburetters, supplied by John Mitchell of Huddersfield and producing something like 65 horsepower. This, of course, does not constitute racing trim, but as the new Marcos is intended as a tractable GT car it is natural that Jem Marsh should run his demonstrator in this form. For the racing driver, a Ford 105E engine, developing anything up to 90 horsepower, can be dropped in, along with a close-ratio gearbox, a magnesium alloy bell-housing, and all the usual 'goodies'.

The important thing is that the Marcos remains fundamentally unchanged when used on the circuits, and in this track test I was particularly interested to try the car in 'road' form to discover how the frame structure, the steering, the suspension and the brakes behaved when given some real work to do. I must admit that I expected to hear a few squeaks and groans as the timber was cornered!

Climbing into the car is not as difficult as it looks. The gull-type doors open high, and although you have to step over a fairly substantial ledge, you can drop down into the seat easily once your feet are in the footwell. The seat grips you well, aided by the side rail on the right and the transmission tunnel on the left, and I found I had ample legroom.

The instruments are arranged sensibly, with matching speedometer and rev counter high up in the centre of the facia, and the all-important oil pressure and water temperature gauges immediately ahead of the driver, where they are clearly visible through the two-spoke wood-rim wheel. The ammeter and fuel gauges are to the left, in a central console between the facia and the transmission tunnel, and this console also houses the direct-acting gear lever.

All holes for the instruments and controls are drilled in the woodwork for left or right hand drive, so it is simply a matter of dropping in the appropriate steering rack and pedal mountings during assembly, the whole car being symmetrical about its axis. I liked the unusual action of the handbrake. This is mounted on the transmission tunnel, but to engage it you have to pull the lever towards you with the left hand (on right hand drive cars). It is a natural action, but the reason for the installation is the practical one of mounting the lever on a reinforced glass fibre surface.

Being a comparatively low-powered engine, I was not surprised to find that it was extremely flexible. Indeed, the Marcos in this form is very much a top gear car, for although the engine will rev to 7,000 rpm if necessary there is little point in using much over 5,000 rpm in the lower gears. But I was not really concerned with power on this test; I was more interested to see how the car would hang on through the bends.

The answer is very well indeed. We were running the tyres with a little more pressure at the front, and the result of this was gentle oversteer. But even using Dunlop Gold Seal road tyres the car held on ex-

The smooth look has come to the Marcos GT which in its previous version had a most unusual, angular styling. As tested, the car was fitted with a Ford 109E engine, but most people interested in competition use will prefer to specify the smaller 105E.

No, Jack Fairman does not smoke a pipe while he is track-testing cars! The illusion is caused by the upright behind the sliding window. These windows can be left open at high speed without causing wind roar or serious cockpit draught. The screen offers an excellent field of vision, though Fairman found some distortion and would have preferred the optional laminated plate glass.

tremely well at racing speeds, and when the back end broke away it did so quite slowly. The steering was very light, with not too much caster action, and although there was a little kick-back on the rough section of Clearways the linkage struck me as positive and the car could be aimed with accuracy.

I found it possible to lift the inside rear wheel when rounding Druid's Hairpin, but this was because road springs were fitted at the rear; with softer competition springs I doubt very much whether I should have been able to lift the wheel off the ground. At the same time I should be fair and say that the car as I tested it was ideally set up for road use, and if I had lifted a wheel on a sharp bend then it would have been my own fault for driving much too fast!

I must say that the suspension, which is partly proprietary and partly original, struck me as being well balanced. The front suspension, with unequal length wishbones, is basically Triumph Herald, but with different steering angles, while the rear axle is located by forward facing parallel radius arms, anchored at the extreme back of the body structure, the suspension medium being Armstrong coil-spring-damper units.

There is a stout anti-roll bar at the front, and this keeps body lean well checked. I found that during cornering there is a small amount of initial body deflection, but this remained constant however much I increased the cornering force.

Two things were a most pleasant surprise. The first was the low level of cockpit noise. This is indeed a quiet GT car, and if I had a passenger with me I should have been able to carry on a normal conversation with him, (or her!), at the 90 mph I was getting on the approach to Paddock Bend. I par-

ticularly noticed that although I had the sliding door windows partly open there was no roar around them, nor did I feel any draught in the cockpit on a day when I should imagine all brass monkeys were indoors!

Jem Marsh has gone to a lot of trouble to make this a quiet running car, and I agree with him that this is an important sales feature for a model intended for road use as well as competitions. The secret seems to rest largely in the shape of the body as far as wind noise is concerned, and in its construction when dealing with the suppression of mechanical noise—wood, it seems, can be a pretty useful insulator!

No wholesale use of additional insulating material has been needed in the cockpit, and although glass-fibre itself is not among the best sound deadeners, it certainly seems to cause no problems when used in conjunction with wood.

The second surprise on the circuit was the almost complete absence of the expected body groans. The structure must be extremely rigid, for even the most violent cornering failed to suggest any weakness in or protest from the framework.

I was also pleased to find that a genuine effort had been made to provide a professional looking interior, with carpeting on the vertical surfaces and over the transmission tunnel, as well as quilted leather on the deep parcels shelf behind the seats. There is also a leathercloth covering for the full-width facia.

One or two points struck me as in need of attention. For example, I thought the anchorages for the stays supporting the gull-wing doors were not all that rigid, but I understand that this is being overcome by

fitting counterbalance springs in the mechanism. The fit of the doors was not perfect, but the trouble here has been caused by working to too fine tolerances; this is also to be rectified on future models.

I was also put off by a small patch of distortion in the curved front screen, and I would advise customers to spend the few pounds extra on laminated plate glass, which does not suffer from this defect.

To me, the little Marcos GT is an intriguing two-seater. I like its originality of design, the more so because it really seems to work out in practice. Apparently the car weighs only about 9 cwt, so it is little wonder that several serious GT competitors are turning to them for the 1962 season—fitted with the 997 cc 105E engine, of course. With a really good engine, a close-ratio gearbox, and the usual racing equipment, they should have a really useful car for the one litre class.

The car's appeal seems to rest in its versatility, for with a quiet but lively road performance, (a maximum of 100 mph should be well within its reach on the motorway with a mildly tuned 105E or 109E engine, and a 4.1 axle), a pair of comfortable seats, a deep luggage boot and quite a lot of useful interior space, it is a thoroughly practical and unfussy road car. It is then quite a straightforward job to rip out some of the trimmings, sort out the rear springs and apply the appropriate engine and gearbox to go motor racing with success.

And this is a car that could be driven to the circuit, raced, then driven home again—assuming you haven't shunted it! If you have, then it will probably have been your own fault, because it is one of the easiest little GT cars I have driven, and I should think one of the safest.

Left: The sensible instrument layout puts the oil pressure and water temperature gauges right ahead of the driver, while a console above the transmission forms a neat housing for the gear lever.

Right: The Forspeed Ford 109E engine, supplied by John Mitchell of Huddersfield, fits snugly between side members of the wood chassis. Suspension units are attached to a pair of metal sub-assemblies bolted to the main frame.

Wooden Winner

by DAVID PHIPPS

From little acorns mighty coupes grow, or so it would seem when the Marcos G.T. takes to the track replete with a wooden chassis.

Notable features of the Marcos body are the gullwing doors, the recessed headlights and the large sectioned windshield.

● So the wooden car, the S.A.A.E.C.V.B. famous from Peter Ustinov's "Grand Prix of Gibraltar" wasn't such an unlikely proposition after all! For some time now, wooden cars bearing the name "Marcos" have been winning races at English club meetings, and having driven a prototype with a 50 bhp engine at over 100 mph on the straight and not much less round the corners I can begin to see why.

The Marcos was designed by Frank Costin—famed for his work on Lister, Lotus and Vanwall aerodynamics—in conjunction with "Jem" Marsh, of Speedex Castings and Accessories, Luton, England. The aim was to turn out a really efficient two-seater coupe at a price comparable with that of small, mass-produced sedans. As the car was intended for racing and rallying as well as everyday road use, high chassis performance was essential, and this is the chief reason for the decision to adopt all-wooden construction. Metal chassis-body pressings were ruled out by tooling costs, resin-bonded fiberglass was considered to require a long development program (as witness the time taken to get the Lotus Elite into full production) and the use of a space frame or conventional chassis and separate body was discouraged by such considerations as weight, fatigue, corrosion and inaccessibility.

By contrast with all this, Costin's experience in the aircraft industry (where wooden construction is widely employed) convinced him that a structure of spruce and plywood offered considerable advantages in terms of strength, stiffness, weight and cost, together with freedom from fatigue and corrosion. In addition, he had already built a wooden-bodied Austin Seven Special for his own use. An indication of the rigidity of the Marcos is given by its claimed torsional stiffness of nearly 3000 lbs-ft per degree, which compares favorably with that of anything previously produced in the automotive sphere. In more practical terms, Costin demonstrates by jumping up and down on the front cross-member both that the plywood structure is considerably stronger than it looks and that, under such loading, any movement of the doors relative to their frames is quite imperceptible.

The whole design is based on two "torsion boxes" which form the side members of the car. These are deep, longitudinal box-section members, made of plywood, with stiffening diaphragms along their length. At the front they are joined by a reinforced transverse member which incorporates suspension, steering gear and radiator mountings. The engine bulkhead forms a central transverse member, and is also linked to the stressed propeller shaft tunnel, while at the rear the seat foundations and the front wall of the trunk provide further reinforcement. The roof is supported by box-section pillars on either side of the rear window, but contributes little to the stiffness of the car due to the use of gull-wing doors.

All joints are glued (and does that glue stick!) and all material is treated with protective and fire-resistant compounds; wise-cracks about woodpeckers and termites are regarded as very good publicity. A certain amount of fiberglass, used for small, double-curvature items like the doors, helps to keep the weight down, so that the whole structure, complete with windshield and all mounting brackets, weighs little more than 200 pounds.

Proprietary mechanical components are used throughout the car, to keep down initial costs and also to facilitate servicing in all parts of the world. The double-wishbone-and-coil front suspension and the rack-and-pinion steering are Triumph Herald, and the rear axle is Austin Metropolitan; the latter is positively located by means of parallel leading radius arms and a Panhard rod. The Girling brakes and Girling hydraulic clutch assembly, together with pedals, pedal brackets and handbrake, are also readily obtainable production parts.

The Marcos is normally supplied with a mildly tuned version of the Ford 105E engine, incorporating a sports camshaft, twin S.U. carburetors (or one twin-choke Weber) and a four-branch exhaust system. For racing purposes a 90 bhp "Formula Junior" engine is available. 4.55 to one final drive gears are fitted as standard, with 4.11 gearing optional. There is also a 1216 cc Climax-engined version in existence, which regularly takes on—and sometimes beats—the Elites.

Frank Costin has never hesitated to give a car an unusual profile if it will obtain optimum aerodynamic efficiency.

A great deal of development work has been carried out since the car's rather premature announcement. The cycle-type fenders of the original prototype were soon replaced by an all-enveloping one-piece front body panel, and production cars are now being fitted with full-width windshields instead of the divided screen shown in the accompanying illustrations. Interior trim has also been greatly improved and is now fully in keeping with the car's price bracket.

Despite the use of gull-wing doors, getting in and out of the Marcos is not particularly easy, for the "torsion boxes" which are the secret of the car's chassis stiffness necessitate a high door sill. Once inside, however, the seats are quite comfortable and provide adequate leg and head room for anyone up to six feet or a little over. In addition, the body sides and deep propeller shaft tunnel provide very good lateral support.

The outstanding features of the car are its performance and its cornering. The "works hack" I tried recorded a genuine 100 mph, reached 50 mph from a standstill in 8 seconds and 70 mph in 15 seconds. Fuel consumption was in the region of 35 mpg. All this is due more to light weight (around 1000 pounds ready to go) and good shape than to power output. Racing versions are capable of over 120 mph.

In the dry, thanks partly to its Dunlop R5 racing tires, the Marcos corners "on rails," with just a suggestion of understeer. There is very little roll, and evidence of the car's chassis stiffness is given by its stability on fast s-bends. The racing tires were less happy in the wet, however, and for everyday use the Firestone tires fitted as standard would obviously be a better choice. The steering is very light and direct, the brakes are more than adequate (they felt in need of adjustment on the test car) and the remote control gearshift has a very short travel but is a little on the stiff side. Instruments and switches are laid out on a central console; on production cars a Smiths electronic tachometer is fitted as standard.

An unusual feature on the Marcos is a complete absence of openable windows. Ventilation is provided by aircraft-type "Punkah louvers," which are more than adequate in mild weather, and by a Smiths Fresh Air Heater, which can also be set to provide cold air. Luggage space in the rear trunk is extremely good for a car of this type; there is also a cubby hole in the dash and a parcel shelf behind the seats.

Sales of the Marcos in the United States are handled by Engine Imports Inc., Broadway Pier, San Diego, California, and the price in standard trim is $2995. As a road car it is definitely "different," and as a racing car it should stand a very good chance of success in the 1000 cc G.T. category (in which it is already homologated). It also makes an extremely interesting design study for would-be chassis builders.

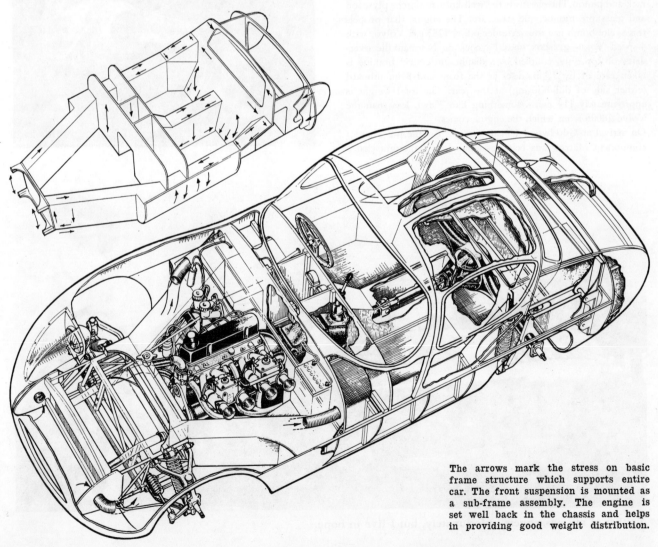

The arrows mark the stress on basic frame structure which supports entire car. The front suspension is mounted as a sub-frame assembly. The engine is set well back in the chassis and helps in providing good weight distribution.

MAGNIFICENT MARCOS

IT MAY NOT HAVE A WOODEN HEART, BUT IT HAS A WOODEN CHASSIS_____

IAN GERRARD

RECENTLY IT FELL TO MY LUCKY LOT to be invited along to Goodwood by Evans of Wimbledon to test the 1800 Marcos coupé. I was in fact invited to the launching but, as I have already seen graunched ones here and there and a couple of secondhand ones, the term "launching" seems a little out of place: I couldn't even get it to aquaplane in the wet on my all-too-brief drive.

I suppose that the unique Marcos wooden construction (á la Mosquito) is too well-known to go rambling on about, but for those who just think of it as that wooden car, here are a few technical details.

All independent suspension, by unequal length wishbones and coil springs at the front, and fixed length driveshafts with two leading links and sliding joint cross brace, with chassis mounted differential suspended by coil springs, at the rear; steering is by rack and pinion. The chassis is the well-known Marcos plywood and glassfibre monocoque structure. The engine that propels this svelte bomb is a four-cylinder o.h.v. 1783 c.c. Volvo, with 4-speed Volvo gearbox with Laycock de Normanville over-drive on top only, coupled by a diaphragm clutch; braking is taken care of by $9\frac{1}{4}$ in. discs at the front and 8 in. inboard (either side of diff housing) at the rear. The total weight is approximately $11\frac{3}{4}$ cwt.—something like 7 cwt. less than the Volvo 1800S from which the engine comes.

On arrival at Goodwood I made straight for the pit where a component Marcos was being assembled, as I thought that a

stage-by-stage description of the assembly would be of interest to our readers. However, apart from bolting on the front suspension, nothing else was done, apparently because of the B.B.C. who were there in force and having camera trouble. Actually, the B.B.C. TV Team were a pain in the neck; they just about monopolised the place for a while, and one could

Neither of my passengers unfortunately, but I live in hope.

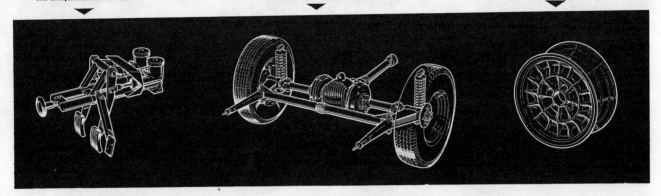

not approach within eyeshot of the component car, without being waved away by some little Hitler. It would appear that ordinary people, especially ones with a job of work to do, are not allowed to appear in the background of any television shots that they take. The B.B.C. must think that apart from them and their audience no one else exists. Anyway, back to the Marcos. I was duly driven around the circuit for two laps and then allowed two whole laps to myself, during which my compulsory passenger turned all shades from pink down to grey/green. Extraordinary. Two laps were not enough to assess any of the characteristics of the car and so I demanded a few more laps, which I eventually got in after refreshments had been served: I found it nearly impossible to stay on coffee— some others succumbed in a big way to the alcoholic refreshments. Then we were let loose, about four at a time, on to the track. I'm afraid I didn't get the name of my second passenger, but he was surely the world's best, because when two of the aforesaid gentlemen pulled straight out in front of us from the pits as we were going past flat out in overdrive top, he didn't turn a hair, even though we eventually had to take to the grass to avoid being killed. But I digress. If anyone thinks of the Marcos as a sort of a special thrown together he couldn't be more wrong. It is beautifully finished and would be a credit to any of the major manufacturers. The doors close as if they are coachbuilt, which I suppose by modern standards they are. One tends to bump one's head getting in if one is tall and not careful—I am both. One also has to get in over a fairly wide sill, which isn't easy for a "lady". Once inside things couldn't be better—the rearward vision, which I had thought would be

of the letter-box variety, is superb. The instruments are comprehensive in the extreme with rev counter and speedo directly in front of one, and viewed through the small two-spoked dished wheel (rim of treewood, of course). The rest are in what I believe is described as a central console and all switches, etc. are readily to hand.

I was instructed to keep the revs down to 5,500 and with this limitation in mind, Goodwood can be lapped flat out in overdrive top, top, and third; in fact, I did one lap in top and overdrive top in the wet, and at no time did the car feel a handful— always remaining responsive and easy to control. The ride in the wet and in the dry seemed remarkably similar, possibly due to the Pirelli Cinturatos, which are really great tyres. The cornering power seemed very high and was accomplished with little or no roll. I thought the brakes a bit of a disappointment; they seemed to be beginning to fade a bit by the time I was through. This could be because they are rather shrouded at the rear, although most probably it was because the cars had done quite a few laps round Goodwood. Speed? Well, the makers claim 115 m.p.h. and I see no reason to doubt them.

To sum up, it was a pleasant run, spoilt only by the two aforesaid idiots trying to kill me and a B.B.C. Mobile Camera Van with a Marcos just behind it crawling round the Circuit nearly always on the wrong line on the corners.

Well, I want one, but at £2,283 2s. 5d. basic or £1,865 in component form, I think I will have to wait a bit. Since this was written we have arranged to have a Marcos for a full extended road test, when performance figures etc., will be taken.

DIMENSIONS

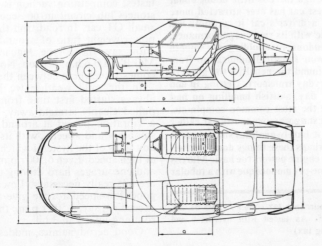

A	Overall Length	160¼"	408 cm
B	Overall Width	63¾"	162 cm
C	Overall Height	45½"	114 cm
D	Wheel Base	89"	226 cm
E	Front Track	49"	125 cm
F	Rear Track	49½"	126 cm
G	Ground Clearance	5"	13 cm
H	Seat Squab Length	18"	47 cm
I	Seat Squab to Roof	37"	94 cm
J	Passenger Seat Width	14"	36 cm
K	Driver's Seat Width	14"	36 cm
L	Front of Seat to Pedals	24"	61 cm

M	Driver's Leg Room (Width)	15"	38 cm
N	Passenger's Leg Room (Width)	15"	38 cm
O	Driver's Leg Room Seat Squab to Wheel	12"	30 cm
P	Passenger's Leg Room Seat Squab to Bulkhead	28"	71 cm
Q	Clearance—Door Opening	30"	76 cm
R	Boot Height	16"	41 cm
S	Boot Length	21"	53 cm
T	Boot Width	32"	81 cm

Road Test No. 25/65

Marcos 1800

FIVE years ago Jem Marsh and Frank Costin built an ugly little car with a wooden monocoque chassis and a hot Ford engine and called it a Marcos—a contraction of their names. Costin is no longer with the company they formed but the name has stuck and Marcos cars of progressively more beautiful shape have since won many races and a reputation for sound if unorthodox engineering. If a specialist manufacturer is to survive in one of the world's most competitive markets his product must have a strong appeal to an enthusiastic (and often wealthy) minority. Hitherto the Marcos has offered competition handling and performance at a reasonable price but the 1800, a much more expensive and ambitious project, breaks fresh ground as fast semi-luxurious road transport—a category in which many other marques already jostle for relatively few orders.

Marcos don't seem to be influenced by compromise or fashion. They wanted a car with striking looks and great driver appeal and built one regardless of the associated penalties. As an eye-catching design there is little doubt about the success of the styling: no test car has ever attracted more attention from bystanders. As a driver's car it certainly has enormous appeal to some people with its raucous performance, F1 driving position and tremendous roadholding on smooth surfaces. These things alone won fanatical admiration from some of our drivers but others found the penalties too great to regard the car as practical everyday transport. Getting in and out, poor ventilation on a hot day, skittish handling on bad roads and excessive noise were the most common complaints. But if you regard the 1800 as a snug way-out sports car rather than a grand tourer (for which it barely qualifies since there is little space for luggage) then perhaps these things don't matter.

A slightly tuned Volvo P1800 engine powers the basic Marcos 1800—which is still a rigid marine-ply monocoque with a tubular

PRICE £1,650 plus £345 6s. 3d. purchase tax equals £1,995 6s. 3d. Component form (no tax), £1,645. As tested with overdrive and magnesium wheels £2,148 (including tax)

sub-frame structure up front to take the conventional coil and wishbone suspension: a semi independent de Dion arrangement suspends the rear wheels with the differential (ex B.M.C.) mounted on the chassis. Glass-fibre panels clothe the very well finished bodywork—the lowest closed coupé we have yet tested standing a mere 3 ft. 6½ in. on its Pirelli Cinturato tyres.

Even after a recent big price cut, the car is fairly expensive at just under £2,000 but you must expect to pay dearly for a vehicle of unique conception.

Performance and economy

Now that many specialist manufacturers are turning to big American V-8s as an abundant source of cheap power it was a bold move by Marcos to retain a less appealing European "four". Yet the performance justifies the choice and there are important fringe benefits of economy and a widespread service network too.

This is a very fast car with a top speed approaching 120 m.p.h. (considerably more with a tail wind) and vivid acceleration that only six test cars in the past two years have bettered to 50 m.p.h.—only one of them by more than a second. The Volvo P1800 engine is normally rated at 96 b.h.p. (net) at 5,800 r.p.m. but new inlet and exhaust porting and a pair of Stromberg carburetters produce a bit more power for the basic Marcos installation. These modifications are necessary anyway to fit the engine in. At extra cost there are various stages of tune above this—the potential output of the sturdy Volvo engine was another reason it was selected—and the fastest competition version is said to have lapped the Silverstone Club circuit in 66 seconds—a prodigious speed for a small GT car. In road trim the 1800 weighs 15 cwt. giving a power/weight ratio of around 150 b.h.p. per ton compared with, say, the E-type Jaguar's 220 b.h.p. per ton and the MG B's 100 b.h.p. per ton. Not surprisingly, the performance comes somewhere between the two.

In the mild weather we had for our test, the engine always started first time from cold without the choke and pulled cleanly straight away. Between the lumpy idling and a vibration period at around 5,500 r.p.m., the engine runs smoothly and sweetly, with its deep-throated roar concealing any signs of the hysteria which afflict some sports car engines at high speed. Even 6,500 r.p.m. feels mechanically unstrained and encourages hard driving though these astronomical revs are not really necessary. Low intermediate gearing and very good low-speed torque give fast acceleration without ever exceeding, say, 3,500 r.p.m.: the same things will send the car romping up a 1-in-3 hill.

Good aerodynamics, modest weight and a high overdrive

A "real" sports car with a roof, luxury trim and a grand prix driving position. Great fun once you have made friends.

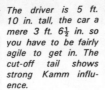

The driver is 5 ft. 10 in. tall, the car a mere 3 ft. 6½ in. so you have to be fairly agile to get in. The cut-off tail shows strong Kamm influence.

top gear account for the excellent petrol consumption which does not drop below 30 m.p.g. until the car is doing 80 m.p.h. or below 25 m.p.g. until you reach 100 m.p.h.—a natural motorway cruising speed. This economy is partly offset by the demand for expensive 100 octane petrol: the engine pinks noticeably on lower grades unless you avoid slogging at low revs.

Transmission

The all-synchromesh Volvo gearbox is a delight to use. A very short central lever, like a big switch, works swiftly and precisely through a well defined conventional gate: only with the snatch changes demanded by performance testing can the synchromesh be beaten. Our test car, like all the earlier Marcos 1800s, had overdrive on top and with a fairly low axle ratio you tend to regard this ratio as top gear of a 5-speed box: direct top is too low for main road cruising without the higher axle ratio now offered (without overdrive) as a cheaper alternative. By sports car standards the ratios are not particularly close together and some drivers would have preferred higher intermediate maxima but, this aside, the transmission—including the short-travel medium-weight clutch—will please the most fastidious enthusiast who probably won't mind dipping the clutch to cushion the abrupt overdrive engagement.

Handling and brakes

The cornering power of the Marcos 1800 is enormously high and it is a beautifully balanced car to hustle along smooth twisting roads, yet there are certain things about its handling we did not like. Poor surfaces can throw it off course and there is a curious and, until you get used to it, disconcerting

Magnesium elektron wheels cost nearly £20 each.

"hip wobble" at high speeds apparently caused by slight changes of camber in the road rather than definite bumps: the car does not seem to like motoring with its wheels at different levels. Even on a motorway there is a tendency for it to dart, almost imperceptibly, from side to side at high speed unless there is no wind: on the other hand, the body is astonishingly stable in pitch and roll and even under the most vicious cornering remains as flat as any production car we have driven.

The sheer speed and adhesion of the car round corners can be very exhilarating and two of our drivers claimed that no previous test car had given them more enjoyment during early Sunday morning outings on deserted roads. It is undoubtedly great fun and familiarity seems to camouflage the faults.

The steering is very positive and transmits so much feel that you could practically draw a relief map of the road from its message. This strong reaction, which not everyone liked to such a marked degree, and a fairly heavy action demands a firm grip on the wheel to hold an accurate line. On bumpy corners you will need concentration too. Very little movement is needed, however, partly because of the high gearing and partly because there is very little understeer. Despite a mere 2¾ turns from lock-to-lock, the turning circle is exceptionally tight (27¼ ft. to the right) and compensates for the poor visibility when manoeuvring in, say, a packed car park.

Our test car had Pirelli Cinturato tyres on special wider-than-standard magnesium wheels (costing nearly £20 each). On dry roads, it was virtually impossible to make them slide and only the hardest cornering would provoke a squeal. In the wet, excessive power would naturally break the back away, and correction needs delicacy but not great skill.

The disc/drum brakes, without servo assistance, need a firm push (which is desirable for heel-and-toeing) but are progressive and very reassuring so long as you never have to resort to the puny pull-out handbrake in an emergency: it scarcely worked at all on our test car and was certainly not strong enough for a 1-in-4 hill. Twenty ½g stops from 73 m.p.h. provoked no fade at all.

Comfort and controls

The Marcos is a very unusual car in many ways but two things at least are unique in our road testing experience—the fixed reclining seats in which you lie more than sit, and the ingenious adjustable pedal assembly that works extremely well. Seat "adjustment" is provided by spare cushions—one

The driving position is tailored by adjustable pedals and steering wheel, and extra cushions for the fixed, very reclining seats. Restricted elbow room dictates long-arm stance. Competition versions of the 1800, which are already winning races, cost about the same as the road car because they are stripped of much expensive equipment.

a thick backrest for small people (which no one used), the other a thin full-length bolster which all but the tallest (6 ft. 4 in.) driver did use. Without it, the transmission tunnel and doorsills are too high for both comfort and adequate vision. This apart, the seats are supremely comfortable with or without cushion once you have got used to driving with your chin on your chest, and passengers were usually very reluctant to move once they had settled down against the built-in headrest. But then the very thought of the contortionist act needed to get out of a car only 3 ft. 6 in. high is no encouragement to quit your seat readily. What is more, the seats remain comfortable for hours on end: because the weight of your body is spread over such a large area—from head to knees—aches and pains are non-existent despite a very firm ride.

The pedal assembly adjusts fore-and-aft by turning a large convenient knob beneath the steering wheel—itself movable for rake and reach by some spanner work under the bonnet. Given a little time to experiment, anyone should be able to find an ideal driving position as akin to a racing car as you'll get without actually driving one. The cockpit is small, almost claustrophobic at first, and half-filled with transmission tunnel which provides a natural resting place for your left elbow but gets in the way when you are twirling the steering vigorously. This tunnel, and the trough-shaped seats, give vice-like side support the value of which can only really be appreciated by driving the car. Never do you have to brace yourself for a corner or cling to the door handles: even nervous passengers found they could relax in the Marcos which suggests that tension is as much the engineers' concern as the driver's.

You sit so low that visibility is poor when manoeuvring or driving in traffic, and the road can disappear completely under the long bonnet when breasting the top of a hill or humpback bridge—disconcerting if there is a corner immediately afterwards. The mirror gives a good view aft but over-the-shoulder glances are distorted by the acutely curved sides of the rear window. Another by-product of the low seating is that you get a tremendous impression of speed when your bottom is only a few inches from the ground. The lights are quite good.

This is a noisy car but if you like the deep roar of sporting engines it isn't particularly tiresome. Surprisingly, there is quite a lot of wind noise too, caused, we suspect, by detail obstructions to the airflow rather than the body shape itself.

The Marcos 1800 is by no means the only GT car we have tested to suffer from poor ventilation. With such a small cockpit, there ought to be cold air outlets at foot level and, ideally, extractors behind to keep the flow moving. Without this refinement, the Marcos gets very hot inside on a sunny day even with the rather crude but easy slide-down windows

The small padded boot (30 in. wide, 41 in. longest diagonal) is half-full of spare wheel leaving room for 3 cu. ft. of test luggage. The low boot lid makes loading awkward.

1, thermostatic fan (extra). 2, radiator filler cap. 3, steering column universal. 4, oil filler cap. 5, pedal assembly cover. 6, twin Stromberg carburetters. 7, dip stick. 8, heater motor. 9, windscreen washer reservoir. 10, distributor. 11, coil. 12, battery.

Performance

Conditions

Weather: Warm and mild, negligible wind.
Temperature: 65°—72° F. Barometer 29.8 in Hg.
Surface: Dry tarmacadam.
Fuel: Super premium (101 octane R.M.).

Maximum speeds

	m.p.h.
Mean of four opposite runs (o/d top)	116.0
Best one way ¼-mile	124.1
Direct top gear (at 6,000 r.p.m.)	105.0
3rd gear (at 6,000 r.p.m.)	77.5
2nd gear (at 6,000 r.p.m.)	52.0
1st gear (at 6,000 r.p.m.)	33.5
"Maximile" speed: (Timed quarter mile after 1 mile accelerating from rest)	
Mean	111.2
Best	118.5

Acceleration times

m.p.h.	sec.
0—30	2.8
0—40	4.2
0—50	6.0
0—60	8.2
0—70	10.7
0—80	13.6
0—90	18.4
0—100	25.7
Standing quarter mile	16.3

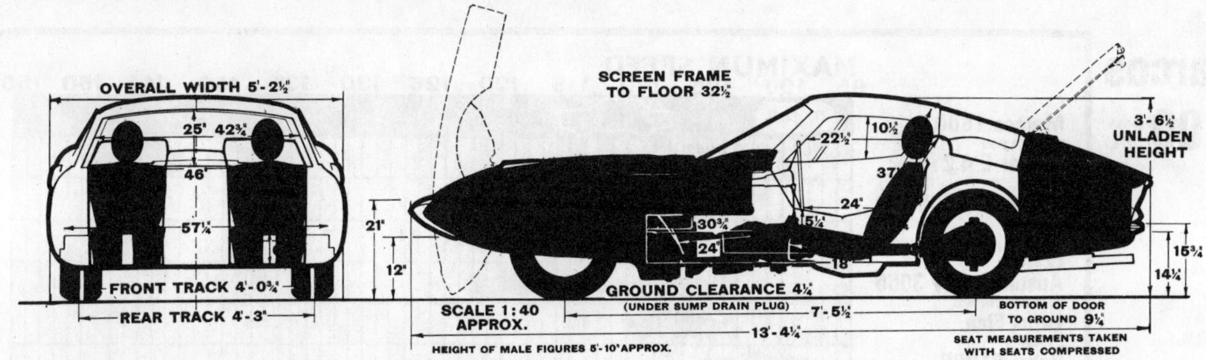
OVERALL WIDTH 5'-2½"
25" 42¾"
46"
57¼"
FRONT TRACK 4'-0¾"
REAR TRACK 4'-3"
21"
12"
SCREEN FRAME TO FLOOR 32½"
22½"
10½"
37"
24"
5¼"
30¾"
24"
18"
3'-6½" UNLADEN HEIGHT
15¾
14¼
GROUND CLEARANCE 4¼
(UNDER SUMP DRAIN PLUG)
SCALE 1:40 APPROX.
7'-5½"
13'-4¼"
BOTTOM OF DOOR TO GROUND 9¼"
SEAT MEASUREMENTS TAKEN WITH SEATS COMPRESSED
HEIGHT OF MALE FIGURES 5'-10" APPROX.

fully open. No one can be really comfortable with sweaty feet. We only had one hot day during our test: at other times, the cockpit remained pleasantly warm and the modest output of the heater seems adequate for cold nights since it has only a small volume of air to cope with.

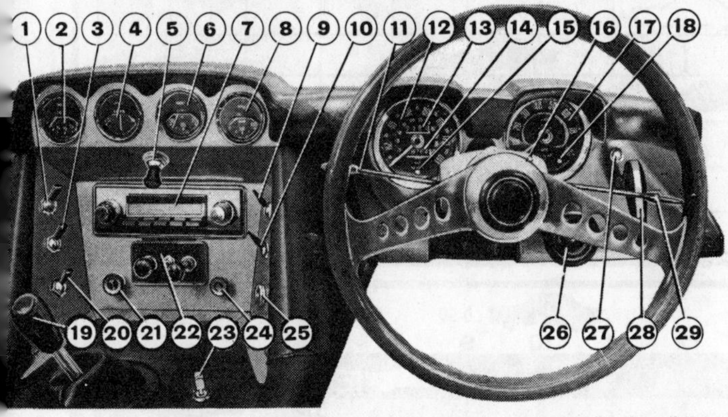
1 2 3 4 5 6 7 8 9 10 11 12 13 14 15 16 17 18
19 20 21 22 23 24 25
26 27 28 29

1 and 3, spare switches. 2, petrol gauge. 4, ammeter. 5, cigar lighter. 6, temperature gauge. 7, radio (extra). 8, oil pressure gauge. 9, panel lights. 10, lights master switch. 11, headlamp flasher and lights switch. 12, speedometer. 13 and 14, mileage recorders. 15, main beam tell tale. 16, ignition light. 17, rev counter. 18, indicator tell tale. 19, gear lever. 20, 2-speed wipers. 21, screen washer. 22, heater controls. 23, overdrive. 24, choke. 25, ignition/starter. 26, pedal assembly adjuster. 27, handbrake tell tale. 28, handbrake. 29, indicators.

Fittings and furniture

Apart from the odd detail, the interior is beautifully finished and neatly, if rather futuristically, styled with a clear and comprehensive set of instruments. A central switch panel is easy to reach but none of the five toggle switches is labelled: a handbook will soon be ready to tell you what they are. Stacked vertically (see picture) they are less easily confused than a horizontal row once their functions are memorised. A particularly handy switch on the transmission tunnel works the overdrive and two stalks for the indicators and lights are within fingertip reach of the small thick wood-rimmed steering wheel.

The doors do not shut very cleanly and there is the familiar resin bonded smell inside—both things are common to most cars with glass fibre bodies—but these are the only obvious faults of otherwise excellent coachwork. Stowage space is confined to a parcel shelf on the passenger's side (there is room to make it much bigger), a high shelf behind the seats that is not too easy to reach, small door pockets, and the transmission tunnel, its slightly lipped sides preventing small odds and ends from sliding off. The boot is small and further restricts the car's potential as a long-distance grand tourer. Neither are there any sun visors (a strange omission) so sun glasses are sometimes essential.

Safety belt anchorages are built in and our test car had neat and comfortable Britax installations.

Continued on the next page

m.p.h.	O/d Top sec.	Top sec.	3rd sec.
20—40	—	7.6	4.9
30—50	10.6	7.0	4.4
40—60	10.6	6.1	4.4
50—70	9.4	6.7	4.6
60—80	9.4	7.3	5.2
70—90	11.4	7.9	—
80—100	15.1	11.0	—

Speedometer

Indicated:

20 30 40 50 60 70 80 90 100 110

True:

19 29 38½ 48 58 67½ 76½ 85½ 94½ 103

Distance recorder . . . . 1% slow

Hill climbing

At steady speed		lb./ton
O/d top	1 in 8.7	(Tapley 255)
Top	1 in 6.3	(Tapley 350)
3rd	1 in 4.6	(Tapley 490)
2nd	1 in 3.4	(Tapley 655)

Brakes

Pedal pressure, deceleration and equivalent stopping distance from 30 m.p.h.

lb.	g	ft.
25	0.27	111.0
50	0.55	54.0
75	0.95	31.5
85	0.98	30.5
Handbrake	0.19	158.0

Fade

20 stops at ½g deceleration at 1 min. intervals from a speed midway between 30 m.p.h. and max. speed (= 73 m.p.h.).

	lb.
Pedal force at beginning	42
Pedal force at 10th stop	42
Pedal force at 20th	42

Fuel consumption

Touring (consumption midway between 30 m.p.h. and maximum less 5% allowance for acceleration) . . . . 30.6 m.p.g.

Overall . . . . 22.8 m.p.g.

= 12.4 litres/100 km.

Total test distance . . . . . . 1,650 miles

Tank capacity (maker's figure) . . . 12 galls.

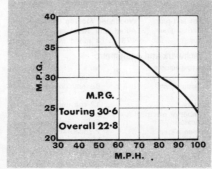

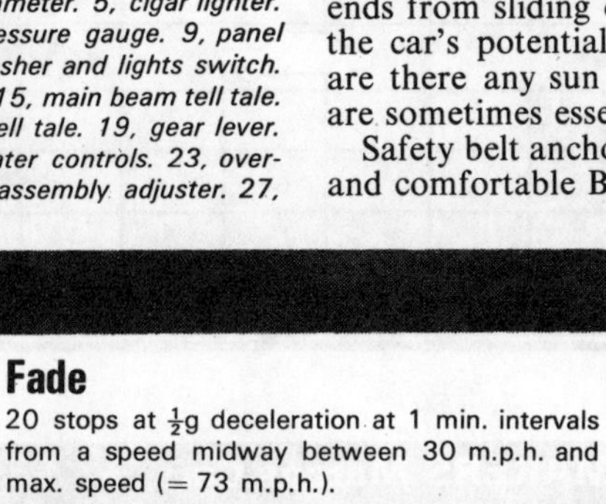
M.P.G.
40
35
30
25
20
30 40 50 60 70 80 90 100
M.P.H.
M.P.G.
Touring 30·6
Overall 22·8

Weight

Kerb weight (unladen with fuel for approximately 50 miles) . . . . 15.2 cwt.

Front/rear distribution 50/50

Weight laden as tested . . . . . . 18.9 cwt.

Steering

Turning circle between kerbs: ft.

Left 29.5

Right 27.2

Turns of steering wheel from lock to lock 2.8

Steering wheel deflection for 50 ft. diameter circle . . . . 0.75 turns

Clutch

Free pedal movement . . . . 0.5 in.

Additional movement to disengage clutch completely . . . . 3.2 in.

Maximum pedal load . . . . 37 lb.

Parkability

Gap needed to clear a 6 ft. wide obstruction parked in front.

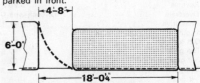

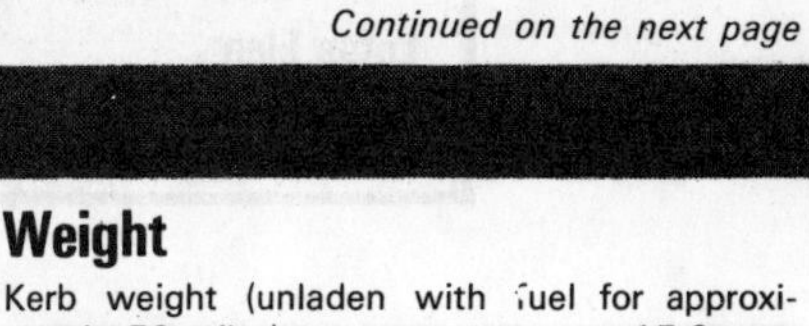
4'-8"
6'-0"
18'-0¼"

Marcos 1800

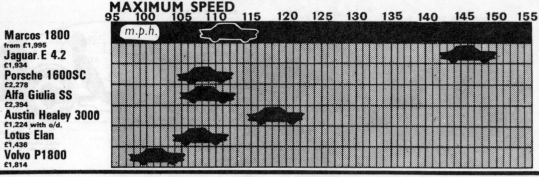

MAXIMUM SPEED *m.p.h.*

| | 95 | 100 | 105 | 110 | 115 | 120 | 125 | 130 | 135 | 140 | 145 | 150 | 155 |

Marcos 1800
from £1,995

Jaguar. E 4.2
£1,934

Porsche 1600SC
£2,278

Alfa Giulia SS
£2,394

Austin Healey 3000
£1,224 with o/d.

Lotus Elan
£1,436

Volvo P1800
£1,814

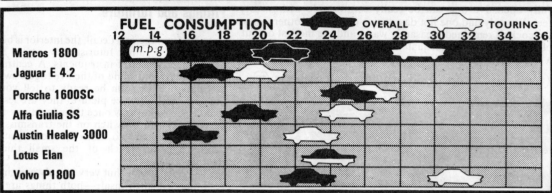

FUEL CONSUMPTION *m.p.g.* — OVERALL / TOURING

| | 12 | 14 | 16 | 18 | 20 | 22 | 24 | 26 | 28 | 30 | 32 | 34 | 36 |

Marcos 1800 · Jaguar E 4.2 · Porsche 1600SC · Alfa Giulia SS · Austin Healey 3000 · Lotus Elan · Volvo P1800

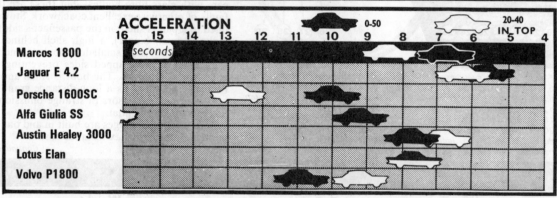

ACCELERATION *seconds* — 0-50 / 20-40 IN TOP

| | 16 | 15 | 14 | 13 | 12 | 11 | 10 | 9 | 8 | 7 | 6 | 5 | 4 |

Marcos 1800 · Jaguar E 4.2 · Porsche 1600SC · Alfa Giulia SS · Austin Healey 3000 · Lotus Elan · Volvo P1800

MAKE Marcos : TYPE 1800 : MAKERS Marcos Cars Ltd., Greenlands Mills, Bradford-on-Avon, Wiltshire.

Engine

Cylinders	4
Bore and stroke	84.14 mm. x 80 mm.
Cubic capacity	1,780 c.c.
Valves	o.h.v. pushrod
Compression ratio	10:1
Carburetter(s)	2 Stromberg CD 175
Fuel pump	AC PEGI
Oil filter	Full flow WIX
Max. power (gross)	114 b.h.p. at 5,800 r.p.m. (90 b.h.p. at wheels)
Max. torque (gross)	110 lb. ft. at 4,200 r.p.m.

Transmission

Clutch	Borg and Beck 8½" diameter diaphragm
Top gear (s/m)	1:1 (overdrive 0.803:1)
3rd gear (s/m)	1.36:1
2nd gear (s/m)	1.99:1
1st gear (s/m)	3.13:1
Reverse	3.25:1
Overdrive	Laycock type D
Final drive	3.91:1
M.p.h. at 1,000 r.p.m. in:—	
O/d top gear	21.8
Top gear	17.5
3rd gear	12.9
2nd gear	8.7
1st gear	5.6

Chassis

Construction	Monocoque structure of marine ply

Brakes

Type	9¼ in. Girling discs at front, 8 in. drums at rear
Friction area	175 sq. in.

Suspension and steering

Front	Independent by unequal length wishbones with coil spring/damper units and anti-roll bar
Rear	De Dion type axle with telescopic transverse link connecting twin leading arms with fixed length drive shafts and coil spring/damper units.
Shock absorbers	
Front and rear	Woodhead Monroe telescopic
Steering gear	Alford and Alder rack and pinion
Tyres	175 x 13 tubed Pirelli Cinturato

Coachwork and equipment

Starting handle	No
Jack	Scissor type
Jacking points	Beneath door sills on each side
Battery	12-volt under bonnet
Number of electrical fuses	2
Indicators	Self-cancelling flashers
Screen wipers	2-speed electric
Screen washers	Hand vacuum pump
Sun visors	None
Locks:	
With ignition key	Both doors
With other keys	Boot
Interior heater	Fresh air heater/demister
Major extras available	Special coachwork finishes; light alloy wheels; overdrive, tuned engine.
Upholstery	Linen backed p.v.c.
Floorcovering	Carpet and rubber matting
Alternative body types	None

Maintenance

Sump	7 pints S.A.E. 10W/30
Gearbox	3½ pints (including o/d) S.A.E. 30
Rear axle	1½ pints 90 EP
Steering gear	Grease
Cooling system	14 pints with heater (2 drain taps)
Chassis lubrication	Every 5,000 miles to 3 points, every 20,000 miles to 6 points
Ignition timing	17° to 19° b.t.d.c.
Contact breaker gap	0.016 to 0.018 in.
Sparking plug type	Bosch N225TI
Sparking plug gap	0.028 to 0.032 in.
Tappet clearances (hot)	Inlet 0.020 in., Exhaust 0.020 in.
Front wheel toe-in	⅛ in.
Castor angle	7½°
Tyre pressures	26 p.s.i. front and rear

MARCOS 1800

A wooden backbone, a Volvo engine and
a fiberglass body add up to the Marcos 1800

BY STEPHEN F. WILDER

MUCH HAS BEEN made, technically and humorously, of the wooden frame of the Marcos. But as you look at the Marcos, its frame is as completely concealed as any car's. This modesty is also evident in the Marcos brochure which mentions the word "wood" only in describing the steering wheel rim. Apparently the jokes fly thick and fast in England too, for the frame is described simply as "race-proven" and "monocoque."

Even without its wood, the Marcos 1800 is memorable for faithfully putting on the public roads the kind of driving

<table>
<tr><td colspan="2">MARCOS 1800
AT A GLANCE...</td></tr>
<tr><td>Price as tested</td><td>$6325</td></tr>
<tr><td>Engine</td><td>4 cyl, ohv, 1783 cc, 114 bhp</td></tr>
<tr><td>Curb weight, lb</td><td>1700</td></tr>
<tr><td>Top speed, mph</td><td>115</td></tr>
<tr><td>Acceleration, 0-60 mph, sec</td><td>9.0</td></tr>
<tr><td>50-70 mph (2nd & 3rd gear), sec</td><td>6.0</td></tr>
<tr><td>Average fuel consumption, mpg</td><td>30</td></tr>
</table>

MARCOS 1800

position and body shape that is contemporary in GT proto-type racing. Although the acceleration is mild in comparison with the shape and the technical features, this should be of little concern to customers who intend to race the car, for naturally they will modify the rugged Volvo 1800-cc, 4-cyl, 5-main-bearing engine up to the rules' limits, which can mean as much as 135 hp instead of 114.

The Marcos is incredible as an attention-getter. It out-draws Ferraris and Maseratis even when painted refrigerator white. The external view is wild and so is the internal. When both driver and passenger are strapped in their over-one-shoulder harness/seat belts, they look and feel ready for a ride in outer space. The seating position is not far from that generated in Formula I, and as befits a car styled in the current racing idiom, there is little waste space in the cockpit. The controls are all within easy reach, partly because there isn't anywhere else for them to get to. All surfaces are completely trimmed and many are padded, immediately conveying an air of luxury as well as purpose.

If you like making a grand arrival, there is nothing to match the Marcos in its ability to bring people out of the house on the run to see it. Even in the rain. The car is astonishingly low (41.5 in.), considering that it really can contain two full-sized people, and the fiberglass reinforced plastic body has magnetic styling which you cannot ignore. Of course, getting out of the car is rather awkward, but there's sweet revenge on those who laugh at your exit. Offer them a chance to sit behind the wheel and watch them struggle in and out. The seating position is reclined at about 45° from the seat cushion to your shoulders, but unlike an open F-I car the Marcos must be entered from the side. Short of extending the doors into the roof, there seems no inexpensive improvement to suggest. The steering column telescopes 4 in.

and adjusts vertically about as much. When raised, it's easier to slip into the car; however, it then has to be lowered so you can see over it, unless you have a very long torso. Backing up is a major visibility problem; our solution was to unfasten the shoulder harness and lean out the door.

The relaxed seating position is extraordinary. Once in the car, it is delightful just to lean back and relax. Rather like when you're shopping for a lounge chair. And with the harness pulled up tight, it feels absolutely secure. While it's certainly a seat in which you could drop off to sleep, you need not worry on that score. You aren't likely to try driving with your head tilted back against the headrest (the Marcos is the first car to exceed the minimum backrest height since we started scoring driver comfort). For one thing, this drops your eyes too low in the cockpit to see well and, furthermore, any bumps in the road are translated into jolts at the headrest, reminders to stay alert.

There are plenty of gauges and controls on the dash and the steering is very quick, so cross-country runs on empty roads induce Mille Miglia euphoria in short order. On smooth surfaces, the Marcos clings fiercely. Body roll is unnoticeable, the high sides of the seats give superb support, and one quickly senses that this car is made to order for racing.

Despite its fully independent—tilt, that's a form of de Dion at the rear—despite its fully light-weight suspension all around, the Marcos betrays its British heritage with far from limber springs. Wheel travel at the rear, for instance, totals only 2.5 in., one-third of usual American practice. And this gives a ride that is firm by any standards but Bugatti's.

The rear suspension eschews the modern GP tradition of trailing upper and lower control arms with pairs of long radius rods running forward, for trailing arms are impossible to pivot on a centrally boxed frame of a 2-seater like this without skewering the occupants. Instead Messrs Marsh and Costin created a novel variation of the de Dion axle. Each hub carrier is mounted on the front end of a welded steel leading arm (it leads forward from frame to wheel). These

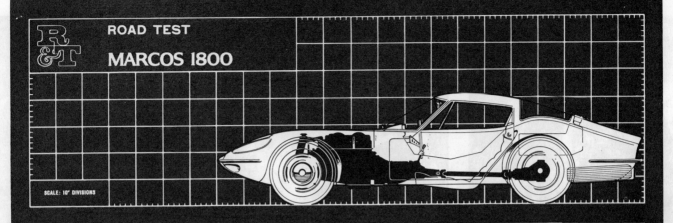

ROAD TEST
MARCOS 1800

SCALE: 10" DIVISIONS

PRICE

List price.................$5997
Price as tested............$6325

ENGINE

No. cylinders & type....4 cyl, ohv
Bore x stroke, in......3.31 x 3.15
Displacement, cc...........1783
  Equivalent cu in........108.6
Compression ratio..........10.0:1
Bhp @ rpm......114 @ 5800
  Equivalent mph...........101
Torque @ rpm, lb-ft. 110 @ 4200
  Equivalent mph...........73
Carburetors.........2 Stromberg
No. barrels & dia....1 x 1.75
Type fuel required......premium

DRIVE TRAIN

Clutch type......single plate, dry
  Diameter, in..............8.5
Gear ratios: o'drive (0.80)..3.14:1
  4th (1.00)...............3.91:1
  3rd (1.24)...............4.85:1
  2nd (1.67)...............6.54:1
  1st (2.62)..............10.25:1
Synchromesh........on all 4
Differential type....hypoid bevel
  Ratio.................3.91:1

CHASSIS & SUSPENSION

Frame type: central torque box of
  wood with metal trusses to carry
  suspension.
Brake type...........disc/drum
  Swept area, sq in.........207
Tire size.................175–13
  Make.........Pirelli Cinturato
Steering type......rack & pinion
  Turns, lock to lock........2.3
  Turning circle, ft.........37
Front suspension: independent with
  unequal length A-arms, coil
  springs, tube shocks, anti-roll
  bar.
Rear suspension: single leading
  arm with cross brace (de Dion
  tube), coil springs, tube shocks.

ACCOMMODATION

Normal capacity, persons.......2
Seat width.............2 x 16.5
Head room..................37.5
Seat back adjustment, deg......0
Entrance height, in..........39
Step-over height.............13
Door width..................30
Driver comfort rating:
  For driver 69-in. tall......90
  For driver 72-in. tall......70
  For driver 75-in. tall......60
  (85–100, good; 70–85, fair;
  under 70, poor)

GENERAL

Curb weight, lb............1700
Test weight...............2020
Weight distribution (with driver),
  front/rear, %..........45/55
Wheelbase, in.............89.0
Track, front/rear......49.0/49.5
Overall length, in........159.0
  Width...................62.5
  Height..................41.5
Frontal area, sq ft........14.4
Ground clearance, in........4.7
Overhang, front/rear......34/37
Departure angle (no load), deg .14
Usable trunk space, cu ft......7.0
Fuel tank capacity, gal......14.1

INSTRUMENTATION

Instruments: 8000-rpm tachometer, 140-mph speedometer, oil
  pressure, water temp, fuel, ammeter.
Warning lights: high beam, ignition, turn signal.

MISCELLANEOUS

Body styles available: coupe as
tested.

EXTRA COST OPTIONS

Pirelli Cinturato tires, shoulder
harness, overdrive, competition
tuning equipment, wheels, etc.

CALCULATED DATA

Lb/hp (test wt).............17.7
Mph/1000 rpm (o'drive)....17.4
Engine revs/mi............3450
Piston travel, ft/mi........1810
Rpm @ 2500 ft/min......4760
  Equivalent mph...........83
Cu ft/ton mi..............107
R&T wear index...........62.4

MAINTENANCE

Crankcase capacity, qt.........4
  Change interval, mi.......3000
Oil filter type...........by-pass
  Change interval, mi.......6000
Chassis lube interval, mi....3000

ROAD TEST RESULTS

ACCELERATION

0–30 mph, sec..............2.9
0–40 mph..................4.3
0–50 mph..................6.7
0–60 mph..................9.0
0–70 mph.................12.7
0–80 mph.................16.5
0–100 mph................31.4
50–70 mph (2nd & 3rd gear)..6.0
Standing ¼-mi, sec........17.1
  Speed at end, mph.........81

TOP SPEEDS

Overdrive (5300), mph.......115
4th (6000)................104
3rd (6000).................84
2nd (6000).................62
1st (6000).................40

GRADE CLIMBING

(Tapley data)

Data not taken.

SPEEDOMETER ERROR

30 mph indicated.....actual 29.4
40 mph.................40.4
60 mph.................58.8
80 mph.................78.0
100 mph................96.0

FUEL CONSUMPTION

Normal driving, mpg.......26–32
Cruising range, mi.......360–450

ACCELERATION & COASTING

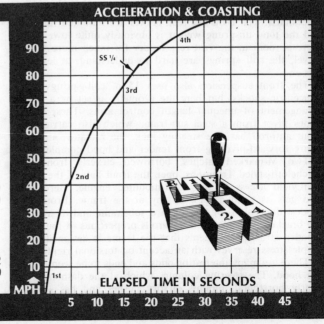

ELAPSED TIME IN SECONDS

arms mount with rubber fittings like a stud-type shock absorber's to the rearmost vertical panels of the frame. The latter take the fore and aft thrusts of the tires. The doubly universal-jointed axle shafts are of fixed length without any splines so all side forces are transmitted into the differential carrier bearings and then reach the frame via the differential case's mounting bolts. Vertical loads are taken by the 15-in. coil springs and concentric shock absorbers which mount on the front side of the hub carriers. To keep the wheel hubs at the chosen degree of negative camber, the two leading arms are connected by a cross-brace or de Dion axle. The latter consists of two unsplined telescoping halves so that it does not act like a giant anti-roll bar and so it does encompass the changes in track dictated by the swinging of the axle shafts. The 8-in. dia rear brakes are mounted inboard and the total unsprung weight is obviously quite low. Since there is room in the vast rear fender for much more wheel travel, the stiff springs are hard to understand, at least at this end.

The front suspension also uses 15-in. coil springs with concentric shocks, but here the geometry is set by a usual arrangement of unequal length control arms. These wishbones pivot from a steel sub-frame which also carries the front anti-roll bar, the steering rack, the radiator, and the entire forward-pivoting front fender and hood complex.

Two M-marked latches, borrowed cleverly from the Michelotti-styled Triumphs, open the front half of the body and yield access to the front-mounted engine. Here one also gets as good a look as any at the frame. From the modest dimensions of the forward sub-frame and its attaching brackets, and from the generous proportions of the deep wooden structure, it seems that the frame is designed with ample stress reserves with an accent on torsional rigidity.

There are many interesting odds and ends to be seen under the hood. The steering column, which at the dashboard is nearly horizontal, mounts on dry bushes and has several U-joints before reaching almost vertically down to the rack-and-pinion in front of the suspension. Those bushes may

be the source of the mild "stiction" noticed in the steering.

Because the seats are fixed in place, being part of the general structure, adjustments have been provided by mounting the three foot-controls and two master cylinders on a platform that can be moved up to 6 in. by turning a hand-wheel on the dash. To prevent drafts and fumes from entering the cockpit, this platform is boxed in.

The carburetors are British-built Strombergs carrying the name Zenith and shaped like the familiar SU. As with all Volvos, Weber carbs are an available option. Though otherwise stock, the Volvo engine has a set of lightweight headers that dump into tandem Triumph TR resonators. The exhaust note is sporty on acceleration, but when cruising at 60 mph or more there is a hard, mechanical resonance that can be tiring.

Attached to the all-synchro Volvo 4-speed transmission is the MG-B version of the Laycock overdrive, the difference from the usual Volvo edition being a step-up ratio of 0.80:1 instead of 0.76:1 and stronger springs and clutch. With the latter items, the OD should be strong enough to be used in third too but it only engages in top.

Unlike some high-production GT cars, the Marcos has a genuine trunk of 7 cu ft, more if you trust the Pirelli Cinturato 175-13 tires implicitly and remove the spare from the trunk's floor. There is lots of "nook and cranny" room as well to the sides of the trunk plus several pockets in the cockpit, including a glove box. A large trough around the trunk opening prevents gas from spilling in if the attendant overfills the 14-gal tank. The filler is a quick-release type. The parcel shelf below the rear window is too shallow to carry more than a magazine or perhaps a book. The door windows open by loosening a knurled locking wheel and pressing down by hand. Little plastic blocks glued to the windows provide purchase for lifting them closed.

For a variety of reasons, the Marcos is more fun to be seen in than it is to drive. It is interesting in the best tradition of special-builder turned pro, but at over $6000 it is hardly a bargain.

'WARE WHITE ANTS

From DAVID OWEN in London

THE trouble with buying expensive cars these days is that people just aren't impressed any more. Everybody seems so blase, even about expensive sports cars. Granted, one's friends may show an agreeable interest, or even a tittilating twinge of jealousy, but these sentiments usually dry up as quickly as the ink on the banker's draft. And as for the street-corner public, even a Jaguar doesn't catch their eyes any more. There's the faintest chance a Ferrari 330P2 might attract a second's languid glance, but anything else may as well be a 10-year-old sedan for all the emotion it provokes. Gone are the days when a well used roadster drew kerbside admirers; nowadays this only happens in Italy, a courtesy even extended to our humble MG Midget last month.

But a few weeks ago we lived through what must be every car-owner's dream. Everywhere we went, heads turned, eyes glittered, hands waved and questions, questions, questions. Barroom conversational openers ranged from "build-it-yourself?" to "it's one of the new Ferraris Maseratis/Iso Grifos/Lamborghinis". The subject of all this controversy? Our test car, the Marcos 1800GT. And only one person spotted it for what it was — the kind of small, bespectacled 12-year-old who always knows everything. He even asked us if it had the new disc brakes on the back wheels, and as we'd been sworn to secrecy about these, all we could do was blush and say we didn't know. But for most people the car was an exotic enigma — even the name made them think in terms of Turin, Modena or Stockholm rather than Bradford-on-Avon, Wiltshire, where the Marcos roots are anchored.

Just who is Marcos? Like Cosworth — the engine-tuning team of Costin and Duckworth who work such wonders on the Ford Formula engines — the name means not one man, but two. In fact the "Cos" part of it is the same name — Frank Costin, even though he's no longer with the company. The "Mar" half stands for racing driver, engineer and driving force behind the firm, Jem Marsh, who looked after the business (design and execution) of getting cars that much faster round the track than anybody else's.

The first Marcos appeared back in 1959, and was just as ugly as the present one is striking. Fitted with a series of Marcos-tuned Ford engines from one litre to 1.5 litres the monster was soon wiping the smiles and sneers off other competitors' faces at club race meetings up and down the country. It wasn't long before stories of the car's unique wooden construction began to leak out, and the Marcos legend was born.

Secret of the car's success, apart from careful engine development, was its fantastic lightness — the combination of the two gave a power-to-weight ratio that made drivers' hearts beat faster, and the suspension let them use it to the full on twisty, rutted club circuits. The basic framework

"Racetrack rumors say the Marcos has been known to outhan<u>d</u>le the L*t*s E**n", says Owen.

Instrumentation is lavish, yet precise, small steering wheel complements road-holding ability.

SPORTS CAR WORLD • ROAD TEST

Engine is a tuned Volvo 1800 cc unit with gearbox (OD on top) selected for quality and strength.

consisted of deep box sections built up from sheets of resin-bonded plywood, covered with plywood body panels, using techniques borrowed from De Havilland's super-light ultra-fast balsawood fighter-bomber, the Mosquito of World War II fame. And the idea seemed to work — apart from cutting the weight to racing figures it was strong enough to stand up to racing stresses too. Even if the driver did hit anything hard, the body had such good energy-absorbing properties that it would either bounce back for more or shatter into tiny bits, leaving the driver safe, sound and flabbergasted, sitting on a heap of splinters.

But it wasn't long before Marcos realised that this purely racing outlet was a very limited one, even though it was great fun and of undoubted help to the firm sales and prestige. So that two years ago the firm (minus Costin, who went with the Ford engines) found itself occupying roomy if bizarre premises in a mellow old woollen mill, locked away down the end of a rutted riverside track near Bradford-on-Avon. Conferences were scheduled to take place inside the honey-colored stone walls of the operational HQ, the town's coaching inn, the Swan. And plans were drawn up for producing a new super-luxury road version of the Marcos.

This time it was decided to use composite construction. The body framing was to be made from marine plywood box-sections as before — the main members form an A-frame with the apex at the differential and the two feet at the outside ends of the dashboard. Bonded to this are built-up undertray, seat pans and front bulkhead. But forward of this bulkhead, engine, steering and front suspension are carried on a steel-tube subframe. And to complete the breakaway from the original design, the body itself is moulded in one piece (with extra fittings and lining panels) from fibreglass. And this body wasn't left to chance and function alone — the styling was done by local lad Dennis Adams, with an undoubted flair for pen and drawing board. He even had his own stand at the last Racing Car Show.

But aesthetic appeal isn't the only reason why the Marcos shape is interesting — there are plenty of small details that show the unusual order of priorities lying behind the design. For instance, look at the seating adjustments. There

aren't any. Instead they're fixed into the bodywork, and the steering column and pedal positions are adjustable. And because the seats themselves are deeply padded and set well back in the bodywork in a very prone (almost Grand Prix) position, there's no problem of inadequate location. What problems do occur stem from the height of the firm's directors, both over 6 ft tall. The seats are therefore designed for tall drivers to fit in under the very low roof, so short drivers are provided with a neat detachable seat

cushion to help them see over the wheel.

One advantage of the steeply raked seating is the low overall height this allows. Combined with high ground clearance, this results in low frontal area. As the car's construction keeps weight down too, quite respectable top speed and acceleration can be provided by a medium-size power plant. So instead of following the lead of some British manufacturers in installing American V8s, Marcos has taken the more moderate path of using a medium-tune 1800 cc unit. But not, strangely enough, the cheap and easily obtainable BMC unit used in the MGB, the original TVR, the Gilbern and other sports and GT cars. Instead they use the engine and gearbox from the 1.8 litre Volvo, coupled to a BMC differential. The reason? Says Jem Marsh: "Reliability, sound design and low stresses, and tuning potential."

But cars are like women. It's not so much what's there, it's how it's held up that counts. And the Marcos suspension is a mixture of the conventional and the off-beat. At the front end there's a fairly orthodox arrangement of unequal-length wishbones with concentric coil springs/damper units and an anti-roll bar. But at the back there's a modified de Dion axle, with the telescopic tube carried on twin leading arms and coil spring/damper units. The wheels are driven through fixed-length drive shafts, and on the latest version inboard discs replace the drums on earlier models. So that for the price of complexity, Marcos gets a suspension that's ideal for track work and fast, hard cornering. And to improve the roadholding, the test car had the special Marcos-designed wide-section magnesium wheels with Pirelli Cinturato tyres.

Now to business. As you walk over to the car, you can't help noticing it's no higher than the average seven-year-old child. The big one-piece lid that covers the engine-room is held down by a couple of over-centre clips a la Spitfire, and as the engine itself squats well back in the huge space provided for it, maintenance should be easy enough. Marcos mods to improve the engine's porting arrangements, added by twin Stromberg carburettors, boost power without taking up space. But in spite of the long, slightly uptilted nose, the geometry of the car means that the steering column follows a very distorted path from wheel to wheels.

The doors are push-button actuated — a raised part of the rear edge serves as a handle. But the difficult part comes after you've got the door open. Low seating combined with high door sills make scrambling in at best inelegant, at worst downright pornographic — the only practical technique seems to require edging in backwards, dropping the backside squarely on to the seat squab and swivelling round with the legs tucked neatly in under the chin. But however you manage it, once you're in it's certainly well worth the effort. The seating is superbly comfortable, the position (though it takes some time before it begins to feel natural) is an extremely relaxing one and the controls are laid out sensibly and conveniently. Speedo and tach are right where they should be — in hooded cowls behind the steering-wheel. Steering-column stalk switches look after headlamp dipping and direction indicating, and to the right of the steering column there's a handwheel to look after the foot-pedal adjustment, a pull-out handbrake and a little yellow reminder lamp that unkind people say is the only way you can tell whether the handbrake's on or not.

All the rest of the controls and instruments live in an elaborate central console — at the top a row of dials (fuel gauge, ammeter, oil pressure gauge and water temperature gauge) squats atop a cigar lighter, below which there's room for a radio. Below the radio come the heater controls and below them two buttons control the choke and screenwashers. On each side of this control complex there is a vertical row of three switches. From the top, the left-hand row controls two fog/spotlamps and the two-speed screenwipers — the right-hand row controls panel lights side/head lights and ignition/starting. Behind the console a raised central box sprouts a tiny overdrive switch and a short, stubby gearshift.

Interior finish is pretty good, with all the fibreglass covered up with pvc or padding, all carefully stitched. The only unfinished surface is that surrounding the dials of the instruments, and as that's a separate moulding from the body proper, it has its smooth side outwards so there's never a bit of the hairy underside of the moulded body to be seen. In fact the only give-away is the characteristic smell of the resin bonding — it's not an unpleasant smell and if it worries you, you could always try a stronger after-shave.

Right, that just about covers the statics — now for the dynamics. Twist the key and the engine starts easily enough, with just a subdued faraway rumble to tell you it's idling. Once you've adjusted the pedals — easy, you just turn the handwheel until they feel right and there you are — and the steering column, which means spanners and lid-lifting, you'll find everything (including you) fits very nicely. The take-off is smooth and easy, even though the clutch is on the twitchy side, and the deep-throated roar the engine pushes out under acceleration is a joy to hear. The Marcos isn't a quiet car — but what noise there is sounds purposeful rather than fussy, fragile or disastrous. There's very little body rattle, but there's heaps of wind noise. The engine sounds a little harsh at high revs (6000 rpm plus) but the noise isn't frightening. There's quite a lot of transmission rumble too, but there's mercifully little tendency for the bodywork to drum on harsh surfaces.

The gearbox, taken as it is from a heavy family sedan, has the ratios spread rather more than you might expect on a car like this. But the beefy, mildly-tuned engine is still flexible enough to have plenty of torque low down the range— plenty enough to push the light body along the road at quite respectable speeds without having to play the gearbox or go up to peak revs in each cog. The overdrive switch is small and handily placed, just to the right of the gearshift. And it's only geared to work on top gear too, so that you don't have any of those agonising over-drive - third - or - normal - fourth dilemmas as you hurtle up to a sudden bend at the end of a long, fast straight. The overdrive on the test car was liable to snatch though, especially when dropping back into normal drive, so a spot of left-foot work is recommended. Gearshift movements are short and precise, and pedal travel and positions are such that heeling-and-toeing is easy.

Visibility is good where it really matters. The long, flat nose gives the driver a good idea where the car's limits lie — even cars like this have to park sometime. But it seems to lift slightly when accelerating hard and steep drops in the road surface sometimes disappear out of sight for a few agonising split-seconds. Taking one of the sections of our test track at speed, we found that one sharp bend after a fairly abrupt rise was blotted out long enough to make avoiding action rather interesting. Windscreen pillars are thin enough to give a good view out to either side, and provided you don't take the rear parcels shelf at its word, the mirror will keep you up-to-date on anything that might be able to keep up with you. But the rear corners of the car are very hard to spot — partly because of the gap between side and rear windows and partly because the sharply cut-off back stops you seeing where the bumpers are.

Steering is quick, light and precise, thanks to the rack-and-pinion system used. The wheel is small and handy too — ergonomics experts say that if you ask someone to turn an imaginary wheel they'll tend to place their hands about a foot apart — far less than the diameter of most steering wheels, which are far too big for the forces they demand. The Marcos wheel is 13 in. across, and if you use the cross-hands technique you'll find you can manage most bends without tying your arms in a knot. But — and it's a big but in a GT car that in other ways seems to be ideally suited to long straight runs — the steering is inclined to wander at high speed in a straight line. Since the system itself is inherently precise in spite of the column's contortions — sometimes it can feel too precise, as it does when it feeds road shocks back through to the wheel on bumpy surfaces — it seems likely it's the fault of the car itself, originating either in the suspension or in the aerodynamics of the bodywork. It tends to be aggravated by any periodic bumps like raised lane markings, so keep off the white lines if you like an easy drive.

Another advantage of having a light car is that the brakes have less work to do in stopping it. The test car still had the old mixture, discs at the front and inboard drums at the back, and even though a series of 60 mph crash-stops produced appreciable fade, there was no question of ever running out of brakes. When really hot they tended to pull to the right, though never enough to swing the car right round — enough to make the final braking distance longer than it need have been. The pull-on pistol-grip handbrake was a bit of a failure. It was awkward to release, almost as awkward to use, and it did no more than hold the car at rest on almost level roads.

Handling is happiness itself. It's very, very predictable and that in itself is half the battle — what a car does in a given moment doesn't matter so much if it's expected. Another factor that helps drivers make the most of the handling is the support they get from the seats. Handling is often such a subjective thing that an astute manufacturer can redesign the seats before meddling with the suspension geometry — most motoring journalists will notice they aren't being bounced around so much and they'll call it superior roadholding. And you can't blame them —you're bound to measure the sharpness of a bend by the sideways force you have to exert to stay in your seat, which is why the Marcos has a head start. You're not so much supported by the seats, you're securely boxed in by door and transmission hump so you can't move. Of course this has its disadvantages — spirited wheel-winding can bang your elbow sharply against one side or the other. But as we said, the small wheel and the sensible steering ratio means this doesn't happen very often.

The actual characteristic is very difficult to describe — largely because it's so nearly neutral. There's a slight trace of understeer on gentle bends, but as the radius tightens the wheel movements become smaller and smaller. There's very little body roll and the only sign of strain comes from the tyres as they begin to protest. On very sharp bends taken fast, it's possible to push the tail out, but this is more of an attitude than a movement, in that it doesn't seem to enter an unstable phase, and it's easily corrected. Race-track rumors say the Marcos has been known to outhandle the L*t*s E**n, which should do more than paragraphs of praise to win over the cynics.

What else is there to say about the Marcos? Its obvious breeding, its looks, its performance, its handling will make it a must for many, whatever its defects. But if you're looking for a practical workhorse kind of transport, don't forget it has a tiny boot, it's definitely a two-seater and climbing in and out takes time and effort. The heater's good, but the car stays hot on a warm day. And it's very expensive, for its size. Though not for its performance — in England the Marcos now costs around $6000 as tested, as against $5600 for an E-type Jag. But people don't turn round like that to look at a Jag.

And there are some practical reasons in favor of laying out the extra for the Marcos. Repair jobs are simple, quick and relatively cheap with fibreglass. The company's still small enough, and enthusiastic enough for after-sales service to mean more than a poor part-exchange offer when you get a break-down — and it's reasonable in a country the size of England to take it down to Bradford-on-Avon if something goes seriously wrong. It's fairly easy on the petrol too, with a thirst about equal to that of the Cortina. But when all's said and done, the best reason for buying one is that you have the means, and the desire, to want to enjoy your driving to the utmost. It's a toy car, in the nicest sense of the word. A car to be enjoyed.

But if you do decide on one, make sure your order goes in early. Mass-production has had little effect on Marcos' painstaking workmanship — they have just reached the staggering output of two cars per week.   #

Sports Car—modern style

... maximum enjoyment in complete safety
... very quick ... extremely sure-footed
... boot space not very grand touring ...

WHATEVER officialdom does in its ceaseless quest to suppress the enjoyment of driving it is encouraging that individuality still exists and that there are people who buy cars expressly designed to give enjoyment in complete safety at all speeds. The Marcos is one of these, yet by sporting standards, it is still fairly practical except for the shortage of internal space for shopping oddments (unless you shop alone) and the difficulty of getting in and out. But as high speed comfortable transport for two there are few cars that can match the Marcos for cross-country journeys; most others feel big and clumsy by comparison when you get going on your favourite twisty road.

Not only is it very quick in a straight line—from rest to 60 m.p.h. in 8.7 seconds—but the roadholding is extremely sure-footed and the handling very safe with no hidden vices. It is really a complementary safety factor that the cornering power is so good because the view from the semi-reclining seating position tends to flatten out all corners, making them look faster than they are. This position

takes some getting used to, but apart from the restricted view over hump-back bridges and out of side turnings, there are no problems with visibility, even to the rear.

We tested a Volvo-engined Marcos in June 1965. The overall design is still the same with the monocoque marine-ply chassis underneath the striking glass-fibre body but the Volvo engine has been replaced for the home market by the Ford 1½-litre in-line four. This is available in approximately Cortina GT form, but our test car was the more expensive 1600 model, employing a 1,650 c.c. 120 b.h.p. version tuned by Chris Lawrence; you also get a sunshine roof with the 1600.

The rear suspension too has been revised to use a well located live axle instead of the near de Dion arrangement with its proneness to bump steering. A change to the ventilation system makes it possible to keep cool inside, although the heater output is not very great, and the engine is rather quieter. In fact the changes have removed our major criticisms of the previous model—that it was tiring to drive for long distances due to noise, too much heat and directional instability on bumps.

PRICE: £1,500 plus £360 1s. 6d. purchase tax and surcharge equals £1,860 1s. 6d. Available in component form £1,450.

Marcos 1600

There is still a lot of low speed harshness and the boot space does not allow very grand touring, but as a well equipped closed sports car, the Marcos can be counted a success. The price of the 1600 at £1,860 is evidence of the high cost of individuality in a nation of sheep; at £1,495 in kit form it is better value.

Performance and economy

The cheapest Marcos GT uses the Cortina GT engine as its basis with a pair of Stromberg CDs and minor installation differences, but many people find even this 85 b.h.p. unit (giving 115 b.h.p./ton inadequate and opt for the 1600. This is, in fact, the 1500 engine bored out to 1,650 c.c. and tuned by Chris Lawrence to produce 120 b.h.p. with a modified head and camshaft plus a compound Solex carburetter in which the second choke opens according to manifold pressure, rather than throttle movement. On the reliability side, the pistons are very much lighter than standard and the pushrods (shorter for the shallower head as well as of thinner section) save reciprocating weight and make high revs less of a strain on the valvegear. An uprated oil pump and Vandervell racing bearings complete the "conversion".

Despite the big increase in output we found this hotter version extremely tractable and well able to hold its tune over many hard driven miles. A lumpy tickover and a couple of dents in the power curve at 2,800 and 5,500 r.p.m.—not flatspots, but just a temporary levelling off of power increase—are the only indications that it is not just a mass production unit.

The choke was not connected on the test car, but a couple of dabs on the accelerator pumped enough fuel through for instant cold weather starting. Keeping the revs over 2,500 r.p.m. for the next

Performance

Conditions

Weather: Dry with very light winds 0-6 m.p.h. Temperature 48°F. Barometer 29.85 in. Hg. Surface: Dry concrete and tarmacadam. Fuel: Super premium 101 octane (R.M.)

Maximum speeds

	m.p.h.
Mean of opposite runs	117.0
Best one-way ¼-mile	120.0
3rd gear	82.5
2nd gear } at 6,500 r.p.m.	57.0
1st gear	39.0

"Maximile" speed: (Timed quarter mile after 1 mile accelerating from rest)
Mean: 110.0
Best 114.0

Acceleration times

m.p.h.	sec.
0-30	3.1
0-40	4.6
0-50	6.6
0-60	8.7
0-70	11.2
0-80	14.0
0-90	18.3
0-100	24.3
0-110	33.9
Standing quarter mile	16.4

m.p.h.	Top sec.	3rd sec.
10-30	—	6.3
20-40	9.1	6.4
30-50	11.0	5.4
40-60	9.9	4.5
50-70	7.7	4.9
60-80	8.1	5.5

70-90	8.9	7.3
80-100	11.0	
90-110	16.0	—

Hill climbing

At steady speed		lb./ton
Top	1 in 6.9	(Tapley 320)
3rd	1 in 4.8	(Tapley 460)
2nd	1 in 3.3	(Tapley 640)

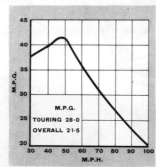

M.P.G.
TOURING 28·0
OVERALL 21·5

Fuel consumption

Touring (consumption midway between 30 m.p.h. and maximum less 5% allowance for acceleration) . . . . 28.0 m.p.g.
Overall . . . . 21.5 m.p.g.
(= 13.1 litres/100 km.)
Total test distance . . . . 1.525 miles
Tank capacity (maker's figure) . . . . . 10 gal.

Brakes

Pedal pressure, deceleration and equivalent stopping distance from 30 m.p.h.

lb.	g	ft.
25	0.12	250
50	0.35	86
75	0.62	48½
100	0.88	34
130	0.98	30½
Handbrake	0.33	90

Fade test

20 stops at ½g deceleration at 1 min. intervals from a speed midway between 30 m.p.h. and maximum speed (=73½ m.p.h.)

	lb.
Pedal force at beginning	71
Pedal force at 10th stop	67
Pedal force at 20th stop	68

Steering

Turning circle between kerbs:	ft.
Left	29½
Right	28
Turns of steering wheel from lock to lock	2.8

Steering wheel deflection for 50 ft. diameter circle . . . . . 0.8 turns

Clutch

Free pedal movement . . . . = ⅜ in.
Additional movement to disengage clutch completely . . . . . . =3½ in.
Maximum pedal load . . . . =28 lb.

Speedometer

Indicated	10	20	30	40	50	60	70	80	90	100	110
True	11	20½	31	41½	51½	61	71	80	89	99	108

Distance recorder . . . . ½% fast

Weight

Kerb weight (unladen with fuel for approximately 50 miles) . . . . 14.8 cwt.
Front/rear distribution 51/49
Weight laden as tested . . . . 18.6 cwt.

Parkability

Gap needed to clear a 6 ft. wide obstruction parked in front

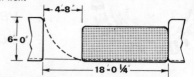

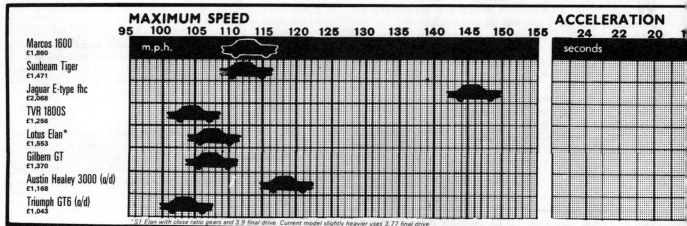

	MAXIMUM SPEED m.p.h.	ACCELERATION seconds
Marcos 1600 £1,860		
Sunbeam Tiger £1,471		
Jaguar E-type fhc £2,068		
TVR 1800S £1,256		
Lotus Elan* £1,553		
Gilbern GT £1,370		
Austin Healey 3000 (o/d) £1,168		
Triumph GT6 (o/d) £1,043		

S1 Elan with close ratio gears and 3.9 final drive. Current model slightly heavier uses 3.77 final drive.

The driver's seat is one of the lower parts of an already low car which stands at 3ft. 6½ins. All round visibility is good on the open road but a bit restricted on humps and in town.

Sunshine roof is standard on the 1600; it folds down well and is sufficiently taut not to chatter. When open it is substantially draught free.

The seats do not look as reclining as they feel; they are extremely comfortable. There are pockets in each door which can take small oddments. The courtesy light is placed between the two seats and is good for map reading. Gear lever is within finger tip reach of the wheel.

(Right) View of the only place inside where you can put any luggage. The seat belt anchorages are exceptionally well placed. The box on the far side is the radio speaker. The fire extinguisher reflects in the rear screen and obstructs the mirror image.

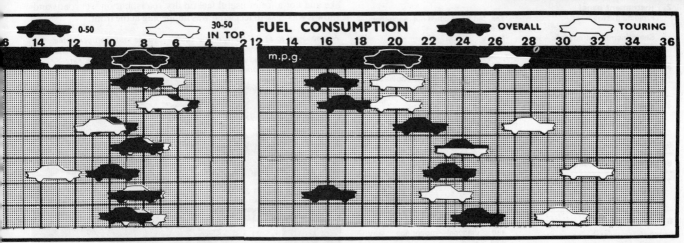

FUEL CONSUMPTION

0-50   30-50 IN TOP   OVERALL   TOURING

16 14 12 10 8 6 4 2   12 14 16 18 20 22 24 26 28 30 32 34 36

m.p.g.

Marcos 1600

The body style is identical with the one tested in July 1965, but there are numerous detail changes; among them is the extractor vent in the rear screen.

mile or so soon brought the engine to running temperature. After that it is as happy to pull from 1,000 r.p.m. in top on part throttle as it is to sing up to the recommended 6,500 r.p.m. at full chat. At a steady 30 m.p.h. there was unpleasant transmission snatch, probably because the carburetter was operating in the region which gives the lumpy tickover (on the idling jet), so low is the rolling resistance.

Our overall fuel consumption of 21.5 m.p.g. is more representative of a Continental freedom from speed restrictions, but in this country we found 25 m.p.g. well within reach on long out-of-town runs, despite making full use of the impressive acceleration. We used 101-octane fuel for our testing, but the engine still ran-on for several seconds after switching off although there was no pinking.

To get the best figures in our standing starts we were permitted to use 7,000 r.p.m., which just allows 60 m.p.h. in second gear, and the unit did not sound overworked at this speed. To reach 60 m.p.h. in under 9 seconds is fast by any standards. Some seven years ago it required well over 3-litres and twin overhead camshafts to do 0-100 m.p.h. in under 25 seconds but the pushrod Marcos can do it quite easily on 1,650 c.c., reaching 100 m.p.h. in 24.3 seconds. For maximum speed we used the high speed banked circuit at MIRA, although in days pre-Castle we tested 100 m.p.h. cars on straight roads. Even so, a lap at 114.6 m.p.h. felt entirely stable and the maximum we have quoted is the mean speed on three straights. On a long flat road the Marcos could probably work up to 120 m.p.h. but this is well beyond its power peak.

Despite the hard driving, oil consumption (which had been rather heavy in development) proved to be a very moderate 490 miles per pint.

Transmission

Several people felt that this was one of the best installations of the Cortina GT box with its uprated second gear. The lever is well placed on the tunnel and the left hand drops on to it naturally; the selection was a little vague, as happens when these boxes get worn, but the current Marcos will have the latest Cortina GT box with the same ratios but a far more positive feel to the lever; on the Corsair 2000E the same gearbox was rated as excellent (road test next week).

In our first attempt at standing starts the clutch slipped without the wheels spinning so we had to use fewer revs, letting the clutch in at nearer 3,000 r.p.m. There was no clutch slip on fast gear changes but it prevented an easy start on a 1-in-3 hill; the Marcos made it, but only just. On a car which has not been used for development there is no reason for the clutch to slip at all. The pedal pressure required is light but the movement is quite long, a controlling factor in fixing the position of the adjustable pedals.

The ratios suit the car well, giving maxima in the gears of 39, 57, and 82½ m.p.h. This makes second a very useful overtaking gear and ease of selection encourages its frequent use. The standard final drive ratio is 3.77/1 (as used on Corsairs and Lotus Cortinas); the car would probably be even faster with higher gearing and a 3.545 ratio is available. The gearbox was quiet, but final drive whine was noticeable at steady speeds up to about 50 m.p.h.

It must be remembered when comparing the performance of the Volvo-engined Marcos 1800 and this car that the former used the lower final drive ratio plus an overdrive, which effectively gave five well-spaced ratios instead of the current four; this made the 1800 slightly faster up to 80 m.p.h. but marginally slower thereafter.

Handling and brakes

If the Marcos didn't handle well there would be little point in having one, since it is designed to be the ultimate in sports cars and handling is just as big a consideration as acceleration and braking. On all accounts the outcome is well up with the design.

If you can get one of the better family saloons through a given corner at 50 m.p.h. when driving fast you can probably take the Marcos through at 60 m.p.h. in the wet and wonder why you took it so gently. Its dry roadholding on fast bends is really beyond the roadgoing limit, except for experts on open corners, and even on tighter corners, where there is just enough surplus power to slide the tail, the car needs no more correction than a premature straightening of the wheel.

Several factors are responsible for such good manners. The centre of gravity is very low, which allows one to select springs which let the suspension work without generating high roll angles, and the live rear axle is very well located, with a Panhard rod and unusual leading arms. Consequently there is no tendency to tramp or hop on bumpy corners nor to dart around on the straights which was a tiresome feature of the previous layout. Also the Marcos is fitted with Pirelli Cinturatos of a useful section which give extremely good adhesion in both wet and dry conditions. Unless the road is greasy, rather than just wet, it is difficult to get wheelspin from a standing start.

High geared steering with radial ply tyres gives immediate response and it is difficult to detect any under- or oversteering characteristic—it just follows a predicted line until the tail eventually comes round. There is more kick-back than we would like and not a lot of useful feel on dry roads, but on wet roads and snow it was easy to feel what was happening at the front.

We managed to fit 2.6 cu.ft. of our square luggage into the uncarpeted boot, which is not very grand touring. The toolkit is of good quality and comprehensive. A lead hammer is used on the three-eared hub nuts— wire wheels being standard.

Safety check list

1	**Steering assembly**	
	Steering box position	Ahead of wheel centres
	Steering column collapsible?	Two universal joints
	Steering wheel boss padded?	No
2	**Instrument panel**	
	Projecting switches?	Yes, but head could not reach them in accident
	Sharp instrument cowls?	No
	Effective padding?	Yes, above and below facia
3	**Door structure**	
	Interior handles, winders, etc.	Door handle projects; windows are sliding
4	**Ejection**	
	Anti-burst door locks?	No
	Child-proof door locks?	No, but two doors only
5	**Windscreen**	Laminated
6	**Windscreen pillars**	Firm cloth covering
7	**Driving mirror**	
	Framed?	Yes
	Collapsible?	Yes
8	**Safety harness**	Anchorage points standard for lap and diagonal—mountings very well placed

14" × 11" × 5"

17½" × 13" × 6"

The brakes were a bit spongy but reasonably light for normal use; we had to use 130 lb. pressure for the best stop, by which time the rear wheels had locked up and the tail started to slew. There was no fade; unfortunately the water splash was empty when we were testing so we cannot comment on their recovery from a soaking but we had no trouble on the road. The handbrake was slightly better than with the previous car, but still would not hold the car on a 1-in-4 hill.

Comfort and controls

The Marcos is unusual in that the seats are fixed; different drivers can be accommodated by adjusting the steering column (with a spanner under the bonnet) and the pedals (bodily with a knurled wheel on the right of the column). The position is very comfortable as you lie back in the seat with arms outstretched; it is even comfortable once you get used to it, to rest your neck on the headrest; since there is no pitching, there is no tendency to jerk your head forward on each bump.

People over 6ft. tall found that they could see forward quite well, but smaller drivers needed the auxiliary cushion/backrest to be able to see comfortably over the high scuttle. This lessened the excellent side and shoulder support, but if you are running your own car it should be quite easy to adjust the cushion height without additional bolsters, although the latter may be necessary if smaller people are also going to drive. The range of steering column and pedal adjustment is good for all sizes.

At speed out of town the ride is good, swallowing up undulations without unpleasant movement but in town every bump is felt and there is a fair amount of radial ply tyre thump at these speeds. On our hard worn test car, there was also a rattle somewhere in the rear but this was never traced.

Despite the very shallow rear window, visibility through it is good with the panoramic mirror, and in traffic the rear quarter is sufficiently narrow not to constitute a blind spot if you are looking

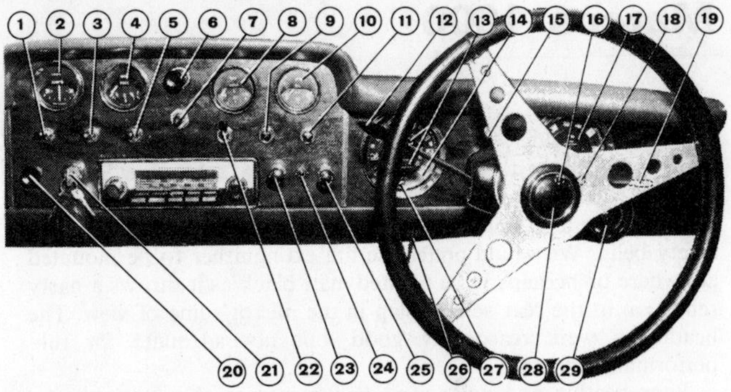
1
2
3
4
5
6
7
8
9
10
11
12
13
14
15
16
17
18
19
20
21
22
23
24
25
26
27
28
29

1, spare. 2, ammeter. 3, spare. 4, fuel gauge. 5, reversing light. 6, cigar lighter. 7, washer button. 8, water temperature gauge. 9, wiper switch. 10, oil pressure gauge. 11, panel light switch. 12, lighting stalk. 13, total and trip mileage recorders. 14, speedometer. 15, reversing light tell-tale. 16, dynamo charge warning light. 17, tachometer. 18, indicator tell-tale. 19, indicator stalk. 20, choke. 21, ignition/starter key. 22, lighting switch. 23, heater air control. 24, blower fan. 25, heater temperature control. 26, trip zero. 27, main beam tell-tale. 28, horn. 29, pedal adjuster.

Specification

Engine

Cylinders	4
Bore and stroke	85 mm. x 72.8 mm.
Cubic capacity	1,650 c.c.
Valves	pushrod o.h.v.
Compression ratio	10.5:1
Carburetter	Solex PAIA 24/28 pressure compound
Fuel pump	AC mechanical
Oil filter	Fram full flow
Max. power (net)	120 b.h.p. at 5,400 r.p.m.
Max. torque (net)	126 lb.ft. at 3,500 r.p.m.

Transmission

Clutch	Borg and Beck 7¼ in. s.d.p.
Top gear (s/m)	1.0
3rd gear (s/m)	1.397
2nd gear (s/m)	2.010
1st gear (s/m)	2.972
Reverse	3.324
Final drive	Hypoid bevel 3.77/1
M.p.h. at 1,000 r.p.m. in:—	
Top gear	17.7
3rd gear	12.7
2nd gear	8.8
1st gear	6.0

Chassis

Construction	Marine ply monocoque chassis with glass fibre body.

Brakes

Type	Hydraulic disc front/drum rear.
Dimensions	9⅝ in. disc, 9 in. drums
Friction areas:	
Front	22.2 sq. in. of lining operating on 197 sq. in. of disc
Rear	48.0 sq.ins. of lining operating on 96.1 sq.ins. of drum

Suspension and steering

Front	Independent with unequal length wishbones and anti-roll bar—coil springs.
Rear	Live axle located longitudinally by two lower leading links and one upper leading link and transversely by a Panhard rod—coil springs.
Shock absorbers: Front / Rear	Woodhead-telescopic
Steering gear	Alford and Alder rack and pinion
Tyres	Pirelli Cinturato 165-13
Rim size	4½J-13

Coachwork and equipment

Starting handle	None
Jack	Scissors type with ratchet handle
Jacking points	One under each door sill
Battery	12 volt positive earth, 38 amp. hrs. capacity
Number of electrical fuses	Two
Indicators	Self cancelling flashers
Screen wipers	Single speed electric
Screen washers	Manual plunger
Sun visors	Two
Locks:	
With ignition key	Doors
With other keys	One for boot, another for bonnet
Interior heater	Smiths fresh air
Extras	Wider mag. alloy wheels, chrome plated wire wheels, radio, safety belts, brake servo, fog lights, reversing light, laminated screen, air horns, supplementary seat cushions
Upholstery	Cirrus and Ambla leathercloth
Floor covering	Carpet
Alternative body styles	None

Maintenance

Sump	6¼ pints S.A.E. 20/50 (Duckhams or Castrol)
Gearbox	1¾ pints S.A.E. 80 EP
Rear axle	2 pints S.A.E. 90 hypoid gear
Steering gear	Castrolease LM or equivalent
Cooling system	13 pints (drain taps 2)
Chassis lubrication	Every 6,000 miles to 3 points
Minimum service interval	3,000 miles
Ignition timing	T.d.c.
Contact breaker gap	0.013 ins.
Sparking plug gap	0.028 ins.
Sparking plug type	Champion N3
Tappet clearances hot/cold	Inlet 0.012/0.015 in., Exhaust 0.012/0.015 in.
Valve timing:	
Inlet opens	36° b.t.d.c.
Inlet closes	70° a.b.d.c.
Exhaust opens	68° b.b.d.c.
Exhaust closes	34° a.t.d.c.
Front wheel toe-in	⅛ in.
Camber angle	0°
Castor angle	6½°
Kingpin inclination	8°
Tyre pressures	24 lb/sq.in. front and rear

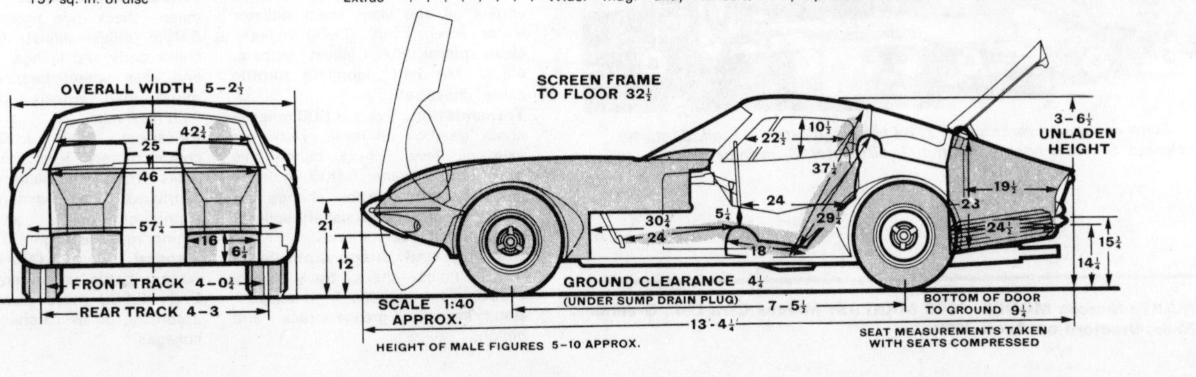
OVERALL WIDTH 5-2½
42¾
25
46
57¼
16
6½
FRONT TRACK 4-0½
REAR TRACK 4-3
21
12
SCALE 1:40 APPROX.
HEIGHT OF MALE FIGURES 5-10 APPROX.
SCREEN FRAME TO FLOOR 32½
22½
10½
37½
24
5¼
30½
24
29½
18
GROUND CLEARANCE 4¼
(UNDER SUMP DRAIN PLUG)
7-5½
13'-4¼
3-6½ UNLADEN HEIGHT
19½
23
24½
15¾
14¼
BOTTOM OF DOOR TO GROUND 9¼
SEAT MEASUREMENTS TAKEN WITH SEATS COMPRESSED

Marcos 1600

over your shoulder, although there is some distortion where the curvature is largest. When emerging from a side street in busy traffic it is possible and useful to lean right forward, as the bonnet sticks out quite a long way, but this is not possible when wearing safety belts. We would prefer the fire extinguisher to be mounted elsewhere or perhaps to be painted matt black as it throws a nasty reflection in the rear screen, slap in the mirror's line of view. The headlights were reasonably good, but not adequate for full-performance driving.

Poor heating and noise were bad points on the previous car. Noise is now much less and the heating not so uncontrolled. Most of the noise comes from the exhaust and obtrudes in hard acceleration and at speeds over 80 m.p.h. or so, but we understand that most of the sound deadening material had been blown out of this exhaust system, and that future production cars should be rather quieter. There is some wind noise which could probably be cured by padding the seals out to press more effectively against the doors; this would also reduce the draughts which appeared only when the sunshine roof was open. Otherwise this roof was very effective without producing buffeting, even at 100 m.p.h., if the side windows were kept closed. At normal cruising speeds the noise level was acceptable and the radio only became difficult to hear at over 100 m.p.h.

The heating modifications are less satisfactory. The stifling heat from the engine on the previous model has been reduced and the interior can now be kept at a reasonable overall tem-

The windows have simple pulls glued to them; they are fastened by thumb screws in the window channel.

perature. But in cold weather our toes froze since the heater outlets are at about knee level and the rather poor supply of warm air goes to the driver's head rather than his feet, making the atmosphere rather stuffy. There is little ram effect as the intake is sited under the bonnet behind the radiator so that the fan is frequently in use—something a private owner might well sort out to his own satisfaction when building a kit car.

Fittings and furniture

The facia has been completely revised in a more traditional wooden style but the switches are still unlabelled; being in rows of three they are difficult to find accurately. As a start we would put an extension on the wiper—the central of the right hand three. The Standard Triumph headlight stalk, with its three positions for side, main and dipped beams is still confusing to some as it is easy to turn off by mistake when coming up on to main beam. The handbrake is reasonably placed alongside the tunnel in front of the driver's seat but we scratched several knuckles on an adjacent screw head until we stopped putting the hand on the left of the lever. The instruments are all well placed, although some of the rev counter figures disappear under the facia top.

There is little room inside the car for more than a briefcase and a few other flat objects, which can be held by the seat backs on the rear parcel shelf, or small items can fit in the door pockets or in the glove locker. The boot will take quite a reasonable size of suitcase together with a soft bag or two, but there should be a flat floor over the spare wheel.

The general interior layout is well planned and the trim attractively finished. The stiff windows have pulls and little finger screws to fasten them; this is a reasonable economy of space to give more elbow room but nevertheless rather crude for such an expensive car.

Servicing and maintenance

The 500-mile service schedule has about the most comprehensive check list we have ever seen, presumably so that home built cars can be thoroughly examined by professional mechanics. Apart from that, servicing every 3,000 miles is well within the scope of the private owner and the hotter engine has no additional requirements. The toolkit is a high quality set of Britool equipment which covers any on-the-road use; a lead hammer is supplied for the three-eared hub nuts. Accessibility is good aided by the forward hinging bonnet, which needs a key to open it.

1, Solex compound carburetter. 2, oil filler. 3, dipstick. 4, coil. 5, starter solenoid. 6, petrol filter and pump. 7, distributor. 8, radiator filler.

Routine service

Engine. Every 3,000 miles—change engine oil and filter, check radiator water level. Every 6,000 miles—clean petrol filter, adjust tappets, adjust fan belt, lubricate throttle cable, choke, etc.

Transmission. Every 3,000 miles—check gearbox oil level, check rear axle oil level, check clutch free movement. Every 6,000 miles—drain and refill gearbox, change rear axle oil, grease propshaft splines, check clutch reservoir level.

Steering and suspension. Every 3,000 miles—check track. Every 6,000 miles—grease front suspension swivels, grease rack and pinion.

Wheels and brakes. Every 3,000 miles—check tyre pressures. Every 6,000 miles—adjust brakes and check pads and linings, check front and rear wheel bearings, change round road wheels, check brake fluid reservoir.

Electrical. Every 3,000 miles—check battery level. Every 6,000 miles—replace plugs, lubricate distributor and dynamo, check distributor points and ignition timing, reset headlights.

General. Every 3,000 miles—refill washer bottle, wash down engine. Every 6,000 miles—lubricate pedal assembly, oil all catches, locks and linkages.

MAKE: Marcos MODEL: 1600 MAKERS: Marcos Cars Ltd., Greenland Mills, Bradford-on-Avon, Wilts.

MARCOS

> **ENGINE CAPACITY** 51.74 cu in, 848 cu cm
> **FUEL CONSUMPTION** 45 m/imp gal, 37.3 m/US gal, 6.3 l × 100 km
> **SEATS** 2 **MAX SPEED** 85 mph, 136.8 km/h
> **PRICE IN GB** basic £ 760, total £ 945

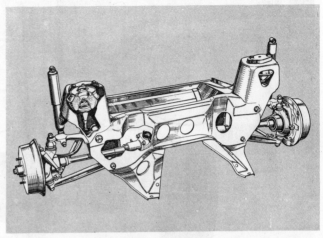

Independent front suspension

ENGINE front, 4 stroke; cylinders: 4, transverse, in line; bore and stroke: 2.48 × 2.69 in, 63 × 68.3 mm; engine capacity: 51.74 cu in, 848 cu cm; compression ratio: 8.3; max power (SAE): 34 hp at 5,500 rpm; max torque (SAE): 44 lb ft, 6.1 kg m at 2,960 rpm; max engine rpm: 5,800; specific power: 40.1 hp/l; cylinder block: cast iron; cylinder head: cast iron; crankshaft bearings: 3; valves: 2 per cylinder, overhead, push-rods and rockers; camshafts: 1, side; lubrication: gear pump, full flow filter; lubricating system capacity: 8.80 imp pt, 10.57 US pt, 5 l; carburation: 2 SU type HS 2 semi-downdraught carburettors; fuel feed: electric pump; cooling system: water; cooling system capacity: 6.25 imp pt, 7.40 US pt, 3.6 l.

TRANSMISSION driving wheels: front; clutch: single dry plate (diaphragm); gearbox: mechanical; gears: 4 + reverse; synchromesh gears: II, III, IV; gearbox ratios: I 3.627, II 2.172, III 1.412, IV 1, rev 3.627; gear lever: central; final drive: helical spur gears; axle ratio: 3.765.

CHASSIS integral in plastic material; front suspension: independent, wishbones, rubber cone springs, telescopic dampers; rear suspension: independent, swinging longitudinal trailing arms, rubber cone springs, telescopic dampers.

STEERING rack-and-pinion; turns of steering wheel lock to lock: 2.25.

BRAKES drum.

ELECTRICAL EQUIPMENT voltage: 12 V; battery: 34 Ah; generator type: dynamo, 240 W; ignition distributor: Lucas; headlamps: 2.

DIMENSIONS AND WEIGHT wheel base: 80 in, 2,032 mm; front track: 47.44 in, 1,205 mm; rear track: 47.87 in, 1,216 mm; overall length: 136.50 in, 3,467 mm; overall width: 56.50 in, 1,435 mm; overall height: 39 in, 991 mm; ground clearance: 5 in, 127 mm; dry weight: 1,176 lb, 533 kg; turning circle (between walls): 31.7 ft, 9.7 m; width of rims: 3.5''; tyres: 5.20 × 10; fuel tank capacity: 6 imp gal, 7.1 US gal, 27 l.

BODY coupé; doors: 2; seats: 2.

PERFORMANCE max speeds: 24 mph, 38.6 km/h in 1st gear; 40 mph, 64.4 km/h in 2nd gear; 62 mph, 99.8 km/h in 3rd gear; 85 mph, 136.8 km/h in 4th gear; power-weight ratio: 34.6 lb/hp, 15.7 kg/hp; carrying capacity: 353 lb, 160 kg; speed in direct drive at 1,000 rpm: 15 mph, 24.1 km/h.

PRACTICAL INSTRUCTIONS fuel: 90 oct petrol; engine sump oil: 8.45 imp pt, 10.15 US pt, 4.8 l, SAE 20 (winter) 50 (summer), change every 6,000 miles, 9,700 km; gearbox and final drive oil: 8.45 imp pt, 10.15 US pt, 4.8 l, SAE 10W-20 (winter) 20W-30 (summer), change every 6,000 miles, 9,700 km; greasing: every 3,000 miles, 4,800 km, 8 points; tappet clearances: inlet 0.006 in, 0.15 mm, exhaust 0.006 in, 0.15 mm; valve timing: inlet opens 5° before tdc and closes 45° after bdc, exhaust opens 40° before bdc and closes 10° after tdc; normal tyre pressure: front 22 psi, 1.5 atm, rear 20 psi, 1.4 atm.

A car which is used entirely around London . . .

Lawrencetune Marcos

IT'S funny how often pre-conceived notions get shattered; we were offered this fuel injected five speed Marcos for test and told that the customer who owned the car was a lady who used it entirely around London. So we got visions of a nice tractable King's Road burner, plenty of low speed torque and of course the eye catching car pottering along the Chelsea highway making contented little burbles to itself. Since then we have driven the car for nearly 500 miles mostly out of town and can't imagine how anyone could treat it as a pure traffic-light dicer. Make no mistake, it's fast furious and fun out of town, but in the commuter jam bottom gear is too high, idling for any length of time is uncertain and to cap it all the car has left hand drive.

Basically the specification is the same as on the Marcos 1600 we tested in April 1967, with the non-Heron headed Cortina engine stretched to 1650 c.c. with a rather special cam and the ability to use around 7,000 r.p.m. This car had the Tecalemit Jackson fuel injection system and a Hewland five speed gear set in its standard Cortina gearbox casing; the injection system certainly gave more power, witness maximile and maximum speeds, but the five speed box has ratios more suited to the track and a rev. limit of 9,000

r.p.m. than to a road car, so the acceleration improvement wasn't quite as great as it might have been, but 0-60 m.p.h. in 8.1 s. does require more horses.

Most T-J systems have a cold start device which supplies more petrol to the continuous flow circuit, but this one didn't, so starting involved quite a lot of churning even after a pause to allow the Bendix pump to prime the circuit. After a while the engine catches but wants to die if you use the throttle so you have to let it tick over at 1,000 r.p.m. or so before blipping, and then suddenly a spit and a splutter and all is clear. Once clear no more choke would be needed even if there were one, so the cold start device would appear to be necessary only for the initial firing up. Warm starting only requires a bit of throttle and rather less churning.

Despite its lumpy tickover—about 2,000 r.p.m. as you come to rest before dropping down to 1,000 r.p.m. after five seconds or so —the unit is really quite tractable. It will hold 20 m.p.h. in top and even pull up to 30 m.p.h. or so, but as on the standard car the cam seems to have a curious flat area at 2,500 r.p.m. which it takes a bit of spluttering to get through. This makes the 30-50 m.p.h. time the slowest of the lot; once through that the engine really develops a lot

of power from 3,500 r.p.m. onwards, the noise changing from a purely mechanical one up to 5,500 r.p.m. to the curious rattle which open intake trumpets seem to generate up to 7,000 r.p.m., a noise which is exhilirating initially but a little wearing on a fast cross country run.

The overall fuel consumption worked out rather heavier than with the standard car partly because testing occupied a greater proportion of the total mileage and partly because the extra performance was certainly used—even with fuel injection you don't get something for nothing. However a shorter spell of hard cross country stuff out of town returned over 20 m.p.g. which was pretty favourable.

Hewland's five speed box takes a little learning. There isn't enough room inside to get five speeds *and* synchromesh so you have to put up with dog clutches which are fine once you get on the move and don't dither between ratios, but can be a little obstructive on the line. If you look at the gate pattern (2,3,4 and 5 in the conventional 4-speed positions with 1st back on the right), you will see that the 1-2 change is a major navigational exercise across the gate, and this is coupled with the fact that these ratios are very widely spaced; in the next

This particular model has lefthand drive.

Left: One of the smallest cross sections on the road.

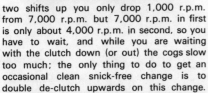

Right: The T-J fuel injection system looks relatively simple.

two shifts up you only drop 1,000 r.p.m. from 7,000 r.p.m. but 7,000 r.p.m. in first is only about 4,000 r.p.m. in second, so you have to wait, and while you are waiting with the clutch down (or out) the cogs slow too much; the only thing to do to get an occasional clean snick-free change is to double de-clutch upwards on this change.

Once into second however, you are into a normal four speed gate of ultra close ratios with the change getting cleaner the faster you move your hand up or down. The only disadvantage of the ultra close ratios is that you frequently have to drop two cogs if you want snap acceleration, or you might get stuck in the dreaded 2,500 r.p.m. band with no power when you want it. All of which seemed to us to make the car far from bird-proof, but great fun to us highly intelligent specimens of homo sapiens. However we understand that madam loves the car and doesn't hang around once she gets going, so perhaps we underrated her. She certainly quoted the maximum speed fairly accurately which we hadn't quite got the nerve to check on a damp banked track at MIRA—our figure is worked out from rev. counter readings seen on the straights. A true maximum may well be 125 m.p.h. plus.

Other fitments in the car included a radio,

tape recorder (not of the instant variety) and sunshine roof (surprisingly draught free). However listening had to be confined to speeds under about 60 m.p.h. due to the combination of mechanical and wind noises.

The only other changes were 175-13 Firestone F100s on 5½J Minilite wheels. It was the first time we had used these tyres on a high performance car and they are certainly well up to the general Marcos roadholding. The car had been used to demonstrate T-J equipment at Silverstone where the pressures were raised to over 30 psi; it wasn't until we dropped them to a more respectable level that we realized that the suspension wasn't so harsh—ride and roadholding have reached really quite a reasonable compromise and the back axle is well enough behaved not to leap around on bumpy corners.

As ever we all thoroughly enjoyed belting around the countryside and playing tunes on the gearbox but driving in town wasn't such fun, particularly when the clutch pedal needs such a long travel. However Lawrence-tune only give the customers what they want, and this one's happy.

■

Performance comparisons

	Marcos 1600TJ	Marcos 1600
maximum	122 mph.	117 mph.
maximile	115.4	110.0
best	118.5	114.0
acceleration from rest		
0–30 mph.	2.9 sec	3.1 sec
40	4.1	4.6
50	6.1	6.6
60	8.1	8.7
70	10.6	11.2
80	13.6	14.0
90	17.4	18.3
100	23.0	24.3
110	29.8	33.9
ss. ¼m.	16.2	16.4
overall fuel cons.	17.9 mpg.	21.5 mpg.

Gear ratios	Standard	Hewland
1st gear	2.972	3.048
2nd	2.010	1.78
3rd	1.397	1.47
4th	1.00	1.21
5th	—	1.00

Prices: Marcos 1500 £1,664. Engine modifications to increase to 1,650 c.c., improved camshaft, etc., £130. Tecalemit Jackson fuel injection system £90. Hewland five speed gearbox £120. Total with performance extras £2,004.

The test Marcos 1600 was fitted with considerable extra equipment. Apart from the standard Webasto sun roof, which made driving more comfortable in hot weather, this included Cibié fog lamps incorporating flashing indicators and side lamps, and magnesium alloy wheels.

MARCOS 1600 GT
1,599 c.c.

Radio suppression equipment (another extra) masks the engine; the fully instrumented cockpit requires a reclining driving position

PERFORMANCE

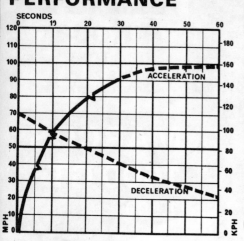

MAXIMUM SPEEDS

Gear	mph	kph	rpm
Top (mean)	109	175	6,120
(best)	112	180	6,300
3rd	80	129	6,300
2nd	56	90	6,300
1st	38	61	6,300

Standing ¼-mile 17.6 sec 76 mph
Standing kilometre 33.3 sec 92 mph

MOTORWAY CRUISING

Error	
(ind. speed at 70 mph)	75mph
Engine	
(rpm at 70 mph)	3,930 rpm
(mean piston speed)	2,000 ft/min
Fuel (mpg at 70 mph)	27.8 mpg
Passing (50-70)	7.0 sec
Noise (per cent silent at 70 mph)	35 per cent

CONSUMPTION

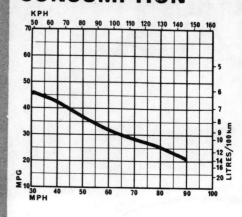

TIME IN SECONDS	3.6	5.7	8.0	11.4	15.0	22.0	29.1
TRUE SPEED MPH	30	40	50	60	70	80	90	100
INDICATED SPEED	35	45	55	65	75	86	100	110

Mileage recorder 1.7 per cent over-reading.
Test distance 891 miles. Figures taken at 9,500 miles by our own staff at the Motor Industry Research Association proving ground at Nuneaton.

SPEED RANGE, GEAR RATIOS AND TIME IN SECONDS

mph	Top (3.77)	3rd (5.27)	2nd (8.86)	1st (11.19)
10-30	—	7.1	4.6	3.1
20-40	11.1	6.3	3.8	—
30-50	10.9	5.8	4.5	—
40-60	9.3	5.8	—	—
50-70	8.4	6.8	—	—
60-80	9.9	10.3	—	—
70-90	13.5	—	—	—

FUEL

(At constant speeds—mpg)	
30 mph	46.5
40 mph	42.1
50 mph	36.4
60 mph	32.3
70 mph	27.8
80 mph	25.1
90 mph	21.1

Typical mpg 25 (11.3 litres/100km)
Calculated (DIN) mpg   30.5 (9.3 litres/100km)
Overall mpg 21.5 (13.1 litres/100km)
Grade of fuel: Premium, 4-star (min 97RM)

OIL

SAE 20/50. Negligible.

HOW THE CAR COMPARES

Maximum Speed (mph)

90 — 100 — 110 — 120 — 130

- Marcos 1600
- Alfa-Romeo GTV (1600)
- Lotus Elan SE
- Reliant Scimitar 3-litre
- TVR Vixen 1600

0-60 mph (sec)

20 — 10 — 0

- Marcos 1600
- Alfa-Romeo GTV (1600)
- Lotus Elan SE
- Reliant Scimitar 3-litre
- TVR Vixen 1600

Standing Start ¼-mile (sec)

30 — 20 — 10

- Marcos 1600
- Alfa-Romeo GTV (1600)
- Lotus Elan SE
- Reliant Scimitar 3-litre
- TVR Vixen 1600

MPG Overall

10 — 20 — 30

- Marcos 1600
- Alfa-Romeo GTV (1600)
- Lotus Elan SE
- Reliant Scimitar 3-litre
- TVR Vixen 1600

PRICES

Marcos 1600 GT	**£1,919**
Alfa Romeo GTV (1600)	£2,248
Lotus Elan SE	£1,902
Reliant Scimitar 3-litre	£1,576
TVR Vixen 1600	£1,387

TEST CONDITIONS: Weather: Dry, cloudy. Wind: 5-10 mph. Temperature: 17 deg. C. (63 deg. F.). Barometer: 29.65in Hg. Humidity: 56 per cent. Surfaces: Dry concrete and asphalt.

WEIGHT: Kerb weight: 14.5cwt (1,630lb-740kg) (with oil, water and half-full fuel tank). Distribution, per cent F, 49.3; R, 50.7. Laden as tested: 18.2cwt (2,042lb-927kg).

TURNING CIRCLES

Between kerbs: L, 34ft 0in.; R, 33ft 2in.
Between walls: L, 34ft 7in.; R, 33ft 9in.
Steering wheel turns. lock to lock: 2.5

PERFORMANCE SUMMARY

Mean maximum speed	109 mph
Standing start ¼-mile	17.6 sec
0-60 mph	11.4 sec
30-70 mph (through gears)	11.4 sec
Typical fuel consumption	25 mpg
Miles per tankful	250

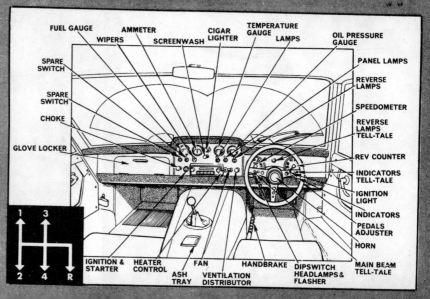

BRAKES

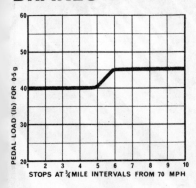

STOPS AT ¾ MILE INTERVALS FROM 70 MPH

(from 30 mph in neutral)

Load	g	Distance
20lb	0.26	116ft
40lb	0.54	56ft
60lb	0.78	39ft
80lb	1.0	30.1ft
Handbrake	26	116ft

Max. Gradient: 1 in 4

Clutch Pedal 35lb and 6in.

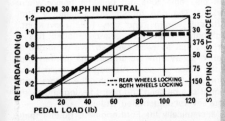

FROM 30 M.P.H IN NEUTRAL

- - - - REAR WHEELS LOCKING
········· BOTH WHEELS LOCKING

SPECIFICATION
FRONT ENGINE, REAR-WHEEL DRIVE

ENGINE

Cylinders	4, in line
Main bearings	5
Cooling system	Water; pump, fan and thermostat
Bore	80.98mm (3.19in.)
Stroke	77.62mm (3.06in.)
Displacement	1,598 c.c. (97.51 cu.in.)
Valve gear	Overhead, pushrods and rockers
Compression ratio	9.0-to-1 : Min. octane rating: 97RM
Carburettor	One Weber 32 DFM compound twin choke downdraught
Fuel pump	AC mechanical
Oil filter	Fram or Tecalemit full flow, renewable element
Max. power	88 bhp (net) at 5,400 rpm
Max. torque	96 lb.ft. (net) at 3,600 rpm

TRANSMISSION

Clutch	Borg and Beck, single dry plate, diaphragm spring, 7.54in. dia.
Gearbox	Ford four-speed, all-synchromesh
Gear ratios	Top 1.0
	Third 1.40
	Second 2.01
	First 2.97
	Reverse 3.32
Final drive	Hypoid bevel, 3.77-to-1

CHASSIS and BODY

Construction	Resin-bonded laminated plywood chassis, separate glass-fibre body

SUSPENSION

Front	Independent, coil springs, wishbones, telescopic dampers
Rear	Live axle, coil springs, radius rods, Panhard rod, telescopic dampers

STEERING

	Alford and Alder rack and pinion
Wheel dia.	13in.

BRAKES

Make and type	Girling discs front, drums rear, no servo
Dimensions	F. 9.6in. dia.
	R. 9.0in. dia. 1.75in. wide shoes
Swept area	F. 190 sq. in.; R. 99 sq. in.
	Total 289 sq. in. (317 sq. in./ton laden)

WHEELS

Type	Cast magnesium, four-stud fixing, 4.5in. wide rim (extra)
Tyres—make	Avon
—type	Radial
—size	165-13in.

EQUIPMENT

Battery	12 volt 32Ah
Generator	Lucas C40 22-amp d.c.
Headlamps	Lucas sealed beam, four lamp system, 220/100 watt (total). Cibié conversion on test car.
Reversing lamp	Extra
Electric fuses	2
Screen wipers	Single speed, self-parking
Screen washer	Standard, electric
Interior heater	Standard, water-valve type
Heated backlight	Not available
Safety belts	Extra, anchorages built in
Interior trim	Leather seats (extra) vyweld headlining
Floor covering	Carpet
Starting handle	No provision
Jack	Screw scissors
Jacking points	One each side, under doors
Windscreen	Toughened; laminated extra
Underbody protection	Non-corroding glass-fibre body

MAINTENANCE

Fuel tank	10 Imp. gallons (no reserve) (45 litres)
Cooling system	12.75 pints (including heater)
Engine sump	7.2 pints (4.1 litres) SAE20/30 or 20/50. Change oil every 3,000 miles. Change filter element every 3,000 miles
Gearbox	2 pints SAE 80EP. Change oil every 6,000 miles
Final drive	2 pints SAE 90EP Check level every 3,000 miles
Grease	4 points every 6,000 miles
Tyre pressures	F. 26; R. 26 psi (normal driving) F. 28; R. 28 psi (fast driving)
	F. 30; R. 30 psi (full load)
Max load	500 lb (227kg.)

PERFORMANCE DATA

Top gear mph per 1,000 rpm	17.8
Mean piston speed at max. power	2,750 ft./min.
Bhp per ton laden	96.5

STANDARD GARAGE 16ft x 8ft 6in.

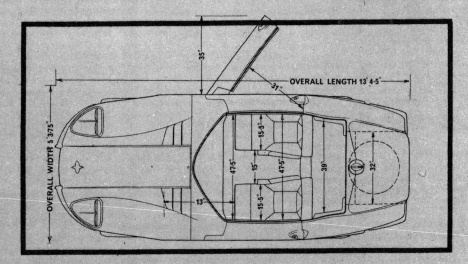

OVERALL LENGTH 13' 4·5"
OVERALL WIDTH 5' 3·75"

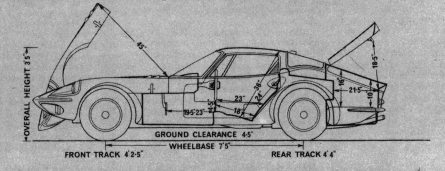

OVERALL HEIGHT 3'5"

GROUND CLEARANCE 4·5"
WHEELBASE 7'5"
FRONT TRACK 4'2·5"
REAR TRACK 4'4"

SCALE
0.3in. to 1ft
Cushions uncompressed

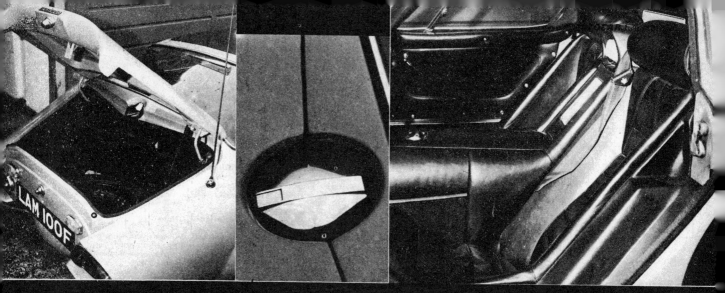

Clever positioning of the rear number plate lamp allows it to double as a boot lamp and there is a quick-release fuel filler just above the boot. Leather upholstery is a £40 extra; headrests are built in.

MARCOS 1600 GT . . .

AT A GLANCE: Plywood-chassis lightweight GT in latest form. Now has 1600 crossflow Ford GT engine. Superb steering and roadholding. Poor ride. Good performance. Extreme lying-back driving position; awkward visibility aft. Excessively noisy in cockpit. Very good fade-free brakes. Expensive, fun and eye-catching.

MANUFACTURER:

Marcos Cars Ltd., Greenland Mills, Bradford-on-Avon, Wiltshire.

PRICES

Basic	£1,500	0s	0d
Purchase Tax	£418	15s	0d
Seat belts	£15	0s	0d
Total (in GB)	£1,933	15s	0d
In Kit form (no	£1,485	0s	0d
Purchase Tax)			
EXTRAS (inc PT)			
Magnesium alloy wheels	£98	0s	0d
Stereo tape player	£42	7s	0d
Push-button radio	£38	0s	0d
Radio suppression kit	£7	10s	0d
Leather upholstery	£40	0s	0d
Cibié quartz-iodine headlamp			
conversion	£20	10s	0d
Special Cibié fog lamps			
(pair)	£11	10s	0d
Reversing lamps (pair)	£7	10s	0d
Twin air horns	£5	19s	6d

IT IS more than three years since we put a Marcos through our road test procedure.

In that time the shape has not changed at all, but instead of the 100 bhp Volvo 1800 engine, a more mundane Ford Cortina GT unit is fitted. Gone is the novel independent rear suspension and the overdrive; fancy cast magnesium wheels are extra. These changes have been a way of pegging the list price against rising costs, and a Marcos today is £50 less than it was in 1965. As then, it can be bought as a kit of parts not liable to purchase tax and as such will carve a £1,485 hole in your bank balance. If you want to drive out of the factory in one, then start thinking in terms of £2,000.

Although the Ford engine is probably much cheaper to install than the Volvo unit, it is much smoother, quieter and develops not very much less power. It has a capacity of 1,599 c.c. and peaks with 88 bhp net at 5,400 rpm. Without overdrive to help it along at high speed, the Marcos 1600 runs out of revs just short of 110 mph, whereas the overdrive 1800 would go to 115 mph. From a standing start the latest car is over 2sec slower to 60 mph and about 8sec slower to 90 mph; it takes 1.1sec longer to cover the quarter mile.

Basically then, as a performance car, the 1600 is not as good. As a road car it is, in contrast, much nicer to drive and there are a whole host of tuning specialists eager to boost the power output for a reasonable outlay, should any owner want to go faster.

As an eye-catcher, the individual Marcos shape has lost nothing at all. Our test car was the personal transport of Marcos' managing director Jem Marsh, who had chosen an exciting orange and black colour scheme and lots of fittings, which all added to the effect. Two we appreciated particularly, the standard Webasto sunshine roof which in hot sunshine converted the little cockpit instantly from a high-bake oven to a habitable living room, and the Slot-Stereo tape cassette sound system which regularly beamed us in on a wavelength appropriate to the car's image—the Beach Boys and Sgt. Pepper alternating in shifts.

It takes a while to get used to the unfamiliar lying back driving position, and the shorter members of our test staff would have liked to sit higher, to raise their eye level above the parked wiper blades. Only one adjustment is provided, for the complete pedal cluster reach, and this is worked by a small handwheel on the facia. Although it is comfortable for the body to be in this reclined position, the neck must be cranked forwards at an unnatural angle or else one tends to look down one's nose at the world ahead. It feels a bit like reading in the bath. When reversing or emerging from an oblique turning, one must pull oneself upright with the steering wheel to see round the blind rear quarters.

Without the roof open, ventilation is not very effective, despite extractors moulded into the Perspex back window. Quarter-lights in the doors are fixed, and to open the main windows a crude thumbscrew must be loosened and the glass pushed down by hand. Getting in and out is a game all of its own, and we were grateful that girls have become much less bashful about showing their legs, or we might have spent all our hours at the wheel alone.

Despite losing the sophistication of independent rear suspension, the Marcos handles superbly and the five-link location for the back axle keeps it well under control all the time. Rack and pinion steering is completely without free play and does not become heavy when parking. The ride though is exceedingly firm with stiff springs and very little movement. With only 4in. ground clearance unladen, this is perhaps just as well; even so, we grounded a silencer every time we bridged the gentle ramp of the office car park. Although the main body structure feels rigid enough, the doors and bonnet can be seen and heard flexing and there were several unidentified rattles.

Mechanically the Ford engine is quieter than the Volvo, but acoustically the plywood and glass-fibre construction seems to be bad, and at speed we had great difficulty in shouting above the general racket and commotion transmitted to the cockpit.

Ford Cortina brakes are bigger now and Marcos wisely use them in this latest car. They work superbly, with light pedal efforts, an emergency potential of 1.0g (at only 80 lb load, incidentally) and virtually no fade during 10 stops from 70 mph in quick succession. Front-to-rear pressure balance was just right, so that when the wheels did lock it was all four together. Being a Ford unit too, the clutch now needs only 35 lb to free it instead of 50 lb.

It is unusual for a model which has seen three years' development in production not to put on weight in the process. Yet, probably because of the lighter engine and gearbox (without overdrive) and the simpler rear end, the Marcos 1600 weighs 60 lb less than the 1800. It has an almost 50:50 weight distribution.

With a car costing so much it was disappointing to find the fit and finish below expectations. Gaps round the complex mating edges were uneven on the test car, the driver's seat cushion split its stitches and there were slight ripples in the panelwork—a characteristic of hand-laid glass-fibre construction. Bumpers, although stylishly slim, are only weak plastic trim strips with no structural strength to withstand parking knocks.

All this apart, it is a great fun car, guaranteed to turn the heads of passers-by and give the driver lots of satisfaction. We would rather it had more of a lion in its heart (why not a Ford Zodiac V6?) so that it could live up to its looks a bit more vividly. As it stands, it is well-tamed and safe.

"YOU CAN'T JUDGE A BOOK...."

MINI MARCOS: FIBREGLASS MINI KIT SOON FOR AUSTRALIA?

MARCOS — the small British specialist sports car builders with a flair for wooden cars — have plans to break into an almost untapped niche on the Australian market.

The vehicle they hope to offer is their wood-strengthened, monocoque fibreglass kit-car for Minis, the Mini-Marcos. At present they are searching for a competent fibreglass firm in either Melbourne or Sydney to manufacture the bodies under licence.

Sold in various stages of finish, starting probably at about $400, the bodies are hoped to be marketed locally to accept all Mini components manufactured in Australia, including the 1275 cc Cooper S engine and hydrolastic suspension.

Mr. Jem Marsh, "Mr. Marcos", gave me the tip-off on this venture when I visited the busy Bradford-on-Avon factory recently.

He has been studying the Australian market closely and feels there is a drastic shortage of kit-cars for BMC components which he hopes his rakish, two-seater "ugly" coupe will fill. "The South African market is very similar", he said, "and we have established a manufacturing set-up there with a local firm. The Australian duty on imported cars makes dealing from our end out of the question, but we are sure we can shake the market from the inside."

In Britain the Mini-Marcos, which tips the scales in road trim at about 2 cwt. less than an ordinary Mini and has much better streamlining, has found its way into the hands of about 300 private owners.

The stages of tune for these cars vary from "cooking" 850 engines from wrecked Minis to the full-house factory-entered car which was the only British car to finish in the 1966 Le Mans 24 hour race.

Driven in part by the company's enthusiastic managing director, Marsh, it reached a fantastic 142 mph down the Mulsanne Straight fitted with a tall 2.9:1 final drive ratio.

Marsh claims that fitting a Marcos body to even standard Mini components will substantially increase performance.

Powered by an ordinary 850 engine, a Mini Marcos will run out of revs at 84 mph, he says — 10 mph faster than the standard car. Fit a stronger set of valve springs and the performance is equal to an early 998 Mini Cooper. A road-going 1275 cc 'S' — powered car will top 120 with the right gearing, he claims.

I watched a "production line" of Mini Marcos bodies being assembled, and the process is remarkably simple.

Separate moulds are made of the fibreglass platform floor section and upper body of the cars, and laid on trestles.

Wood strengthening pieces are bonded into the structure, as are sub-frame attachment points. Finally the two halves are joined like an Easter egg, and the finishing work begins. Careful bracing and double-skinned panels make for a sturdy structure that will accept a sun-roof without loss of rigidity.

At which of five offered stages you take delivery of your car depends on your skill as a handyman — and your pocket.

Really, at no stage of the process could the Marcos be considered an attractive car. The completed, but untrimmed, body shell looks like a refuge from a hairdresser's shop, the rear end looks as though it's had an argument with a bus and the bottom photo looks like nothing on earth — yet, it sells well and goes hard!

Stage one (£199 stg.) includes the body-chassis unit in clear Gelcoat finish. The doors, incorporating polished alloy window frames and sliding windows are unfitted. The windscreen, complete with rubber mounting and filler strip, is also supplied.

All that is needed is to trim the body-chassis down to accept doors, windows etc. and then bolt on you own Mini components.

By buying a wrecked 850, it is estimated you could have a complete car assembled for $700 (Aust.).

The final stage five (£349 stg.) includes full interior trimming, soundproofing and exterior painting. Doors, windscreen, etc. are all fitted and only front and rear suspension assemblies and the engine-transmission unit need to be fitted.

While at the factory, I had an opportunity to drive a "hot" Mini Marcos around the neighbouring country lanes.

What suprised me was the little car's rigidity and even hard driving over some rough sections failed to produce any pronounced scuttle shake. The car would appear tough enough for Australia. Inside, it is very roomy, but strictly for two. Behind the seats is a large luggage shelf, but if used would block the rear window. Entry and exit is very easy. The car's looks are certainly controversial, to say the least, and it attracts plenty of attention wherever it goes.

But the looks have always been a controversial point with Marcos.

Their first ever plywood-bodied racing prototype they freely admit was "probably the ugliest car ever produced", but it did its job very effectively and put the little firm on the map.

Now the Mini Marcos's big-brother stablemate, the Marcos 1600, powered by a cross-flow Cortina engine, is winning wide praise as a "looker".

Unfortunately though there are no plans to bring this car to Australia. "Full importation is out of the question", said Marsh, "and the production techniques are too complicated to hand over to anyone locally."

However the Mini Marcos is a serious venture "down under". Marsh is waiting for an Australian firm to take up his challenge.

MARCOS 1600 GT

To a plywood monocoque, attach various running gear,
add fiberglass body and, presto, a modern British sports car!

RECENT DEVELOPMENTS in U.S. law that make it possible for small manufacturers to apply for exemption from certain parts of the vehicle safety regulations mean that once again there's a chance for really crazy specialty cars like the Marcos to be sold in America. Meanwhile, however, the Marcos is available in Canada; it's certainly an interesting car and the current 1600 version of it is different enough from the 1800 we tested in 1965 to make it worth a fresh look.

Marcos got its start from Jem Marsh and Frank Costin in England just a few years ago. The small company is one of many British specialty car builders that seem to be able to survive by building and selling a handful of cars each year—in Marcos' case fewer than 500 of them. Costin was well known for his association with Lotus and for building light aircraft, and both these bits of background show through clearly in the conception and execution of the Marcos.

Like Lotus cars, the Marcos is a unique design that still makes maximum use of available proprietary components —from its Ford Cortina engine to its Triumph hood releases. And, like many light aircraft, it has as its basic structure a shell of plywood. Unusual as this may seem, the wood

seems to make an adequate structure; front and rear suspension systems are attached to steel subframes which in turn bolt to the wood chassis. The 1600 is lower in price than 1965's 1800; it has a mildly tuned Ford Cortina 1600 engine in place of the 1800's Volvo engine and an unusually located live axle in place of the former De Dion-like rear suspension. Fully independent suspension was used for a time but has been discarded by Marcos. Other detail refinements have been made too, but basically the Marcos 1600 is the same car as the 1800.

And what is the Marcos 1600? Well, it occurs to us that it's a modern sports car. Not a GT, because it's not comfortable enough or practical enough. And not a traditional sports car like an MGB or a TR-250, because—well, because it's modern. In fact, you might reason that if the British had several inexpensive cars of this type in production today, instead of the relatively dull and old-fashioned sports cars they are selling, they wouldn't be in the sales trouble they're in. But the Marcos isn't inexpensive, so it's not a real threat—and we're sure it would take a real threat, probably more, to shake loose the British.

What's great about the Marcos is that it's exciting. It's got the most prone driving position we can recall in a road car. Some of our drivers actually found themselves using the built-in headrests while driving—that's how prone it is. It's an extremely low car—45.5 in. low—and yet it has headroom enough for an over-six-footer. This isn't to say, however, that the 1600 is a comfortable car for any and all. It's pure hell to get in and out of the car. And if you're less than six feet tall, we defy you to see what's going on behind you—you just can't see over the ledge behind you to find out if you can change lanes, and our test car had no outside mirror.

The seats are fixed and, like the Ford Mustang I, the Marcos has adjustable pedals. Brake, clutch and throttle pedals are all on a frame that moves back and forth about 6 in. by means of a knurled crank knob to the left of the steering column, but we couldn't get them close enough for our shorter drivers. We found the seats of the test car too confining for large drivers because of their pronounced bucket shape, but we understand there is some choice of seats when ordering the car. A leather-rim steering wheel is standard, which is great, and though it seemed miles away in the test car it can be adjusted for reach by some fiddling under the hood. Obviously some custom tailoring is in order. Instruments are nice white-on-black, proprietary Smiths and Lucas units, set into a real wood panel with padding top and bottom (the left top padding obscures the top of the tachometer slightly).

To complete the feeling of a race-car-trimmed-for-the-road, there's a huge center console making for claustrophobia; the windows slide up and down rather than cranking, the windshield is very steeply raked and the gearshift lever is in exactly the right place. Irvin Morris inertia-reel harnesses anchor to the package tray behind the seats and are extremely convenient to hook up, though we couldn't get them to lock up by jerking forward as we usually can with inertia reels.

If you're a nitpicker about finish, stay away from the Marcos. There are nice touches here and there, but the general level of finish is mediocre. The fiberglass body panels are wavier than most, the paintwork only fair. Bumpers are painted plastic, similar to those of the Lotus Elan. The trunk is tiny (3 cu ft) and Spartan—we believe there was a plywood floor panel missing from it. You can see the headlight adjusting screws through the plastic covers over the quad lights. The doors didn't fit well either. On the other hand, some of the interior work—particularly the door padding, the center console and the seats themselves—are outstanding, and one cannot help but appreciate the cost of things like inertia-reel belts and varnished wood.

Marcos chassis is of marine plywood sheets bonded together.

GORDON CHITTENDEN PHOTOS

MARCOS 1600 GT
AT A GLANCE

Price as tested (Canadian dollars) $5722
Engine .... ohv 4-cyl, 1599 cc, 100 bhp
Curb weight, lb 1638
Top speed, mph 101
Acceleration, 0-¼ mi, sec 17.5
Average fuel consumption, mpg 26
Summary: Impractical, noisy and rough-riding but lots of fun under the right conditions . . . docile but willing engine . . . race-car seating . . . very good brakes . . . good handling on smooth roads.

SCALE: 10" DIVISIONS

PRICE

Basic list $5250
As tested $5722

ENGINE

Type . . . . 4 cyl, inline, ohv
Bore x stroke, mm . . . 81.0 x 77.6
  Equivalent in . . . . 3.19 x 3.06
Displacement, cc/cu in . . 1599/97.7
Compression ratio 9.6:1
Bhp @ rpm . . . . 100 @ 5500
  Equivalent mph 89
Torque @ rpm, lb-ft . . 105 @ 3600
  Equivalent mph 60
Carburetion. one Weber 32DFM 2V
Type fuel required . . . . . . premium

DRIVE TRAIN

Clutch diameter, in 7.5
Gear ratios: 4th (1.00) 3.70:1
  3rd (1.39) 5.13:1
  2nd (2.01) 7.42:1
  1st (2.97) 11.00:1
Synchromesh . . . . on all 4
Final drive ratio 3.70:1

CHASSIS & BODY

Body/frame: plywood chassis-body
  structure with steel reinforce-
  ment & fiberglass outer panels
Brake type: 9.60-in. disc front,
  9.0 x 1.7-in. drum rear
  Swept area, sq in 207
Wheels . . . . . . cast alloy, 13 x 4½
Tires . . . . Dunlop SP41 165-13
Steering type . . . . . . rack & pinion
  Turns, lock-to-lock 2.8
  Turning circle, ft 29.0
Front suspension: unequal-length
  A-arms, coil springs, tube
  shocks, anti-roll bar
Rear suspension: live axle on lead-
  ing arms, upper torque reaction
  rods & panhard rod; coil springs,
  tube shocks

OPTIONAL EQUIPMENT

Included in "as tested" price:
  radio, alloy wheels, backup
  lights, air horns
Other: wire wheels, stereo tape
  player, fog lamps, special paint,
  leather upholstery

ACCOMMODATION

Seating capacity, persons 2
Seat width 2x19.5
Head room 39.0
Seat back adjustment, deg 0
Driver comfort rating (scale of 100):
  Driver 69 in. tall 70
  Driver 72 in. tall 55
  Driver 75 in. tall 45

INSTRUMENTATION

Instruments: 140-mph speedo, 8000-
  rpm tach, oil pressure, water
  temp, ammeter, fuel level, 99,999
  odo, 999.9 trip odo
Warning lights: ignition on, high
  beam, directional signals, backup light

MAINTENANCE

Engine oil capacity, qt 4.0
  Change interval, mi 4000
Filter change interval, mi 4000
Chassis lube interval, mi 3000
Tire pressures, psi 24/24

MISCELLANEOUS

Body styles available: coupe only
Warranty period, mo/mi.12/12,000

GENERAL

Curb weight, lb 1638
Test weight 1985
Weight distribution (with
  driver), front/rear, % 48/52
Wheelbase, in 89.0
Track, front/rear 50.5/52.0
Overall length 160.5
  Width 63.8
  Height 45.5
Frontal area, sq ft 16.2
Ground clearance, in 5.0
Overhang, front/rear . . 34.2/37.3
Usable trunk space, cu ft 3.0
Fuel tank capacity, gal 11.9

CALCULATED DATA

Lb/hp (test wt) 19.8
Mph/1000 rpm (4th gear) . . . 16.7
Engine revs/mi (60 mph) . . . 3600
Piston travel, ft/mi 1835
Rpm @ 2500 ft/min 4910
  Equivalent mph 81
Cu ft/ton mi 102.5
R&T wear index 66
Brake swept area sq in/ton 208

ROAD TEST RESULTS

ACCELERATION

Time to distance, sec:
0–100 ft 2.8
0–250 ft 5.7
0–500 ft 9.4
0–750 ft 12.3
0–1000 ft 14.7
0–1320 ft (¼ mi) 17.5
Speed at end of ¼ mi, mph . . . 76
Time to speed, sec:
0–30 mph 3.6
0–40 mph 5.4
0–50 mph 7.6
0–60 mph 10.5
0–70 mph 14.5
0–80 mph 20.5
0–100 mph 36.2
Passing exposure time, sec:
To pass car going 50 mph . . . 6.6

FUEL CONSUMPTION

Normal driving, mpg 26
Cruising range, mi 300

SPEEDS IN GEARS

4th gear (6400 rpm), mph 101
3rd (6400) 76
2nd (6400) 53
1st (6400) 36

BRAKES

Panic stop from 80 mph:
  Deceleration, % g 81
  Control . . . . good
Fade test: percent of increase in
  pedal effort required to maintain
  50%-g deceleration rate in six
  stops from 60 mph . . . . ni
Parking: hold 30% grade . . . . yes
Overall brake rating . . . . very good

SPEEDOMETER ERROR

30 mph indicated . . . . . actual 27.4
40 mph 37.7
60 mph 56.5
80 mph 74.5
100 mph 92.1

ACCELERATION & COASTING

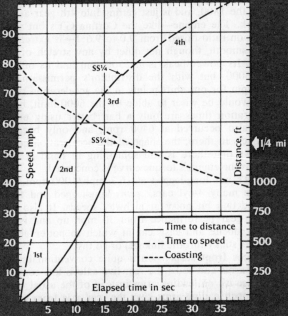

Time to distance
Time to speed
Coasting

Elapsed time in sec

MARCOS 1600 GT

In performance the 1600 is no match for the earlier 1800, but it gets better fuel economy and of course costs less. It covers the standing quarter-mile in 17.5 sec, just 0.4 sec slower than the 1800, and is just getting into 4th gear at the ¼-mile mark. The engine—like the Cortina GT's but with its compression ratio raised from 9.0 to 9.6:1—is extremely willing and smooth, though not quiet by any stretch of the imagination. Its power peak is at 5500 rpm and its official redline at 6000, but with the distributor's permission we used 6400 rpm for our shift points in the acceleration runs. The owner would be wiser to abide by the 6000 limit, however; acceleration times are only a hair better using 6400. Top speed also occurred at 6400 rpm, and only because valve float sets in there; the shape of the acceleration curve plainly shows that there is still something in hand at 101 mph as far as the engine's torque curve is concerned.

Though it's not long-legged at 16.7 mph/1000 rpm, the Marcos, like many 4-cyl cars, *seems* long-legged and feels quite relaxed if a bit noisy at highway speeds. It also has passable top-gear performance from 30 mph up and is, in fact, a very docile and easy car in which to potter about (except for its sticky throttle linkage) or go fast.

The Marcos front suspension is quite conventional with the usual A-arms and coils; the rear live axle is less conventional because it's on leading arms instead of the usual trailing ones. Upper leading arms keep the rear axle from winding up unduly and a Panhard rod keeps it in place laterally. But, frankly, there is nothing really outstanding about the way the 1600 handles other than its exceptionally flat cornering attitude (due to the low center of gravity) and its great adhesion on smooth roads (due to generous tires for the weight). Steering is light and quick, and response to it is truly neutral. On rough surfaces, things go to pot quickly: the rear axle steers considerably on bumps, and limited suspension travel causes bottoming which can skitter the car sideways just when you want it to hang on. The ride is downright harsh on any but the silkiest of roads, and one must exercise great caution not to ground out the muffler. Add to these things a high wind noise level (aided by the fabric sunroof) and really terrible ventilation and you have a car that does little to pamper its passengers.

The 1600's brakes, the usual British disc/drum combination, do a nice job at light pedal efforts, without a power assist. They came through our fade test with an actual decrease in effort, did well in the panic stop and operated without excessive squeal and without any unevenness in daily use. In hard braking the nose dips and the front wheels chafe against the back sides of the headlights.

We only spent a couple of days with the Marcos, but even a ride around the block left anyone who drove it with profound impressions—most of them wildly enthusiastic or positively antagonistic. Alan Crocker, the Canadian distributor of Marcos cars, drove it all the way down from Richmond, B.C., for us to test it—an indication of his individual enthusiasm for the car. He also intends to help Marcos apply for the exemptions from U.S. safety regulations so that it can be sold here in the near future, and there should be no problem at all in meeting the anti-smog rules with the Cortina engine. At $5000-plus (Canadian) the Marcos is anything but a bargain, but it sure is fun.

MOTOR TESTED

Three litre fireball

Striking closed two-seater with tremendous punch; outstanding roadholding; very hard ride but superb seats; well appointed; poor luggage accommodation

IT LOOKS different, it feels different and it really *is* different from just about any other car on the road, in all sorts of ways. First things first. The striking looks of the Marcos have now been familiar for nearly five years yet the Adams styling has lost none of its appeal; if anything, sports car fashion has begun to catch up with it so it is probably slightly less outré than when it first appeared—the car is still strictly a two seater and was among the first of that now accepted breed, the hard-top sports car. Then there is the chassis (to which the glass fibre bodywork is partially moulded) of high quality marine-ply wood with the front suspension loads fed into a bulkhead by a steel sub frame. No other manufacturer has yet followed suit even though time has shown that the construction loses nothing to conventional all-steel cars in strength and longevity.

The car feels different the moment you slide into its semi-reclining fixed seats and adjust the pedals to suit your legs. It is a position which seems awkward for your first forays into rush-hour traffic, particularly if you have just climbed out of an upright saloon; but most people get used to it very quickly and placing the car on the road soon becomes a matter of

accurate intuition. It is designed as a driver's car and concessions to grand touring with luggage and oddment space are meagre.

The Shape first started with a Volvo 1800 engine, followed by a standard Cortina GT unit that gave a performance which hardly matched the car's looks; so a modified version of 1,650 c.c. (the last one we tested) was offered with 120 b.h.p. The 1,600 c.c. Cortina GT cross flow unit replaced both these, but performance was still well down on that of the early Volvo engined cars (and other competitors) so with the minimum of shoehorning the 3-litre Ford V-6 unit was slipped in. Throughout this work development had taken place in other departments—interior refinement, ride and roadholding, ventilation, etc., and the final outcome, as tested, is a dramatic overall improvement and by far the best Marcos yet.

The cumulative weight penalty of a heavier engine and gearbox, the inclusion of overdrive and more luxurious trim and sound deadening has added 2½ cwt. so that, laden for testing, the Marcos tops a ton. But this doesn't seem to have any drastic effect on performance because the car is very fast reaching 60 m.p.h. in 7.8 seconds. It might be even better were it not handicapped by the standard Ford Zodiac ratios, some of which are utterly unsuited to sporting machinery. Its overall top gearing with overdrive is just right, however, for good high-speed cruising and a maximum of around 125 m.p.h.

Where the Marcos excels even more is in its fantastic roadholding, probably the best of any production car we have driven. Its superb, lurch-free cornering makes it extremely fast across

PRICE: £1,790 plus £560 purchase tax equals £2,350. In component form £1,770. 5½J Marcos alloy wheels £55 extra. Total as tested £2,405. Insurance: AOA group rating 7, Lloyd's on application.

Marcos 3-litre

country, and its progress viewed from above would look like a squat arrow darting, swooping, squirting its way round mobile and static chicanes. And it's safe as well with good handling, and powerful anchors. There are faults too, though. The ride is bad, bumpy and noisy, on anything but good surfaces and wind roar at speed is fairly high. Its gradual refinement inside has produced an attractive array of instruments and controls and the fixed seats are really very comfortable, and help to mask the poor ride by distributing the shocks over your back and bottom.

Once you start paying more than £2,000 for a sporting toy, value for money has little meaning. But the Marcos does not seem outrageously priced for its extreme individuality and excellent roadability and you can, of course, build one yourself for less than £1,800. Fast and striking, this car is an extrovert among sports machinery and we all found it tremendous fun to drive and we readily tolerated its failings.

Performance and economy

Ford seem to have a chance habit of producing potentially ubiquitous engines, but few can have expected that the low revving, albeit powerful and torquey, V-6 would have been quite so widely received by the specialist manufacturers. Marcos

Performance

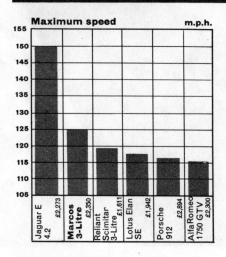

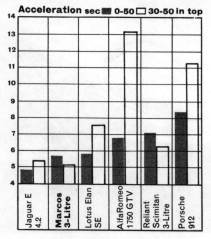

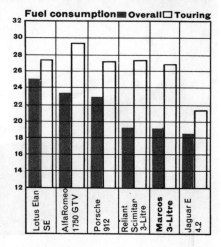

Performance tests carried out by *Motor's* staff at the Motor Industry Research Association proving ground, Lindley.

Test Data: World copyright reserved; no unauthorised reproduction in whole or in part.

Conditions

Weather: Dry, wind 5-10 mph
Temperature: 36-40°F
Barometer: 29.90in. Hg.
Surface: Dry tarmacadam and concrete
Fuel: Premium 98-octane (RM) 4-star rating

Maximum Speeds

	m.p.h.	k.p.h.
Estimated maximum (see text)	125	202
Direct top gear	107	174
O/d 3rd gear	83	135
3rd gear ⎫	68	110
2nd gear ⎬ at 5,500 r.p.m.	44	71
1st gear ⎭	31	50

Acceleration times

m.p.h.		sec.
0–30	. . . .	2.6
0–40	. . . .	4.1
0–50	. . . .	5.7
0–60	. . . .	7.8
0–70	. . . .	10.3
0–80	. . . .	13.4
0–90	. . . .	17.0
0–100	. . . .	20.9
Standing quarter mile	. . . . . .	15.8
Standing kilometer	. . . .	28.9

	O/d Top	Top	3rd
m.p.h.	sec.	sec.	sec.
10–30	—	—	4.5
20–40	9.0	5.9	3.6
30–50	8.7	51	3.6
40–60	7.6	51	3.5
50–70	7.6	5.0	4.0
60–80	7.9	5.2	—

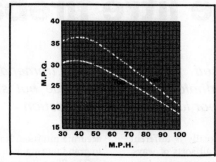

70–90	8.7	6.0	—
80–100	10.4	7.2	—

Fuel Consumption

Touring (consumption midway between 30 m.p.h. and maximum less 5% allowance for acceleration)   26.9 m.p.g.
Overall   19.2 m.p.g.
(=14.7 litres/100km)
Total test distance   1,090 miles

Brakes

Pedal pressure, deceleration and equivalent stopping distance from 30 m.p.h.

lb.	g.	ft.
25	0.42	71½
50	0.70	43
80	1.00	30
Handbrake	0.47	64

Fade Test

20 stops at ½g deceleration at 1 min. intervals from a speed midway between 40 m.p.h. and maximum speed (=82 m.p.h.)

	lb.
Pedal force at beginning	 30
Pedal force at 10th stop	 26
Pedal force at 20th stop	 27

Steering

Turning circle between kerbs: ft.
Left 31¼
Right 31½
Turns of steering wheel from lock to lock . . 2.6
Steering wheel deflection for 50ft. diameter circle . . . . 0.8 turns

Clutch

Free pedal movement . . . . = ½in.
Additional movement to disengage clutch completely . . . . = 2¾in.
Maximum pedal load . . . . = 25lb.

Speedometer

Indicated 10 20 30 40 50 60 70 80 90 100
True   8 18 28 39 48 58 67 77 86 95
Distance recorder 3% fast

Weight

Kerb weight (unladen with fuel for approximately 50 miles) . . . . 17.4 cwt.
Front/rear distribution 52/48
Weight laden as tested . . . . 21.1 cwt.

Parkability

Gap needed to clear 6ft. wide obstruction in front

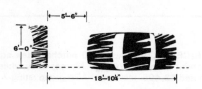

are one of many to take advantage of this compact 3-litre unit. Its installation in the Marcos is very neat and its mountings are well chosen to insulate most of the lumpiness which sometimes occurs when these lazy engines are revved hard. Up to 4,000 r.p.m. (all you really need on the road) it feels almost like a straight six and sounds much more like an Aston Martin; beyond that it obtrudes more and more, but still sounds safe to 6,000 r.p.m. which we used during our acceleration tests.

The engine starts first time, with the choke preset by flooring the accelerator, though it occasionally spits back through the gauze-type air filter during the first few miles. Torque is the really impressive feature; it pulls really lustily from 20 m.p.h. in top and, out of town, top and overdrive are really quite

sufficient for all overtaking; most of the time one starts in second, which loses very little in acceleration times. The Marcos is now the fastest 3-litre production car we have tested and its full performance is very impressive and easily used—50 m.p.h. in 5.7 seconds from rest is very quick by any standards and its top gear acceleration from 30 to 100 m.p.h. actually betters that of an E-type. In fact, the Marcos isn't far behind the E-type in acceleration through the gears, reaching 100 m.p.h. in 20.9 seconds against the E-type 4.2 at 17.2s. It seems that at long last after eight unchallenged years the E-type has a rival on performance/cost ratio.

Maximum power of the V-6 is developed at the very conservative peak of 4,750 r.p.m. which calls for quite high gearing

Still the same classic Adams lines virtually unaltered over five years apart from the V-6 power bulge.

The neat, snug cockpit is nicely finished in leathercloth and carpet, with rubber heel inserts. Window lift switches are in front of the ash tray.

New Marcos alloy 5½ J wheel shows the Marcos insignia in the centre and brake cooling slots.

Adjusting the pedals to suit all leg lengths. Entry into the low car is not too difficult; getting out is a lot harder and scarcely decorous with dresses this length.

Back end shows the cut-off tail and very flimsy bumpers. Central fuel filler takes petrol at a good rate.

Enough for a weekend. The unlined boot took 3 cu. ft. of our test cases with room for soft bags to spare. A supplementary cushion would be required by those under 5ft. 8ins.

14" X 11" X 5"

24" X 18" X 8"

Marcos 3-litre

to get an ideal maximum speed; we lapped MIRA's banked circuit at around 120 m.p.h. with power still in hand, so 125 m.p.h. is a fair flat-road estimate that we did not have the chance to confirm. We wouldn't feel like taking all 120 m.p.h. cars round MIRA at that rate, indicating that the Marcos is impressively stable at speed.

The unstressed power unit is quite happy to run on four-star fuel and will generally return around 22 m.p.g. with only slightly moderated driving and sensible use of the overdrive. At this rate its 10 gallon tank doesn't give a very large range.

Transmission

If you accept a complete power package from another manufacturer you are stuck with the gear ratios that might be suitable for the parent vehicle, but not for your installation. Thus the ratios of the Marcos are too widely spaced and the lower ones much too low. The maximum potential in second of only 47 m.p.h. when 60 m.p.h. should be nearer the mark suggests that better ratios would give even quicker acceleration. Good torque overcomes this to some extent, though, and on the road third gear provides plenty of acceleration and becomes the usual roundabout gear. Most of the time one starts in second leaving first in a rather pre-war fashion as the hill-start ratio—acceleration from rest up the 1-in-3 hill was quite impressive and few cars could leap away up this incline with quite such vigour. The clutch responded quite happily to heavy treatment and gripped quickly and smoothly during our rushed changes; it has a rather long travel but only the first 3½ inches of it are generally needed—there is nowhere to put the clutch foot, though, apart from underneath the pedal.

A much shorter lever than on the Zodiac and the removal of the spring loading seem to have improved the gearchange; the lever can be slid around quickly with the minimum of effort though a deliberate dog-leg movement is needed when changing down to second. An overdrive switch is mounted on the side of the lever in a position which is well suited to a double-change from, say, overdrive third to direct top (a manoeuvre more useful in theory than practice). But for normal engagement it requires an awkward movement of the left thumb or hand; an extension would make it easier to flick with the heel of the hand. The overdrive change on our car was very smooth and didn't require assistance from the clutch. The gearbox is generally quiet but there is some lever chatter when accelerating hard from low revs in top.

Handling and brakes

If you have ever driven a well set-up production car on racing tyres, say a modified MGB, you will have some idea of the cornering power of the Marcos on normal 175-13 Avon radials. The response to steering movement really is in the low-slip racing tyre category, and the roadholding that goes with it is very much in the top class of production cars. Lying back in the reclined racing-style seat you get tremendous satisfaction from an exhilarating cross-country drive; it's not the sort of car you chuck about so much as aim through corners with delicate pressure on the steering and throttle. The fact that the car seems completely roll free (it must roll a bit but the splendid seats don't let you notice it) means that even the most Rolling English Road is an open door to high speed travel. The steering is a bit stiff and sticky, probably as the ratio varies because there is only one UJ in the column, running through 30°. But it is pleasantly high-geared and weighted to get heavier as cornering forces rise. It also gives a good wet-road feel though there is some kick-back as well.

On MIRA's road circuit, which is particularly well surfaced, the tendency on 50-60 m.p.h. corners was for the nose to run wide under power; lifting off brings it back in again in gentle oversteer. But on the open road where surfaces generally have a lower coefficient of friction extra power can be used to slip the tail out in a limited oversteer way which doesn't require correction so much as a premature unwinding of lock—still accompanied, of course, by fantastic roadholding. The Avon

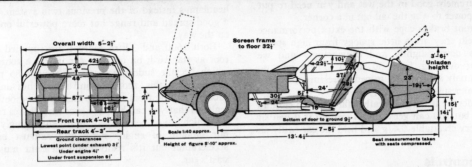

3-litre V-6 engine, rear wheel drive; wooden monocoque chassis, plastic body; live rear axle

Engine

Block material	Cast iron
Head material	Cast iron
Cylinders	V-6
Cooling system	Water, pressurised
Bore and stroke 93.67mm. (3.69in.) x 72.42mm. (2.85in.)	
Cubic capacity	2,994cc. (182.7cu. in.)
Main bearings	Three
Valves	Pushrod o.h.v.
Compression ratio	8.9:1
Carburetter	Weber 40DFN-1
Fuel pump	AC Delco mechanical
Oil filter	AC Delco full-flow
Max. power (net)	136 b.h.p. at 4,750 r.p.m.
Max. power (gross)	144 b.h.p. at 4,750 r.p.m.
Max. torque (gross)	192.5 lb.ft. at 3,000 r.p.m.

Transmission

Clutch	Borg and Beck 9in. dia. s.d.p.
Internal gear ratios:	
Top gear	1.000
overdrive top	0.82
3rd gear	1.412
overdrive third	1.16
2nd gear	2.214
1st gear	3.163
Reverse	3.346
Synchromesh	1, 2, 3, 4
Overdrive type	Laycock LH
Final drive	Salisbury hypoid bevel
M.p.h. at 1,000 r.p.m. in:	
O/d top gear	23.8
Top gear	19.5
O/d 3rd gear	15.1
3rd gear	12.4
2nd gear	7.9
1st gear	8.5

Chassis and body

Construction	Marine ply monocoque chassis with steel sub frames and glass-fibre body-work

Brakes

Type	Girling disc/drum
Dimensions	9.7in. dia. discs, 9in. dia. drums
Friction areas:	
Front	22.2 sq. in. of lining operating on 197 sq. in. of disc
Rear	48.0 sq. in. of lining operating on 98.8 sq. in. of drum

Suspension and steering

Front	Independent with double wishbones, anti-roll bar and coil springs
Rear	Live axle located by upper and lower leading links and transversely by Pan-hard rod; coil springs
Shock absorbers:	
Front	Telescopic
Rear	Telescopic
Steering type	Rack and pinion
Tyres	Avon radials, 175-13
Wheels	Marcos alloy (optional fitting)
Rim size	5½J-13

Coachwork and equipment

Starting handle	No
Tool kit contents	Wheelchanging equipment
Jack	Scissor screw
Jacking points	Under each door sill
Battery	12-volt negative earth, 38 amp. hour capacity
Number of electrical fuses	Two
Headlamps	Rectangular quartz-iodine
Indicators	Self-cancelling flashers
Reversing lamp	Optional
Screen wipers	Two-speed electric
Screen washers	Electric
Sun visors	Two
Locks:	
With ignition key	Ignition/starter
With other keys	Door and boot
Interior heater	Freshair
Upholstery	Leathercloth
Floor covering	Carpet
Alternative body styles	None
Maximum load	Two and luggage
Maximum roof rack load	Not recommended
Major extras available	Wire wheels, alloy wheels, roll-bar, laminated screen, stereo tape, radio

Maintenance

Fuel tank capacity	10 galls
Sump	9.5 pints S.A.E. 10W/30
Gearbox (inc. overdrive)	3.75 pints S.A.E. 80
Rear axle	2 pints S.A.E. 90 E.P.
Steering gear	S.A.E.90
Coolant	21.8 pints (2 drain taps)
Chassis lubrication	Every 6,000 miles to 3 points
Minimum service interval	3,000 miles
Ignition timing	12° b.t.d.c.
Contact breaker gap	0.015 in.
Sparking plug gap	0.025 in.
Sparking plug type	Autolite A622
Tappet clearances (cold)	Inlet 0.012 in.; Exhaust 0.020 in.
Valve timing:	
Inlet opens	20° b.t.d.c.
Inlet closes	56° a.b.d.c.
Exhaust opens	62° b.t.d.c.
Exhaust closes	14° a.t.d.c.
Front wheel toe-in	⅛ in.
Camber angle	0°
Castor angle	6°
Tyre pressures:	
Front	26 p.s.i.
Rear	26 p.s.i.

Safety check list

Steering assembly

Steering box position	Rack in front of engine
Steering column collapsible	Yes
Steering wheel boss padded	No
Steering wheel dished	No

Instrument panel

Projecting switches	None
Sharp cowls	No
Padding	Top and bottom of panel

Windscreen and visibility

Screen type	Zone toughened
Pillars padded	No
Standard Driving mirrors	Interior
Interior mirror framed	Yes
Interior mirror collapsible	Yes
Sun visors	Soft

Seats and harness

Attachment to floor	Fixed
Do they tip forward?	No
Head rest attachment points	Built-in headrest
Safety harness	Inertia reel

Doors

Projecting switches	Door handle
Anti-burst latches	Yes
Child-proof locks	No

1, fuel gauge. 2, fog light switch (spare). 3, ammeter. 4, panel light. 5, cigar lighter. 6, lighting switch. 7, water temperature gauge. 8, windscreen washer. 9, oil pressure gauge. 10, heater fan. 11, speedometer. 12, spare. 13, indicator tell-tale. 14, rev. counter. 15, indicator stalk. 16, spot light switch (spare). 17, ignition/starter key. 18, window lift switches. 19, overdrive switch. 20, windscreen wiper. 21, heater temperature control. 22, heater volume control. 23, main beam tell-tale. 24, lighting stalk. 25, ignition warning light. 26, horn. 27, spare tell-tale. 28, pedal adjuster.

Marcos 3-litre

Radials are also extremely good in the wet and you need to put down quite a lot of power to wag the tail out of a corner.

Slightly larger front brakes cope with the extra performance and weight very well; they are a little spongy from high speed, but the nose dips down slightly and convincingly and we recorded a stop of over 1g from 30 m.p.h. There was no noticeable fade and only a slight rise in pedal pressure after two trips through the water splash.

The pull-up handbrake is mounted rather far forward close to the central tunnel, but you can get a useful grip on it if you sit up. It recorded a very creditable 0.47g and held the car easily on a 1-in-3 hill.

Comfort and controls

If the previous section was an eulogy on handling and roadhold-ing, this one has to be an indictment of the consequent sacrifice—the resulting ride, which is very hard. Solid enough for some people, perhaps, to consider the Marcos only as a trunk road car; on bumpy roads there is considerable jolting and vibration—good for the liver maybe—accompanied by lots of "bonking" as the loads are absorbed in the wooden chassis. Despite this, the wheels stay firmly on the road and adhesion is still first class but, even so, it would almost certainly be a bit wearing to travel far on bumpy, badly cambered French roads. Normal surface humps and hollows are swallowed fairly well with no pitch or lurch and hump-back bridges (provided that you can see what's over them) can be taken surprisingly quickly and smoothly—a sign of good damping. However, you have to be very careful of stray bricks and gate stops as the ground clear-ance below the very vulnerable sump is disturbingly small.

A feature on the Marcos has always been its fixed seat; a shaped supplementary cushion can be used to give extra height and a slightly less reclining back, but the only built-in adjust-ments are to the pedals which all move together on turning a knob under the facia, and to the steering column for reach which requires some 30 second spanner work. On the latest models the seat has been raised slightly and none of us above 5ft. 8in. needed the cushion and we all found it extremely comfortable. The raised seat also improves rearward visibility so you can see all with a quick glance over the shoulder at an angled junction. The mirror gives a good view aft through the shallow screen and the only visibility problem is when reversing; it is then difficult to know exactly where the end is. And it is easy to misjudge the length of the nose.

One of the reasons for raising the seat is to give a better view over the new power bulge in the bonnet; this could do with a

depressurising outlet at the rear because the bonnet centre lifts about $\frac{1}{2}$ inch at 100 m.p.h.—more disconcerting than dangerous, because it is firmly held at the sides by substantial clips. A further change at the front is the use of single rectangular headlamps instead of the previous twin system. They gave quite a good spread and range but more powerful ones are said to be on the way.

Both 1600 and 3-litre Marcos are supplied with a sunshine roof as standard; on our test car it was a source of wind noise which became suddenly worse at around 85 m.p.h. At steady speeds below this, though, wind roar is not unpleasant—just a subdued burble from the exhausts and a whooshing at the door seals, so that you can hear the excellent Philips radio (the speaker for which is just behind your head) surprisingly well. There is a fair amount of engine noise and exhaust bark under hard acceleration but it's really quite pleasant music to an enthu-siast's ear.

The heating is a little primitive but still fairly effective, keeping the interior warm, if rather stuffy at times. There are just two controls, one (very stiff) for temperature, the other for air volume; flaps beneath the scuttle regulate distribution between foot wells and screen. There are no cold air vents, but for fresh air fiends the sunshine roof is very usable in most weather; it is remarkably buffet-free and the only serious draughts it induced were through the door seals—draughts that disappeared when the roof was closed. The side windows are now electrically operated from switches rather far forward on the transmission tunnel but it is a bit too noisy to cruise quickly with them open to all.

Unpleasant exhaust fumes somehow seeped into the cockpit of our car when the roof was open—perhaps through some poor sealing in the boot.

Fittings and furniture

Gone is the rather bitty effect of the wooden facia of earlier Marcos models; the whole interior is now in black leathercloth and looks extremely smart and professional. The instruments are spread across the facia but one sits far enough back to scan them easily without straying too far from the straight ahead position. There is a battery of seven neat rocker switches across the centre of the facia, but the farthest three, two spares for the spot and fog, and a panel light, need hardly ever be touched, so it is only the nearest three that need learning for frequent use on the move, the central one being for the lights. The dip/flasher stalk is a Standard Triumph unit which we never like because you can so easily plunge the road into darkness by mistake.

There isn't a lot of space in the boot, but it is quite square, and it was easy to load our 3 cu. ft. which should be enough weekend luggage for two. Inside the car there is very little oddment space, just one glove locker and a shelf behind the seats where the belt reels are. If you chose to have a stereo tape recorder installed, it fits in the glove locker and then you have even less space.

The interior is designed to comply with American safety regulations, so there are no projections apart from the door handles which it would be virtually impossible to get caught up on in the event of an an accident.

Servicing and maintenance

There are 10 Marcos main dealers scattered throughout the country, each with mechanics who have had a course at the Bradford on Avon factory. Since most of the parts are ex-Ford or Triumph the local garage should have no difficulty in providing service which the car needs every 3,000 miles; the private owner could do this himself without getting very dirty but the 6,000 mile service is a little more comprehensive. The bonnet hinges forward, but without a stay it can blow shut if you park into a headwind; it gives good accessibility round the engine, but if a radio is fitted the plugs are hidden beneath metal shrouding.

The toolkit is now confined to substantial wheelchanging equipment, but no more; the spare wheel sits in the bottom of the boot, and there is room for the odd soft bag around it.

1, steering column adjuster. 2, starter solenoid. 3, oil filler. 4, battery. 5, box housing sliding pedal assembly. 6, coil. 7, dipstick. 8, petrol pump/filter bowl. 9, radiator filler cap. 10, windscreen washer reservoir.

MAKE: Marcos. MODEL: 3-litre. MAKERS: Marcos Cars Ltd., Greenland Mills, Bradford-on-Avon, Wilts.

We visit the factory & drive the groovy V6

IT WAS a multi-car day when we went down to Wiltshire for a look around the Marcos factory — a collection of well converted mills in ye olde sandstone. First we — reporter plus photographic Colin Brown — set off in a Viva van along the M4. At the end of the motorway we met our managing director and 3-litre V6 Scimitar. Having deprived him of that, we were all set for a quick and silent thrash down to the works and a rendezvous (rendezvooze?) with the 3 litre V6-powered Marcos. A sort of instant comparison test, you might say. As soon as we arrived, we went straight in to see their sales director, Nick Harrison, for an inquisition on what the firm(s) are doing.

There are now three companies under their wing at the Bradford-on-Avon works. They are Marcos Cars, Marcos Components and Novaplas. The latter make industrial glassfibre and bodies for the parent company. The components firm supply all body/chassis parts, while the other branch is to deal with every piece of running gear that any type of Marcii may need.

They are making three models at present: the Mini-Marcos, which is all glassfibre construction with metal stays to take subframes: this is sold in kit form only, in three stages of build starting with a bare shell at £230 and working up to a sprayed and trimmed (bucket seats too) body at £380. Next comes the ever so sleek 1600 GT, powered by the Ford engine of that name and a real two-seater. Top of the line is the V6-propelled GT which is based on the 1600 and feels like it's propelled by a Polaris missile! The V6 and the 1600 GT are sold in kit or ready-built form: from what we saw the kit looks very worthwhile, being extremely easy to assemble and exceptionally well finished.

A dash round the manufacturing departments gave us a chance to appreciate the care that's gone into the design of the two bigger-engined GTs. We managed in our short stay to look at the assembly of the 1600 GTs and V6s in logical order; starting with a flat wooden board!

The main chassis/body construction is made from wood, built up on a jig. At this stage the Marcos looks like one of those balsa wood model aeroplane kits — but there's no doubting the strength and lightness of the complete unit. At the front they attach a steel tubing space frame to accommodate the engine mountings and Standard-Triumph GT6-based suspension. Then comes the tricky bit (not you Clive!): they gradually lower a glassfibre shell over the wooden construction, and the shell has to be "sprung" apart to clear the body/chassis. During this stage they have made perfectly sure that the glassfibre and wooden parts are mated up in exactly the right place. After this the complete bodyshell is sprayed in a separate department — final polishing is usually left to the owner,

though to the casual eye it looks beautifully finished anyway. The factory departments all seem to be on different levels, so that the car drops from the top of the buildings to the bottom, as it nears completion. By now we are almost at ground floor level where the car is trimmed, wire, instrumented, fitted with the standard sun roof, steering apparatus and doors checked for instant shutting (they're fitted after the glassfibre shell has been installed, using steel hinges with nylon bushes.) Also at the same stage they fit the standard electric windows and make sure that the remaining wiring and connection of brake pipes and so on is foolproof. "Impossible", you say. Well you could be right, but the firm do everything they can to make sure the kit building job is easy: the wiring that we saw could only be connected up one way because the sockets and connections were all different sizes, so they only mate with what they're supposed to! The front suspension is assembled with the disc brake, so all you have to do is bolt it up and connect the brake piping — an excellent kit feature, we think. By far the biggest task in assembling the kit would be the installation of the engine and gearbox; but even this is only a problem of weight — so get plenty of Rugby players in and buy 'em a pint — a barrel, or even a brewery!

From this final assembly stage we went on to see the Mini-Marcos shop. In there we found three bodies in various stages from just bare glassfibre to a fully-trimmed shell. Marcos do not do a factory-built version, so you have to supply all the necessary Mini running bits. Then we had a brief look at the glassfibre moulding department and found that they were in the process of changing over Mini-Marcos moulds — very strange they look too with lines of enormous "staples" along all the joints.

From that resin-soaked atmosphere we passed into fresh air and the company of Jem Marsh, the boss of the whole outfit. He whisked us off to lunch in the V6, the first time that we'd even sat in one. To say that it was a shattering experience as passenger just isn't enough. For a start you lie back, about four inches from the road, being hurled through every traffic gap by 140 b.h.p. that's only carrying less than 17 cwt. about.

More about that later; meanwhile this is what we found out about the technical side of the 1600 GT and the V6. Both cars use a common body, but there are minor differences to the V6's styling, because it uses a re-shaped bonnet to clear the engine and rectangular headlamps instead of the 1600's twin round lamps. Both cars have a sun roof and electric windows as standard — though very few of the so-equipped 1600 GTs have been sold. Suspension for both is by S-T based unequal length wishbones, coil springs and dampers at the front; at the back there's a live axle that's efficiently located by twin radius arms to the top and bottom of the axle on each side, a Panhard rod for sideways forces plus coil springs and dampers. The only alteration Marcos have had to make for the V6 has been to stiffen up the coil springs, to cope with extra weight. Brakes are identical in both cases, $9\frac{5}{8}$ ins. discs for the front and drums to the rear. Talking about the running gear, Jem Marsh emphasised that they had tried to keep to standard bits, so that service was easy to get at any Ford dealer. The smaller-engined version uses a standard GT Cortina cross-flow motor with a new fabricated exhaust manifold, re-jetted Weber (that's not so easy on current models, because the jets are fixed) and a wire mesh air cleaner. The gearbox is left standard as is the rear axle which has a 3.7 final drive ratio; propshaft is made specially for Marcos. On the V6 models the same approach is used, a completely new exhaust system is fitted with top manifolds by Jan-speed and separate pipes leading out to the rear. In this case they also had to change the settings on the standard twin-choke carb and fit a wire mesh filter. The Zodiac gearbox and overdrive are also used (standard) with a Salisbury back axle that has a 3.5 diff fitted.

Interior gadgets are common to both of 'em, with a neat line of rocker switches — all to current safety requirements — and dials for speed, revs, oil pressure, amps and water-temperature. This is strictly a two-seater, but Marcos have made sure that those are well trimmed and very snug to use. An interesting point about the seats is that because they give a lying-back position, neither driver or passenger are disturbed by flat-out acceleration.

Lowering yourself in is easy, just so long as you plan it out and make sure your feet get in there first. The seats aren't adjustable, but the foot pedals are; all you do is wind a knob and they come forward to meet you. After a wriggle we felt very comfortable and started to explore the mod cons. Jem Marsh had left the Slot Stereo system in action with a four-track tape of the Beach Boys motoring type songs, so we just turned that up and pressed the button until we found "Little 409," which seemed the right mood music to start two hours thrashing round Wilts. The gear-lever is tiny and had the overdrive switch mounted on it. We say *had* because three gearchanges later we broke the switch off! It didn't really spoil our enjoyment though because of those windy roads we were quite happy squirting up to the ton, coming down through the gears and pushing pedals — without worrying about an extra two cogs. The gearchange was a bit stiff on the demo car and we found it hard at times to select second from third. Apparently this is common to all Zodiac gearboxes, when the gearlever has been shortened — this sort of baulking also happens on the Scimitar. Still, the gearbox action isn't really that important, because the engine has plenty of poke right down to 1500 r.p.m. in top; it's quite possible to start

from rest in third and still have more acceleration than you need, after a few seconds build-up! Really first gear is completely redundant, save for restarting on a one in three hill. After five minutes or so, we began to relax and get used to the low-level seating. Jem Marsh had said that we wouldn't notice the bonnet's power bulge, and he was quite right; our driver for the occasion was only 5 ft. 9 ins. but he had no complaints about seeing where it was going — though he confessed that the view at times was pretty hair-raising. You know the sort of thing; you're pounding along a country lane when an incredibly huge concrete lorry hurtles into view, using his road, your road and plenty of the verge! It's in that sort of moment that you appreciate the Marcos's ability to swop direction quickly, simultaneously braking or accelerating. As you might expect, and as you'll certainly enjoy, there's flashing acceleration up to the rev limit of 5500 or 6000 r.p.m., if you're desperate. As you push the go-pedal down there's a hearty roar from the dual exhausts (they'll probably be quieter in later cars . . . A great shame!) and the next piece of solid scenery flies towards you like it's on an elastic band. The theme to all the controls, brakes, clutch, accelerator and steering is instant response; which is how it should be when you think that Marcos claim a top speed of at least 130 m.p.h. and 0-60 m.p.h. in seven seconds. The live rear axle doesn't tramp during acceleration, but it does betray itself when pressed to the limit on a bumpy curve by hopping ever so slightly, but always controllably. We gave the brakes a really hard caning during the descent of a long hill, liberally scattered with hairpins (I knew he'd drag girls into the copy SOMEHOW — ed.)and found that after ten vicious applications they were beginning to feel the pace, as the smell of hot pads and lining had begun to pervade the cabin and there was a slight pull to the left. Really we'll have to get the car on our test track to try proper braking and acceleration runs; as Marcos are selling all they can make of the V6 this is a delight that'll probably have to wait. While on the subject of full road tests we were a little disappointed that we couldn't borrow a 1600 GT version for test; the reason for this is that Marcos have only recently changed the model's trim and general fittings (including the electric windows), so that they haven't a current model to loan. A Minor difference between V6 and 1600 GT is that the big engined one has a padded black dash while the 1600 gets a wooden one.

However back on the driving scene all was happiness, with both Slot Stereo's superb sound and the V6's equally moving roar combining to dispel the effect of depressing weather and the thought that we'd have to give it back!

Altogether a completely unforgettable afternoon: the V6 is a very quick car and is definitely the best model that Marcos have ever produced — which is saying a lot, even at the asking price of £1770.

JEREMY WALTON

MARCOS $6730 WEST COAST P.O.E.

Hardtop two seater sports car with tremendous appearance appeal and performance to match. Suspension delivers superior road holding but at the expense of an extremely hard ride, seats are excellent, however. Interior well appointed, minimal luggage accommodations. Manufactured by Marcos Cars Ltd., Greenland Mills, Bradford-on-Avon, Wiltshire, England.

The Marcos has been a familiar sight on English roads for about five years now but only recently has it begun to make its appearance in the U.S. The striking looks of the Marcos are enough to set it apart anywhere but coupled with its many unique features it can be a conversation piece even among the cognoscenti.

One of the most notable features of the early Marcos was its chassis of high quality marine plywood. Time has shown the strength of this construction which gained additional rigidity by being partially bonded to the fiberglass body. It has another advantage in weight reduction (Jim Hall builds high powered Chap-

arralls with fiberglass chassis).

However, Americans, being a superstitious lot, haven't taken kindly to the advantages of high strength wood so tubular steel frames are available for U.S. buyers. Either way the weight will come in close to 2350 lbs. ready to go. The Marcos is built on a short wheelbase, just 89.5 in. with an overall length of 160 in. This makes for a very cozy package especially considering the height of 42.5 in. and the width of 62.5. There are narrower sports cars but not by much.

Early Marcos cars were fitted with Volvo P1800 engines with displacement of 116 cu. in. and horsepower of 118.

These were later replaced by the Cortina cross-flow GT unit but performance wasn't quite up to that of the cars with Volvo power so 'go' was sought from another source. The engine finally decided upon (and one which will fit) is the 3 liter Ford V-6 which measures out to 182.7 cu. in. This is a conventional water cooled unit with the overhead valves operated by pushrods. Both the block and cylinder head are cast iron. Compression is 9 to 1 and breathing is through a single Weber 40 DFN-1 carburetor.

Power is taken to the all synchromesh four speed gearbox with overdrive

Excellent accessibility is provided by front hinged hood. Engine used is the six cylinder English Ford. Sun roof is standard, provides fresh air without drafts.

Marcos rear treatment is distinctive, simple yet businesslike. Thin blade bumper makes minimum concession to rear protection.

through a 9 in. diameter Borg and Beck single dry plate clutch. The Laycock overdrive is operational on third and fourth gears only.

The three liter engine employed in the Marcos is really the standard unit in the English Ford Zodiac and for simplicity the Zodiac gearbox is used as well. In the case of the engine this works out rather well for even though the V-6 is normally a slow revving lazy lump it can be induced to wind up to 6000 rpm without breaking. With automatic choke the Marcos-Zodiac starts with a twist of the key and with its lusty torque, once warm, will pull away in fourth gear at 20 mph.

The Zodiac gearbox is rather a disappointment. The ratios are fine in the vehicle from which it sprang but are too widely spaced for sports car application. First gear is suitable for setting tires on fire or for pulling stumps. Second is all used up at about 47 mph when 60 or 65 would have been more reasonable. Third gear is about right though and with the gobs of torque available makes for a very fine acceleration gear as well as a most useful, all around traffic gear. The clutch responds well to heavy use. It grips quickly and smoothly on fast changes but those fast changes are complicated by unnecessarily long pedal travel. There is

nowhere to put your left foot between gear changes other than beneath the pedal. One definite improvement has been the _____ ng of the gear lever and changes can be made quickly and positively. The overdrive switch is on the side of the shift lever. For normal engagement the switch position is a bit awkward even though changes using overdrive are smooth when made.

Checking out the Marcos for its power and performance, the first time tester is in for a surprise. In the same price class as the Jaguar XKE the Marcos with 1200 cc less engine displacement comes very close to matching the E in impressive straight line performance. We had no opportunity to do 100 mph tests but

according to our European correspondents the Marcos actually tops the E in 30 to 100 mph acceleration. From a standing start the E wins the 0 to 100 mph test but only by 3.7 seconds.

Where the Marcos really excels, however, is in its truly remarkable roadholding. It is one of the best handling production cars we have ever driven. Across country on secondary roads its superb, lurch free cornering makes it extremely fast while imparting a feeling of solid security. There is nothing particularly. unique about the suspension to account for its good manners, the front is independent with double wishbones, anti-roll bar and coil springs. At the rear there is a live rear axle located by upper and lower

Small trunk has little space remaining with spare in place. Luggage should have soft corners.

Marcos cockpit makes best possible use of dashboard area. A different arrangement of gauges might be in order but necessary information is provided. Overdrive switch is on right of gearshift lever.

leading links and transverse Panhard rod and coil springs.

The Avon 175 SR 13 radial ply tires make a definite contribution to the cornering power of the Marcos.

Lying back in the Formula I type racing seat the appreciative driver gets tremendous satisfaction from the kind of drive the Marcos offers. It's not so much the kind of car you fling about and hurl into the corners as it is aimed and guided with a delicate touch on wheel and throttle. Steering is a bit on the stiff side but with only 2.6 turns lock to lock there is excellent response.

All is not perfection however. The short wheelbase and stiff suspension of the Marcos results in a choppy ride. On anything but smooth surfaces there is a good deal of bounce. The non-adjustable seats however are deeply cushioned and very comfortable and do much to damp out the poor ride by distributing the jolts across your back and thighs.

The brakes are Girling discs at the front and conventional drums at the rear. For the weight of the car and with the radial ply tires fitted the combination is effective. The usual spate of federally required safety devices is in evidence but there is one item that we recommend even though it is an extra cost option. That is the competition type, inertia reel, double shoulder harness. At $50 it's a bargain. With this harness you may want to invest in the optional roll bar which will set you back another $100.

We've discussed virtually all aspects of the Marcos except perhaps the most important, what it's like to live in while you are enjoying its handling and road-holding.

One item we mentioned was the fixed seat. That is true, the seats are immobile.

However, the pedals and the steering wheel are adjustable. The wheel in about 30 seconds with a wrench, the pedals by turning a knob just under the dashboard which moves all the pedals either forward or back. For drivers under five ft. eight in. a shaped supplementary seat cushion is offered. None of the ROAD TESTers needed the cushion but it appears as though it would be comfortable. The seats are finished in red or black vinyl. There is wall to wall carpeting in the office. A sun roof is standard which can be very helpful in warm weather for there is no other ventilation except the windows where the noise level is high.

The heating system is only fairly effective. It can keep the interior warm but being unvented things can become rather stuffy.

The Marcos dash is now finished in black vinyl with the instruments spread out toward the center. Dials are still easy to read because the driver sits well back from them. Needless to say, all information usually sought is provided. Controls are rocker switches above the center console and are marked with international symbols.

The less said about luggage space the better. There is a trunk of sorts but it is best suited to smallish soft cornered bags. Enough luggage for two for a week-end can be carried but that's about it. There is a small glove box in the cockpit but if you elect to have stereo tape that's the only place to put it.

The Marcos has a lot going for it. It looks different, it feels different and by golly it goes like darn few other cars on the road. It is an enthusiasts car that responds to enthusiastic driving. It has faults like its oddly spaced gear ratios and its choppy ride on rough surfaces. It's not an inexpensive car, West Coast P.O.E. is $6730.00 and there is no East Coast P.O.E. The only place in the U.S. you can buy the Marcos is at Prestige

Motors in Beverly Hills, California. However, you needn't worry about service, any place that sells the Ford Cortina will be able to take care of your Marcos.

For many men the sports car is an expensive toy, an extension of his ego. For an ego prop you won't find on every block you might just try the Marcos. ♠

Marcos 3 Liter

Data in Brief

DIMENSIONS

Overall length (in.)	160.0
Wheelbase (in.)	89.5
Height (in.)	42.5
Width (in.)	62.5
Tread (front in.)	48
Tread (rear in.)	51
Fuel tank capacity (gal.)	12
Luggage capacity (cu. ft.)	5.0
Turning diameter (ft.)	31.3

ENGINE

Type	OHV V-6
Displacement (cu. in.)	182.7
Horsepower (at 4750 rpm)	144
Torque (lb./ft. at 3000 rpm)	192.5

WEIGHT, TIRES, BRAKES

Weight (as tested lb.)	2352
Tires	radial 175 SR 13
Brakes, front	disc
Brakes, rear	drum

SUSPENSION

Front . . . . . Independent with double wishbones coil springs anti-roll bar

Rear . . . . . Live axle upper and lower leading links. Panhard rod. Coil springs

ONE WEEKEND

The story of 48 hours in which a Marcos kit was turned into a new car

Saturday, 9 a.m.: The body assembly, on its delivery trolley, awaits the start

The rest of the delivery on the garage floor, with the small parts in plastic bags

Saturday, 6 p.m.: On its own wheels and with brakes bled and steering working

Sunday, 1 p.m.: The Ford V6 engine is lowered into place in the Marcos chassis

If you ever have the opportunity of examining, very closely, Marcos AMX 81 H, you might find, around the suspension and the engine bay, small circles of dried salt. Because the weekend that we chose to build a Marcos turned out to be the hottest August weekend for many years, with the temperature climbing to 91 deg. F. at one stage, and the car is literally marked with the sweat of its constructors. But it was sweat well expended, for the weekend brought the enormous satisfaction of bringing to life a new car (and saving several hundred pounds in the process).

THE kit was delivered by Hexagon Motors of Highgate late on Friday afternoon. Off the back of a flat trailer rolled the castored trolley carrying the entire body assembly, and out of the back of the towing Land-Rover came a collection of bits and pieces ranging in size from a rear axle to a horn button. The engine and gearbox assembly came out last, its massive weight of about 4½ cwt being taken on a chain hoist suspended from a steel joist in the garage roof. We decided to do no more on Friday evening other than to look at the bits, try to decide how they could possibly fit together, and to marvel at the body.

On Saturday morning, at 9 o'clock, we

got started. We slid in the rear axle (after removing one brake drum to get the assembly through the steel framing) and started bolting up the radius rods. We found, to our pleasure, that all nuts, bolts and locking washers had been loosely assembled in their right holes, so there was no identification problem, but the rubber-mounted ends of the rods proved to be a very close fit in their housings on the frame and axle, and it was necessary to give them a preliminary pinch with a Mole wrench to get them to slide into place. Fore-and-aft axle alignment was checked and set by locking the one adjustable radius rod, while sideways alignment was checked and

Saturday, noon: The author connects the brake lines; the jack supports the axle—not the car

Saturday, 4 p.m.: Front suspension installed, but the Marcos is still on its delivery trolley

Sunday 6 p.m.: A tense moment as the V6 engine coughs into life for the first time

Monday, 10 a.m.: Bonnet on, registration plates fitted—and the Marcos is ready for her first run

The bulge on the bonnet indicates that this is the 3-litre V6 version. Below left: Cast magnesium wheels are standard, and the bonnets now lock. Below right: Rectangular headlamps are fitted under the Perspex covers

ONE WEEKEND...

set by the adjustable cross rod between axle and frame.

Using a small jack to support the axle, we slipped the rear spring and damper assemblies into place and bolted them up. While we were down at that end, we connected the flexible brake pipe to the chassis frame and to the steel pipe waiting for it on the body, and loosely connected the handbrake cable.

At the front end, a similar procedure took place on both the front suspension assemblies, although here we found the fits between the wishbone ends and the frame to be even tighter. The wishbones needed some heavy shoving to get them

into place so that the fixing bolts could be slipped through. Springs and dampers slid into place, the brake connections were made, and the track rod ends were connected, to await later adjustment for toe-in.

By 4 p.m., the four wheels had been bolted into place, and the car was ready to come off its trolley. Realizing that we were going to be stuck with a car with all its wheels six inches off the ground, and disliking the practice of multiple jacking and blocking to get it down, we had made previous arrangements to borrow the services of a local mobile hoist, which arrived at 4.30 With bonnet off, the hoist hook round the front lower frame member, and with five men giving an almighty heave at the back end, one brave wife was coerced

into giving the trolley a sideways shove from below, and out it came. The rear wheels descended, very quickly, followed by the front, more sedately, as the hoist let it down.

By 6 p.m., the handbrake had been adjusted, the braking system had been filled and bled (three times to get a "good pedal"), and the steering wheel had been slipped on to its splines, so that the car could be manoeuvred and stopped. At this stage, four tired constructors decided to call it a day.

Sunday morning, at 9 o'clock, saw two of the team preparing the engine for hoisting, removing the carburettor and heater water valve from the top of the block to avoid their being damaged by the lifting sling

Above: The new steel chassis looks very similar to the older sub frame on the wooden-based cars. Below: The boot lid forms a deep lip over the rear lamp clusters

when the engine was to be tilted during insertion. From then until nearly 2 p.m. the crew were engaged in a long, slow process of lifting, lowering, tilting, manoeuvring, and checking and re-checking clearances—and made their only mistake. They had decided to fit both exhaust manifolds on to the block while it was on the ground and, knowing the Zodiac engine, had fitted the manifolds in the usual way, with the down pipes of the manifolds at the rear end of the engine. Later, as the engine was two-thirds of the way in, they saw to their horror that the manifolds should have been fitted the other way round, with the down pipes at the front end, because another inch of lowering would send the manifold ends straight through the sides of the scuttle. Recriminations were quickly silenced as they reviewed the situation, finally deciding that the manifolds could be removed and fitted after the engine was in, which subsequently proved to be true.

This mistake cost them, perhaps, an hour but, finally, just before 2 o'clock, they had the joy of hearing, from each of the two men guiding the block down on its mounts—"I'm in!"—"I'm on!" while, from down below, the man guiding the tail end into the transmission tunnel called that the tail had engaged with the frame and that he'd slipped one of the bolts in.

After a quick, but celebrative lunch, the rest came easily. Engine mounting bolts at front and tail. Carburettor and water valve back. Manifolds on. Radiator on. Gear lever mounted on the rear of the overdrive unit through an access panel in the transmission tunnel. Gear knob on. Speedo drive cable coupled into the rear of the overdrive. Overdrive electrical connections made. Prop shaft slid on to its splines and bolted to the differential nose. Exhaust pipes bolted to the manifolds and the body. Couple the throttle cable to the top of the pedal assembly, heater water valve hose and control cable, water pump hose, top radiator hose, bottom radiator hose, oil pressure nylon tubing to block, water temperature lead to block, petrol pump feed pipe, petrol return pipe, distributor lead to coil, clutch cylinder hose to chassis and pipe from reservoir, fill and bleed (once), heater trunking (uncoupled because it had got in the way during engine insertion), steering wheel locked up, horn button assembly, windscreen wipers connected and, finally, battery earth leads.

With the rear axle and gearbox already filled with oil before assembly, there remained only engine oil and water to put in, and a gallon of petrol in the tank.

A final check of every connection—battery charge state checked—gear lever in neutral. The key was turned at 6 p.m. Anxious eyes watched for the flow of petrol through the clear plastic feed pipe as the engine cranked over. Petrol through. Stop cranking. Now try. Press the pedal once to set the automatic choke; ignition—starter—fire once—stall. Try again. Ignition—starter—firing—quick push on the pedal to hold it—need 2,000 rpm to keep it—not firing on all six yet—amps OK—oil pressure OK—one minute gone—it will hold at 1500 now. One more minute and all six cylinders are firing smoothly.

Try a gear. With no bonnet, and with its front wheels still splayed with a 1-in. toe-out, this new machine comes to life, moves, and *drives* five yards.

We've built a car

There can be few Marcoses that have been christened with champagne poured over their hot radiator caps. After all, the owner is a restaurateur. And there can be few occasions on which a dirty, sweaty crew of amateur mechanics may be seen swigging the same champagne straight out of the bottle. But this was an occasion on which they had the right to celebrate, having built a car in 16 working hours.

There was no more work that night. The next morning saw the remaining two of the team setting the toe-in, re-fitting the bonnet and mounting the number plates. At 10 o'clock AMX 81 H was driven out for her first trial, which showed immediately that the gearbox would offer only third, top and overdrive. Adjustment of the running nuts on the main selector rod at the side of the gearbox settled that.

That drive, again on one of the hottest days of the year, showed that the engine was overheating, the temperature gauge staying up against its stop all the way. When the car was taken to Hexagon Motors the following day, for the standard "kit check" advised by Marcos Cars, that problem was cured by fitting, at no charge, the bigger truck fan to the main pulley, and an auxiliary Kenlow fan in front of the radiator. The kit check, in which the weekend's work was examined by Hexagon mechanics, gave the car a clean bill of health, and AMX 81 H has already carried its first long-legged passenger in one of the astronaut couches in which the Marcos envelops its occupants.

The dramatic new 2 plus 2 Mantis poses outside the new Marcos factory at Westbury.

41-12-1

An exciting new car from a new factory

When we last visited Marcos Cars Ltd, ultra-modern sports coupés were being built in a rambling mill of immense antiquity. Now, Jem Marsh has moved the whole operation from Bradford-on-Avon to Westbury, Wiltshire, where a beautiful new factory houses the enterprise. Everything is on one floor, which makes organisation infinitely easier, and the formerly separate service department has been incorporated in the main structure, which also contains the office block; there is ample room for planned expansion.

Marcos cars were originally based on a wooden monocoque, but recently it has been found possible, after much development work,

The body shape is the work of Dennis Adams.

41-12-2

to design a steel chassis which has great production advantages. The cost of skilled labour is rising all the time and the wooden structure has virtually priced itself out of a job. The steel chassis, CO_2-welded from square-section tube, causes no significant weight increase and there is no loss of rigidity.

The chassis frames are welded up on jigs and there are three complete plants for simultaneous operation. The bodies are made in a large glassfibre shop, a form of construction in which Marcos are specialists. There is a woodwork shop alongside, for this material is still employed at some

strategic points, and all the upholstery and interior trim are made in an adjacent area. The paint shops are most impressive and employ the latest techniques; a separate paint shop and woodwork section is incorporated in the large service department, to avoid interference with new car production. The well-organised stores ensure that no delays shall affect production and Marcos are proud of the rapidity with which orders for spare parts are handled, to the tune of £2000 a month.

The existing 3-litre two-seater coupé is being built at the rate of seven per week, although the 2-litre version may eventually be phased out. The well-known Mini-Marcos body shells have recently been improved by the addition of an opening rear door to the luggage boot; two per week are supplied to do-it-yourself enthusiasts. The new 2 plus 2 Mantis has recently started a production run of two per week which will be stepped up to about seven per week, the proportion of two- and four-seaters produced eventually depending on orders from customers.

The Mantis is considerably more roomy than other 2 plus 2 cars and has as much leg space as the average four-seater saloon. It is not advertised as a full four-seater, however, because the sweeping roof-line does impose a limit on head room for tall rear passengers. The very spectacular body design is the work of Dennis Adams, but it is not just a pretty face. Indeed, it repays the closest attention because it has so many practical details. For a car of this quality, doors that close easily with an expensive sound are a *sine qua non*, and this is achieved by mounting the cast aluminium hinge blocks directly on a chassis member instead of on the body. Because this entirely new car was designed from the outset to have a separate steel chassis, the body does

not have to be completed on the chassis frame but can be constructed separately on a jig. Its styling is as "way out" as the two-seater was when it first appeared, but the size of the body and the boot have been chosen by the customers—some extensive market research has been going on.

The engine is carried well back in the chassis and ahead of it is a radiator with a fully ducted air exit through the top of the bonnet, as is Formula 1 practice. To ensure rigidity, the propeller shaft tunnel is of stressed-skin construction and carries the centre bearing of the divided prop-shaft. The rear axle is located by an A-bracket above the differential housing, with nylon bushes and a large forward ball-joint. Beneath the axle at each end, long trailing radius arms have rubber bushes to give the necessary compliance and reduce road noises. The suspension has much longer travel than that of the two-seater Marcos.

The front suspension is by upper and lower wishbones, the suspension medium front and rear being coil springs and telescopic dampers. Rack and pinion steering is employed, as would be expected, and the servo-assisted disc and drum brakes are by Girling. The bolt-on light-alloy wheels carry 185 by 13 radial ply tyres; in production form, they will be machined and polished with contrasting black centres.

The engine is the fuel-injection, six-cylinder Triumph of 2498 cc, developing 150 bhp at 5500 rpm. It can be supplied with either a four-speed all-synchromesh gearbox or the Borg-Warner Type 35 automatic transmission; like other manufacturers of specialised cars, Marcos are experiencing an increasing demand for automatics. There is, in any case, ample space in the central tunnel for any future transmission option. The electric pump for the fuel injection is on the left of the slab-shaped tank and incorporates an inertia switch to cut off the petrol in the event of an accident. The battery is on the right and 10 cu ft of luggage are carried behind the 17½ gallon tank, with a useful tool kit cunningly concealed and the spare wheel wound up underneath the boot.

The bonnet is entirely separate from the body as it is found that after the average traffic accident, the mere replacement of this relatively cheap component will put a car back on the road without any delay or expensive work. For the more trivial encounters, the black-painted glassfibre bumper also forms the front grille and is considered to be expendable. Nobody anticipates having an accident, but it is nice to know that there are plenty of spare bumpers and bonnets at Westbury in case the improbable happens.

Although this is an entirely new car, it incorporates no untried components and many of the chassis parts are interchangeable with the two-seater Marcos. Nevertheless, its exciting shape and appearance will cause a furore and its performance is not in doubt as it is appreciably lighter than the TR6, while the body has been developed in the wind tunnel. Such a car is inevitably costly, but the price will be below £2550 in kit form.

My dictionary says that a mantis was originally "one who utters oracles while in a state of divine frenzy." Jem Marsh has uttered his oracle and the result is this dramatic new Marcos.

Car reviewed: Marcos Mantis 2+2.
Engine: Six cylinder, 74.7 mm x 95 mm (2498 cc). Pushrod-operated overhead valves. Compression ratio, 9.5 to 1. 150 bhp at 5500 rpm. Lucas fuel injection.
Transmission: Single dry-plate clutch. Four-speed, all-synchromesh gearbox with central gearlever, ratios: 1.0, 1.33, 2.01, and 3.14 to 1. (Borg-Warner Type 35 automatic transmission also available.) Divided propeller shaft. Hypoid rear axle, ratio 3.23 to 1.
Chassis: Separate square-section tubular steel frame. Glassfibre body. Independent front suspension with wishbones and anti-roll bar. Rack and pinion steering. Rigid rear axle on trailing arms and A-bracket. Coil springs and telescopic dampers all round. Girling dual circuit servo-assisted drum rear and disc front brakes. Bolt-on light-alloy wheels, fitted 185 x 13 radial ply tyres.
Equipment: 12-volt lighting and starting with alternator. Speedometer. Rev counter. Ammeter. Water temperature, oil pressure, and fuel gauges. Heating, demisting and ventilation system. Two-speed windscreen wipers and washers. Flashing direction indicators. Reversing lights. Cigar lighter. Extra: electrically heated rear window, sunshine roof, radio.
Dimensions: Wheelbase, 8 ft 6 ins; track, 4 ft 9 ins; overall length, 15 ft 6¾ ins; width, 5 ft 11 ins; weight, 1 ton 60 lbs.

The Mantis has very striking lines, as had the Repco-engined racing prototype of that name (above). The production Mantis uses the 2.5 PI Triumph engine (below). 41-12-3/41-12-4

The interior lay-out is very neat and exceptionally well planned (below). 41-12-5

AUTOTEST

MARCOS 3-LITRE VOLVO (2,978 c.c.)

AT-A-GLANCE: Larger-engined version of well-established sports car. Performance extremely good, with outstanding flexibility and modest fuel consumption. Poor ride but good seating. Noisy if driven hard, but very high handling limits. Heating and ventilation poor.

MANUFACTURER

Marcos Cars Ltd., The Ham, Westbury, Wilts.

PRICES

Basic	£1,970.00
Purchase Tax	£604.23
Total (in G.B.)	£2,574.23

EXTRAS (inc. P.T.)

Sun roof*	£58.80
Supplementary cushion*	£10.50
Radio	£73.20
Laminated screen	£45.70

* Fitted to test car

PRICE AS TESTED £2,643.53

PERFORMANCE SUMMARY

Mean maximum speed	120 mph
Standing start $\frac{1}{4}$-mile	15.9 sec
0-60 mph	7.5 sec
30-70 mph through gears	7.4 sec
Typical fuel consumption	24 mpg
Miles per tankful	290

THE last Marcos tested by *Autocar,* well over two years ago, was the 1600GT. This version is no longer made, but the eye-catching Adams-designed shape has been carried across more or less unchanged to the current versions. Under this skin, however, the car has changed considerably. One important difference is that the original wooden chassis has gone, to be replaced by an equivalent structure in welded square-section steel tube.

Following on from the 1600, Marcos produced their 3-litre with the Ford vee-6 engine, and then the 2-litre with Ford's vee-4. They then produced another 3-litre, this time using the in-line 6-cylinder engine from the Volvo 164. This version was originally intended for American consumption, but Marcos found the constantly proliferating safety regulations too much for them and finally gave up in disgust. The effort was not wasted, however, because the Volvo-engined car was favourably received in Britain and now forms the bulk of 3-litre production. Marcos of course, are no strangers to Volvo power units, since the car originally used a 4-cylinder B18 engine from the Swedish firm; so the wheel may be considered to have come full circle.

Although it may seem a bit of a lump to shoehorn into a small, light car like the Marcos, the Volvo engine has several good points. It is undeniably a quality engine with a good sporting background, and in fact is hardly any heavier than the Ford vee-6. Installation in the Marcos is no problem, for it is easier to find length than width under that graceful bonnet. Perhaps above all, the Volvo engine comes with a Volvo gearbox, with excellently spaced ratios contrasting greatly with the appalling ones in the Zodiac box which has to be used with the Ford vee-6 engine.

Vivid performance

Apart from the removal of some of the anti-pollution plumbing and the subsequent retuning of the carburettors, the Volvo engine is used in standard form. Thus its power output is far from exceptional for 3 litres, but it has an abundance of torque over a very wide rev range.

Starting was always a first-time affair, even though the choke control acts only on the aft carburettor, but it was a mile or so before rich mixture could be completely dispensed with. After that, the engine showed almost no sign of temperament, except for a slight tendency to "hunt" when trundling along at 30-40mph in top gear. Flexibility was outstanding, and with a little throttle feathering we were able to record figures from 10 mph in top, equivalent to little more than 400 rpm. Normal idling speed was 800 rpm, with the red line on the rev counter set at 5,500.

A check on the accuracy of the rev counter showed it to be over-reading by 10 per cent, which meant taking the car to 6,000 rpm indicated—as far as the rev counter went—for the acceleration runs. With the 3.22 German Ford final drive (as used in the Capri 3000) the Marcos is a little undergeared in theory, with intermediate gear maxima of just under 40, just over 60 and exactly 90 mph. Maximum speed is rev-limited to 120, and the car will reach this without a great deal of trouble; with an overdrive or a higher final drive ratio, it would obviously go faster. Unfortunately the Volvo driveline does not permit the use of overdrive in the Marcos, while the present final drive is the highest there is which is readily available, cheap, strong and quiet.

In fact, the car feels very nicely geared for use in Britain, cruising at 70-80 mph at well under 4,000 rpm. It is only on Continental motorways that one would really feel the need for higher overall gearing. Acceleration with the present final drive is most impressive. One particularly fierce start produced a short bout of axle tramp, but a slightly less abrupt clutch engagement avoided it and added only 0.1sec to the time to 30 mph. There is a second squeal

Near right: The Volvo engine is long but quite slender—just right for the Marcos installation. The air cleaners are reduced to simple pancakes. The fan is fixed, and the radiator uses a Jaguar E-type core

Centre right: The cockpit is a snug fit for two, but there is plenty of legroom for the tall driver. The massive gear lever belies the light and precise gearbox, and the tray surrounding it is very useful

Far right: The smooth shape of the Marcos has lost none of its appeal. The vestigial bumpers are lightly moulded in GRP, giving little protection

MARCOS 3-LITRE VOLVO (2,978 c.c.)

AUTOCAR 15 April 1971

ACCELERATION

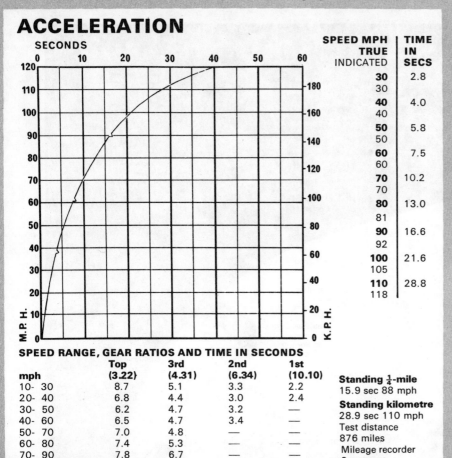

SECONDS

SPEED MPH TRUE INDICATED	TIME IN SECS
30	2.8
30	
40	4.0
40	
50	5.8
50	
60	7.5
60	
70	10.2
70	
80	13.0
81	
90	16.6
92	
100	21.6
105	
110	28.8
118	

SPEED RANGE, GEAR RATIOS AND TIME IN SECONDS

mph	Top (3.22)	3rd (4.31)	2nd (6.34)	1st (10.10)
10- 30	8.7	5.1	3.3	2.2
20- 40	6.8	4.4	3.0	2.4
30- 50	6.2	4.7	3.2	—
40- 60	6.5	4.7	3.4	—
50- 70	7.0	4.8	—	—
60- 80	7.4	5.3	—	—
70- 90	7.8	6.7	—	—
80-100	8.8	—	—	—
90-110	11.4	—	—	—

Standing ¼-mile
15.9 sec 88 mph
Standing kilometre
28.9 sec 110 mph
Test distance
876 miles
Mileage recorder
3 per cent
over-reading

PERFORMANCE
MAXIMUM SPEEDS

Gear	mph	kph	rpm
Top (mean)	120	193	5,500
(best)	120	193	5,500
3rd	90	145	5,500
2nd	61	98	5,500
1st	38	61	5,500

BRAKES

(from 70 mph in neutral)
Pedal load for 0.5g stops in lb

1	45-30	6	40-35
2	40-35	7	37
3	40	8	35
4	40-35	9	30
5	43-38	10	30

RESPONSE (from 30 mph in neutral)

Load	g	Distance
20lb	0.23	131ft
40lb	0.63	48ft
60lb	1.05	28.7ft
Handbrake	0.35	86ft

Max. Gradient 1 in 4

CLUTCH

Pedal . . . . 32lb and 6in.

MOTORWAY CRUISING
Indicated speed at 70 mph . . . . 70 mph
Engine (rpm at 70 mph) . . . . 3,210 rpm
(mean piston speed) . . . . 1,685ft/min.
Fuel (mpg at 70 mph) . . . . 29.0 mpg
Passing (50-70 mph) . . . . 7.0 sec

COMPARISONS

MAXIMUM SPEED MPH
Lotus Plus 2S 130	(£2,616)	121
Marcos 3-litre Volvo	**(£2,554)**	**120**
Triumph TR6 Coupé	(£1,498)	119
Reliant Scimitar GTE	(£2,145)	117
Broadspeed Bullitt	(£1,995)	115

0-60 MPH, SEC
Lotus Plus 2S 130	7.4
Marcos 3-litre Volvo	**7.5**
Triumph TR6	8.2
Broadspeed Bullitt	8.8
Reliant Scimitar GTE	10.7

STANDING ¼-MILE, SEC
Lotus Plus 2S 130	15.4
Marcos 3-litre Volvo	**15.9**
Triumph TR6	16.3
Broadspeed Bullitt	17.1
Reliant Scimitar GTE	17.4

OVERALL MPG
Lotus Plus 2S 130	23.3
Marcos 3-litre Volvo	**22.3**
Triumph TR6	19.8
Reliant Scimitar GTE	18.5
Broadspeed Bullitt	17.3

GEARING (with 175—13in. tyres)
Top	21.8 mph per 1,000 rpm
3rd	16.3 mph per 1,000 rpm
2nd	11.1 mph per 1,000 rpm
1st	6.9 mph per 1,000 rpm

TEST CONDITIONS:
Weather: Overcast. Wind: 0-5 mph. Temperature: 7 deg. C. (44 deg. F.). Barometer: 29.3in. hg. Humidity: 70 per cent. Surfaces: Damp concrete and asphalt.

WEIGHT:
Kerb weight: 18.1 cwt (2,028lb—920kg) (with oil, water and half full fuel tank). Distribution, per cent F, 52.8; R, 47.2. Laden as tested: 22.0 cwt (2,472lb—1,121kg).

TURNING CIRCLES:
Between kerbs L, 35ft 3in.; R, 34ft 1in. Between walls L, 36ft 5in.; R, 35ft 3in., steering wheel turns, lock to lock 2.5.

Figures taken at 13,500 miles by our own staff at the Motor Industry Research Association proving ground at Nuneaton.

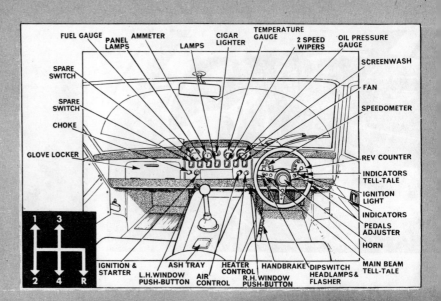

MARCOS 3-LITRE VOLVO (2,978 c.c.)

CONSUMPTION

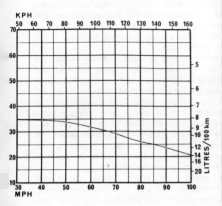

FUEL

(At constant speeds—mpg)

30 mph	35.0
40 mph	34.8
50 mph	33.9
60 mph	32.0
70 mph	29.0
80 mph	26.3
90 mph	23.8
100 mph	20.8

Typical mpg 24 (11.8 litres/100km)
Calculated (DIN) mpg 26.4 (10.7 litres/100km)
Overall mpg . . . 22.3 (12.7 litres/100km)
Grade of fuel . Premium, 4-star (min. 98 RM)

OIL

(SAE 10W/40) . . . Consumption negligible

SPECIFICATION FRONT ENGINE, REAR-WHEEL DRIVE

ENGINE

Cylinders . . .	6 in line
Main bearings .	7
Cooling system .	Water; pump, fan and thermostat
Bore	88.9mm (3.50 in.)
Stroke . . .	80.0mm (3.15 in.)
Displacement. .	2,978 c.c. (181.7 cu.in.)
Valve gear . . .	Overhead, pushrods and rockers
Compression ratio	9.2-to-1. Min. octane rating: 98RM
Carburettors .	2 Zenith-Stromberg 1.75CD 2SE
Fuel pump . .	Pier- urg mechanical
Oil filter	Full flow, replaceable carttridge type
Max. power . .	130 bhp (DIN) at 5,000 rpm
Max. torque . .	152 lb.ft. at 2,500 rpm

TRANSMISSION

Clutch	Diaphragm-spring, hydraulic operation
Gearbox	4-speed, all-synchromesh
Gear ratios . .	Top 1.0
	Third 1.34
	Second 1.97
	First 3.14
	Reverse 3.22
Final drive . . .	Hypoid bevel, ratio 3.22-to-1

CHASSIS and BODY

Construction .	Steel tube chassis, glassfibre reinforced plastic bodywork

SUSPENSION

Front	Independent, double wishbones, coil springs, telescopic dampers, anti-roll bar
Rear	Live axle, upper and lower trailing links, Panhard rod, coil springs, telescopic dampers

STEERING

Type	Rack and pinion
Wheel dia. . .	13¾in.

BRAKES

Make and type .	Girling disc front, drum rear
Dimensions . .	F 9.6in. dia., R 9.0in. dia., 1.75in. wide shoes
Swept area . .	F 197 sq.in., R 99 sq.in., Total 296 sq.in. (269 sq.in./ton laden)

WHEELS

Type	Cast alloy, 4-stud fixing, 5.5in. wide rim
Tyres—make . .	Avon
—type . .	radial ply tubed
—size . .	175-13in.

EQUIPMENT

Battery	12 Volt 39 Ah
Alternator . . .	Bosch 35 amp a.c.
Headlamps. . .	Lucas rectangular, 80/90 watt (total)
Reversing lamp .	Extra
Electric fuses . .	4
Screen wipers .	Two-speed
Screen washers.	Standard, electric
Interior heater .	Standard, water valve type
Heated backlight	Not available
Safety belts . .	Extra, mounting points standard
Interior trim . .	Pvc seats and headlining
Floor covering .	Carpet
Jack	Screw scissor type
Jacking points .	1 each side under sill
Windscreen . .	Toughened (laminated optional)
Underbody protection . .	Chassis painted, GRP body

MAINTENANCE

Fuel tank . . .	12 Imp. gallons (54 litres)
Cooling system .	21½ pints (including heater)
Engine sump . .	10.6 pints (6.0 litres) SAE 10W-40. Change oil every 3,000 miles. Change filter every 3,000 miles
Gearbox	1.1 pints SAE 90EP. Change oil every 6,000 miles
Final drive . . .	2.75 pints SAE 80EP. Check level every 6,000 miles
Grease	No points
Tyre pressures .	F 26; R 26 psi (normal driving) F 30; R 30 psi (fast driving)
Max. payload. .	500 lb (227 kg)

PERFORMANCE DATA

Top gear mph per 1,000 rpm	21.8
Mean piston speed at max. power .	2,625 ft/min
Bhp per ton laden	118 (net)

STANDARD GARAGE 16ft x 8ft 6in.

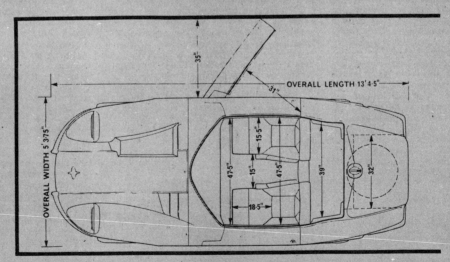

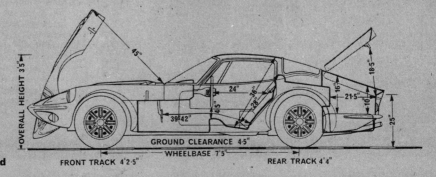

**SCALE 0.3in. to 1ft
Cushions uncompressed**

AUTOTEST MARCOS 3 LITRE . . .

from the tyres as the snatch change into second is made at 40 mph, and this gear takes you on to 60 mph in 7.5sec, more or less matching the time taken by the much higher-revving Lotus Plus 2S 130. The quarter-mile comes up inside 16sec, 90 mph (and the change into top) less than a second later, 100 mph in 21.6sec, and the kilometre is passed in well under the half minute, just as 110 mph appears. This is performance indeed, yet the Marcos does not have to be rowed around with the gear lever; it proved possible to run from 10 to 110 mph in top gear in the length of the MIRA one-mile horizontal straights, without leaving the braking desperately late.

The brakes themselves were absolutely faultless, with plenty of feel and remarkable ultimate stopping power. They were very light despite the absence of a servo, and actually showed a drop in pedal pressure during our fade test.

The Volvo gearchange looks as though it ought to be clumsy, for the cut-down stub of the 164 gear lever is almost an inch in diameter. It comes as something of a surprise to find that the change is actually light and precise, with a light spring loading into the third-top plane which helps the sometimes-awkward change from second to third. There is no trace of baulking, except into reverse, and the clutch—again the standard Volvo article—is strong and yet pleasantly progressive.

Impressive handling

With its wide tyres (Avon radials on the test car), low centre of gravity and good suspension geometry, there is every reason why the Marcos should handle well, and it does. One sits so close to the road that even 60 mph seems fast, but 100 mph seems little faster. The driver must therefore learn a new set of visual references as he creeps up on the handling limits. The Marcos can be thrown into corners at seemingly impossible speeds and go round without fuss, but even so it has its limits. On a smooth surface all four wheels will eventually slide sideways at the same time, correction being a matter of simply lifting-off without having to move the steering wheel at all. On a rougher surface, it is more likely that the back wheels will break away, sometimes fairly smartly. Even in this case recovery is no

problem, for the steering boasts only 2½ turns between extremes of quite a respectable lock, and its directness gives the driver every chance. At the same time, this directness is a drawback because it must contribute to the considerable amount of fight-back through the steering wheel on anything but a very smooth surface. On a poorly surfaced B road it takes a strong man to hold the wheel still at high speed, although one eventually realizes that the car stays pretty much on course even with the wheel jerking wildly some 20-30deg either side of centre. By the same token, stability on motorways is normally excellent, but is upset a little by gusty sidewinds.

Poor ride, good seating

By any standards, the Marcos has a poor ride, although recent improvements in the dampers have got rid of the initial stiction and made the first inch or so of movement softer. Single large bumps are now smoothed out better (helped, no doubt, by the greater sprung weight of the bigger-engined car), but there is still an underlying high-frequency harshness which eventually makes the driver's eyes tired, especially if he is driving fast over secondary roads.

That this is almost the only physical effect of the ride is explained by the excellence of the seats. These are virtually unchanged, giving a semi-reclining driving position which is very relaxing and provides good insulation from the sharp vertical movements of the suspension. The seats are fixed, with the pedal cluster adjustable for reach to suit drivers of different leg lengths. With the pedals fully forward, drivers over 6ft tall can drive the car comfortably. For short drivers (or passengers) there is an optional extra combined cushion-backrest which gives a higher, further-forward sitting position. Sideways location—a matter of being jammed between the door on one side and the massive transmission tunnel on the other—is excellent, and not nearly as uncomfortable as it sounds.

There is enough room down the "pedal tunnel" to allow a driver with large feet to work without the risk of treading on two pedals at once, but there is nowhere to rest the clutch foot when it is clear of the pedal. A positive throttle stop might also be an advantage, because our throttle-bending efforts during the acceleration runs eventually caused the accelerator cable to fray and jam the throttle open. More positive location of the fixed end of the very long cable might also help.

The small steering wheel is set near vertically, just as it should be to go with the driving position. The minor controls are all mounted in the centre of the facia, and are

within the driver's reach. Safety-type rocker switches have replaced the toggle switches of the previous test car. The instruments remain the same, with a large, clear speedometer (dead accurate at low and medium speeds) and rev counter in front of the driver, and the four smaller auxiliary dials above the switches in the centre of the facia.

For tall drivers at least, visibility is not the problem it would appear from outside. The most important thing to remember is that, as in the Jaguar E-type, there is a lot of nose you can't see. It is also rather more difficult to judge the width than in many cars. Wing mirrors would be a help, especially in dense traffic, but a look "over the shoulder" is quite possible. The two-speed wipers clear a good area of screen but were rather smeary and noisy on the test car, and there are no sun visors.

At night, the small Lucas rectangular headlamps do not give anything like enough light to enable the performance to be fully used, and anyone who wishes to drive fast at night will have to investigate the chances of fitting something better. Night driving can also be a bit of a misery because of the driver's low eye level, which is below the height of many lorry headlights.

Heating and ventilation

One point about the Marcos which really deserves further attention is the heating and ventilation. At the moment, the heater is still a simple water-valve affair with a push-pull control on the facia, along with another which controls the air intake. It is possible to get the interior of the car extremely warm, but too much of the warmth emerges at head level. Much more of the hot air needs to be ducted to the footwells, and there should surely be provision for direct fresh-air ventilation in a car whose quarter-lights don't open.

In other respects, the Marcos is quite practical. The boot is by no means large, but will take a fair amount of soft luggage. Inside, there is a map pocket in each door, a large and useful oddments tray built into the centre console, a glove box, and a shelf behind the seats. Entry to and exit from the car varies according to one's height and girth—it is not really a car for the tall and fat.

Noise level is about what one would expect in this sort of car. It can be trickled along very quietly, but when driven hard it makes conversation well-nigh impossible. Induction and fan noise are the main culprits at lower speeds, while higher up the scale there is a good deal of wind noise, especially from the sunroof which was fitted to the test car.

Fuel consumption varies widely according to how the car is driven. We saw as low as 18 mpg on a very hard drive from the West Country; on the other hand the drive up to the MIRA track, deliberately taken fairly gently, returned no less than 30.1 mpg. We would expect most owners to obtain a figure mid-way between these two extremes. Oil consumption on the test car was negligible.

Expensive but fun

For a strict two-seater with a "cooking" engine, the Marcos looks expensive. One has to consider, though, that the engine gives the car extremely good performance, and its standard state of tune should promise long life and great reliability. The chassis gives a good driver the opportunity to explore handling limits well beyond those of most road cars, and the Adams shape has lost none of its eye-catching magic over the years. For these reasons, the car must appeal to the keen extrovert—and it could well be that the car's appeal has been widened by the use of the Volvo engine to give real performance and a touch of the quality image.

The Marcos still looks impressive with everything open. Access to the engine is extremely good, but the massive bonnet is not very rigid; its centre lock helps to keep it in place as well as preventing pilfering from the engine compartment. The boot now has a wooden false floor covering the spare wheel

1971 Models

Marcos Mantis

An upward move from the world of the strict two-seater

By J. R. Daniels, B.Sc.

Triumph TR6 injection engine powers 2-plus-2 car with exciting looks. Tubular metal chassis, reinforced glassfibre body; conventional suspension with live back axle, but much more suspension movement to give better ride

AFTER several years spent producing strict two-seaters, Marcos are at last entering the 2-plus-2 market with their new Mantis. It is a bigger car than anything Marcos have built before, and it uses a new power plant: the Triumph 2.5PI engine as fitted to the TR6 sports car.

The Mantis is a big car by European standards. Compared with the Jaguar E-type 2-plus-2, which is the most nearly comparable car in this respect, Marcos' new car is 3in. longer and 6in. wider—but 4in. lower. The Jaguar has 3in. more wheelbase, but the Marcos has 7in. more track, front and rear. Despite the similarity in size, the Mantis is claimed to have a kerb weight of 2,300 lb, which is 6cwt less than the E-type.

Marcos' use of the Triumph 2.5PI engine represents a complete break with tradition, for they have used Ford engines for years. The Ford vee-6, as used in the Marcos 3-litre, is a good engine in many ways and has some particular attractions for the small, specialized builder. On the other hand, it is relatively heavy and is not exactly renowned for its sporting character.

Having had some experience of big six-cylinder in-line engines (installing the Volvo B30 engine in the 3-litre chassis to meet the American pollution regulations), Marcos decided that the Triumph unit would be more suited to the Mantis. This decision was taken at a late stage, when the chassis had already been designed to take the Ford engine. Fortunately, it was found that very little work was needed to effect the change.

Above: Styled, like the two-seater before it, by Dennis Adams, the Mantis is quite a big car. It is, however, only 3ft 10in. high, and the 13in. wheels do not look too small. Rectangular headlamps are used to keep the wing line low while adhering to the legal minimum lamp centre height

Left: The nose treatment is perhaps the most controversial feature of the styling. Beneath the black snout is the intake for fully ducted radiator, with an electric fan to assist cooling when required

Below: The massive central chassis member is built up into a large console on which almost all the minor controls are mounted, well within the driver's reach. Engine and gearbox are sufficiently far back in the car to allow the comfortable placing of the direct-acting gear lever

Marcos changed from their famous wooden chassis to a fabricated metal-tube one at the end of last year. The change coincided with their move from their old premises at Bradford-on-Avon to the new factory at Westbury, Wiltshire, laid out with a large metal-working area but only a small carpentry shop. The design of the metal chassis for the two-seater was constrained by the existing shape of the car, leading to some awkward production stages. But the Mantis chassis was designed from scratch with metal in mind, and its manufacture has been made very simple: two sub-assembly jigs produce pieces which are laid straight into a final jig, from which the complete chassis emerges after a simple welding operation. Square-section tube is used throughout, and most of the joints are square-cut to ease production. Extra strength is provided at strategic points on the Mantis chassis by tack-welded plates, building up a partial box-section.

The Mantis body is formed from two large and complex glassfibre mouldings, top and bottom. It is completed with the fitting of two massive (and very rigid) doors and the boot lid. Although the greater part of the factory is given over to moulding and body finishing, the body shell is still the production bottleneck. There is only one set of body moulds, and Marcos will want to see how things go with the Mantis before doubling-up their production capacity. As we have already said, the mouldings are quite complex. Marcos are convinced that styling plays the biggest part in selling a car like this, and they were not prepared to compromise the styling for the sake of production convenience. As a result there are (for instance) rebates round the window frames so that all the glass may be flush-fitted, while the roof flares up into sculptured edges with multiple curvature.

When the Mantis body has been finished, it will be painted before being fitted to the chassis—another simplification of production, and a change from their previous practice. A substantial amount of insulating felt is sandwiched between body and chassis at this stage to form one line of defence against noise. Interior layout is conventional, with fixed pedals and moving seats, again in contrast to the smaller Marcos cars.

The Triumph engine is mounted to the chassis on its standard mountings—Marcos are great believers in not bodging the mountings to fit the chassis, which might give rise to considerable problems. Compared with the TR6 installation, the only change is that the air cleaner has been moved from the front of the induction plenum chamber to a sideways-on mounting in the middle. Two Marcos engineers have just completed Lucas' course on the injection system; one of them will be responsible for setting up the engines in the factory, while the other will liaise with Marcos distributors. The Triumph TR6 gearbox is used, with overdrive on the top three gears as standard. Borg-Warner 35 automatic transmission will be an option.

The Mantis suspension follows well-proven Marcos principles, but differs greatly in detail. Triumph Vitesse double wishbones (and steering rack, with the track rod ends suitably extended) are used at the front, together with an anti-roll bar, but the coil spring/damper unit is much longer than on the two-seater, giving a longer travel and a softer ride.

The same principle applies at the rear. Here, the German Ford 3.22 live axle (as used in the Capri 3000) is located by a central A-bracket, massively mounted in the chassis, and two substantial trailing arms. Again, concentric coil spring/damper units are used, and the suspension movement is

Above: The full-fastback rear panel sweeps down to a tail reminiscent of the Aston Martin DB6. A single filler cap feeds the massive fuel tank which is placed forward of the boot and behind the back seats. Note the flush-fitting door handles, of Marcos' own design

Right: The front seats fold forward to give access to those in the back. The latter are small and rather upright, but shaped to give splendid sideways location. Headroom is the main problem for tall back passengers. Not the rearward extension of the centre console; the interior of the tray will be covered by non-slip material in production cars

Below: Claimed capacity of the boot is 10 cubic feet. The loading sill is low, and the lid is self-supporting. A trim panel on the left covers the injection pump, while the battery is on the right and the spare wheel lives in a carrier underneath

no less than 7in.—a good deal for this sort of car.

The brakes add to the list of Triumph parts used on the Mantis, with large front discs and wide rear drums. A split-circuit hydraulic system is used. At the time of writing, the final form of the cast alloy wheels was still being decided. Marcos would like to use really wide tyres on the Mantis, but are limited to 185 section as long as they use 13in. wheels. Apparently no wider tyres than this are made for wheels of this diameter.

One major innovation is the use of a fully ducted radiator, taking in air beneath the edge of the snout and exhausting through a cast alloy grille in the middle of the bonnet. A single electric fan is used, although Marcos are going to keep an eye on any vehicles headed for warmer climes in case doubling-up is needed. Advantages claimed for the ducted installation include the ability to get away with a smaller radiator, and elimination of the hot air flow down the transmission tunnel, which can make the interior uncomfortably warm. Under-bonnet temperatures apparently do not become excessive, even with the airflow ducted away.

Low body drag

The body is reckoned to have a drag coefficient of about 0.35, based on model tests. It is thought that the full-size car may be a little better, having been slightly refined since the wind tunnel model was built. Engine power is 150 bhp (net), a little higher than Triumph's own figure, thanks to the fabricated Janspeed exhaust system used in the Mantis. Jem Marsh reckons he has seen 125 mph in the course of testing; the test programme also included a good deal of time spent on the pavé circuit at MIRA.

Despite its low drag, the body is massive. There is certainly enough room inside to make the Mantis quite a comfortable 2-plus-2, and the back seats are shaped and upholstered to give excellent location. The area of glass used is very large indeed; Marcos say that a full hundredweight of the car is Triplex-produced. The petrol tank is large at 17½ gallons—always a welcome feature—and the boot, with a low loading sill, is really large. The spare wheel lives in a carrier beneath its floor, while the injection pump is on the left and the battery on the right.

Production of the Mantis is already under way at the Westbury factory. Apart from the two development cars, we saw four others in final assembly early this month. Asking price has still to be decided. □

The engine drops neatly between the main chassis members, and the only change needed has been the moving of the air cleaner from its usual position at the front end of the plenum chamber. Note the built-up top mountings for the spring-damper units, which pass through the Vitesse upper wishbones to act on the lower ones. The radiator and its exhaust ducting can be seen

SPECIFICATION FRONT ENGINE, REAR WHEEL DRIVE

ENGINE

Cylinders	6, in line
Main bearings	4
Cooling system	Water; pump, electric fan and thermostat
Bore	74.7mm (2.94 in.)
Stroke	95.0mm (3.74 in.)
Displacement	2,498 c.c. (152 cu.in.)
Valve gear	Overhead; pushrods and rockers
Compression ratio	9.5-to-1 Min. octane rating: 100RM
Fuel injection	Lucas Mk II port-type
Fuel pump	Lucas, electric vane
Oil filter	AC full-flow, renewable element
Max. power	150 bhp (net) at 5,700 rpm
Max. torque	158 lb.ft. (net) at 3,000 rpm

TRANSMISSION

Clutch	Borg & Beck, diaphragm spring, 8.5 in. dia.
Gearbox	4-speed, all-synchromesh
Gear ratios	Top 1.0 OD top 0.82
	Third 1.33 OD third 1.08
	Second 2.01 OD second 1.65
	First 3.14
	Reverse 3.22
Final drive	Hypoid bevel, 3.22-to-1

CHASSIS and BODY

Construction	Fabricated steel tube chassis with moulded glassfibre body

SUSPENSION

Front	Independent; double wishbones, coil springs, telescopic dampers, anti-roll bar
Rear	Live axle, A-bracket, trailing arms, coil springs, telescopic dampers

STEERING

Type	Rack and pinion
Wheel dia.	15.0 in.

BRAKES

Make and type	Girling disc front, drum rear
Servo	Girling vacuum
Dimensions	F 9.6 in. dia., R 9.0 in. dia., 2.0 in. wide shoes.
Swept area	F 197 sq.in., R 113 sq.in. Total 310 sq.in. (188 sq.in./ton laden)

WHEELS

Type	Cast alloy, 4-stud fixing, 5.5 in. wide rim.
Tyres—make	Avon or Goodyear
—type	radial ply tubeless
—size	185-13 in.

EQUIPMENT

Battery	12 Volt 59 Ah
Alternator	Lucas 15AC 35 amp a.c.
Headlamps	Lucas rectangular sealed-beam, 150/150 watt (total)
Reversing lamp	Standard
Electric fuses	4
Screen wipers	2-speed
Screen washer	Standard, electric
Interior heater	Standard, water-valve type
Heated backlight	Extra
Safety belts	Standard in front seats
trim	Ambla seats Cirrus headlining.
Floor covering	Carpet
Jack	Screw scissor type
Jacking points	2 each side under body
Windscreen	Toughened
Underbody protection	Primed chassis, glassfibre body

MAINTENANCE

Fuel tank	17.5 Imp. gallons (80 litres)
Cooling system	11 pints (including heater)
Engine sump	8 pints (4.5 litres) SAE 20W/50. Change oil every 6,000 miles. Change filter element every 12,000 miles.
Gearbox and overdrive	3.5 pints SAE 90EP Change oil every 6,000 miles.
Final drive	1.5 pints SAE 90EP. Change oil every 6,000 miles
Grease	No points

DIMENSIONS

Wheelbase	8 ft 6 in. (259 cm)
Track: front	4 ft 9 in. (145 cm)
Track: rear	4 ft 9 in. (145 cm)
Overal length	15 ft 6¾ in. (474 cm)
Overall width	5 ft 11 in. (180 cm)
Overall height (unladen)	3 ft 10 in. (117 cm)
Ground Clearance (laden)	4 in. (10 cm)
Turning circle	34 ft 0 in. (10.4 m)
Kerb weight	3,200 lb (1,450 kg)

PERFORMANCE DATA

Top gear mph per 1,000 rpm	22.1
Overdrive top mph per 1,000 rpm	27.0
Mean piston speed at max. power	3,553 ft/min.
Bhp per ton laden	91 (net)

What's a Marcos?

As a fiberglass driveway decoration there's nothing near the Marcos 3L at the price. Incidentally, it's a pretty good car.

Imagine a lower E-Type Jaguar. Picture a stretched-out Ford GT40. Believe it to be the latest creation of a famous Italian body builder. That's why the Marcos is spectacular. Almost nothing else on the street attracts such slack-jawed amazement and admiration.

Let's clear up one or two questions you may have about what exactly a Marcos is. It's made in England at a rate of one or two a day, a fiberglass body on a steel squaretube frame. Its name is a compound of Jeremy MARsh, who backed the first car commercially in 1960 and who still heads the firm today, and Frank COStin, who designed the marine plywood frames of the first Marcos cars but hasn't had much to do with them since.

Unlike many of the overseas special-car makers Marcos has done the work needed to qualify its coupe for the U.S. market, plastering it with the usual lengthy placard of exemptions. Under the hood is a fully desmogged engine, the new 182 CID Volvo six. For further details you'll want to talk to your nearest Marcos dealer if you can find him. If not, Marcos International, St. Gabriel's Court, 202 East 35th Street, New York, N.Y. 10016, the importer, may have the dope. Their pride and joy lists for $4,495, which includes the hairy alloy wheels, sunroof, airhorns, electric windows, and your choice of manual or automatic box. Only a radio is extra.

Free-lance designer Dennis Adams did the shape of the Marcos coupe back in 1962, and it hasn't changed much since, which is to say it was ahead of its time then and remains today one of the most professional and most successful sports car styling jobs done in England in the last decade. During the switch from wood to steel construction, the car acquired a not-too-flattering ridge below the rocker panels. Otherwise, it's unmarked and unabashed by the passage of time.

There's one feature of the 43-inch-high Marcos that's distinctly unfashionable in this age of mid-engine mania: you can see out easily all around. Because of a wrap-down rear window, visibility is very good to the rear quarters. You can't see where the nose is any more than you can in a Corvette, so it's an unhappy package to handle in town, both in traffic and parking. It's so low that when a Checker taxi rolled right into the rear of the Marcos, its driver protested, "I just didn't see it!"

Jeremy Marsh is a tall man, luckily, so his Marcos is a roomy car for both driver and passenger. The seats slope back at a 45-degree angle, one that's extremely comfortable. They're fixed in place; a big black wheel on the left side of the dash is turned to swing the suspended pedals back and forth to vary the leg room. Getting into anything this low is not easy. Getting out again is a challenge to youth and agility, a battle to keep from falling out and smashing your expensive bridgework on the pavement. A lateral crawl and scramble is the recommended drill.

Some features of the Marcos are very British. Among them are the round white-on-black instruments, the row of rocker switches on the padded dash, the pull-up hand brake lever, and the incredibly tiny ashtray. Amazingly non-British are the keys: one type of key fits the ignition and all the locks, including the glove box (very narrow) and the trunk (surprisingly roomy). That's an almost unheard of convenience on an English car.

The Marcos surely looks like a sports car. Does it also go like one? ZL-1 Corvettes are not in danger. The Volvo's 145 bhp at 5,500 rpm give the 2,000-pound coupe good performance, such as acceleration to 60 in 7.6 seconds and a top speed of just over 110 mph. But it doesn't give it gladly. The Volvo six may be a good engine in a sedan but it's not as lively and sharp as you'd like in a sports car.

The engine makes a lot of noise, not from the exhaust or the valve gear, but a windy *vrooming* noise, as from the fan. It doesn't encourage you to rev it much over 4,000 rpm. Then there's the throttle travel, which Marcos has made extremely long, so long that it's not easy to stretch your right leg out that far. It may be required by the adjustable-pedal scheme. Anyway it makes it awkward to use full throttle.

There's one thing about the Marcos that's just like a Ferrari GTO: the shift lever, up so high on the central tunnel

Only 43 inches high, the Marcos 3L is essence of the long hood/short tail gran turisimo look. The chassis originally had wood components. Springs are coils, and front brakes discs.

From the rear, the chopped "Kamm" tail can be appreciated. Marcos body is all fiberglass. The standard power plant is a Volvo Six. In England, some are being sold with Ford V6 power plants.

Row upon row of gauges and rocker switches tell you that the Marcos is a real driver's car.

that it's almost at ear level. It's a very nice four-speed shift, smooth, fast and easy. It matches the best side of the Marcos — its responsive, agile handling. There are only 2⅔ turns from side to side on a good steering lock that allows a 30-foot turning circle — quick steering that the small leather-trimmed wheel makes feel even quicker. You just lean back in the all-enveloping seat, strapped in by one of the best diagonal harnesses I've used, and tweak your wrists to aim the Marcos around a corner.

Its handling is very nice for the highway — balanced, neutral and quick to respond. Disc front brakes do a smooth job of stopping. There are coil springs all around, with an unusual parallel leading arm control system for the live rear axle. Its strong suit isn't the ride, which is relentlessly firm. The quick steering came in handy for dodging New York's potholes, a good thing because bumpy surfaces are worth avoiding in a Marcos.

Rough roads do show up one of the car's good features: it gives you the impression that it's been around a while — that most of its bugs and small irritations have been eradicated by its years in production and by the personal attention that Jeremy Marsh gives to the cars he builds. You don't often get that reassuring feeling from a limited-production car, not even from the most costly ones. Pieces don't fall off and they don't feel like they're going to. That may not sound like much of a recommendation but believe me, these days it is. /MT

Classic choice
Marcos

Jonathan Wood looks at what is involved in buying and running one of these stylish wooden chassis two seaters from Bradford on Avon.

MARCOS was derived from two names: Jem Marsh, who originated the company, and Frank Costin an aerodynamicist from De Haviland, who brought with him the idea of a car with a wooden chassis.

Marcos cars were built in significant numbers over an eight year period, 1068 examples of the classic two seater were built. However, despite (and perhaps because of) this comparatively short production life, enthusiasm for the marque is kept buoyant by the 450-strong Marcos Owners Club. In view of this, it seemed sensible to gather together a number of members of the aforementioned club, so I could glean as much practical information as possible about the purchase and running of these cars. My thanks must therefore go to the energetic Colin Feyerabend, who produces the club's bulky and fact filled magazine, and owners Mike Libby and Richard Walden.

But first a historical excursion to put the Marcos into perspective. The vital meeting between Marsh and Costin took place in a pub in Hitchin in 1959. The result was that the first Marci (I am assured that this is the correct plural!) were built, on Lotus 7 lines of a coupé top and gullwing doors, cycle-type mudguard wings and a 100E Ford engine.

By 1960 Dennis and Peter Adams had joined the team, the former being involved on the mechanical side, having arrived via Lister Jaguars, and Peter to "chip in" on the wooden chassis construction.

The cars initially appeared on the race track driven by such notables as Jackie Stewart and Bill Moss. These distinctive cars had four piece windscreens, and contained plenty of plywood and their slightly lumpy appearance resulted in them being known as the "Ugly Duckling". Late 1960 saw the departure of Frank Costin to the boat building industry, while the "factory" moved from cramped premises in Luton to an industrial estate at Bradford-on-Avon in Wiltshire.

With rather more elbow room, the car was developed as a two seater and later the classic Marcos shape, evolved, the car having a monocoque wooden chassis with glass fibre body panels. Although a steel chassis replaced the wood in 1969, the purpose of this article is to deal with these earlier cars of a marque that stopped production in 1972. All the models in this survey are Ford engined, with the exception of the first production model that featured a Volvo 1800 power unit. The following production figures will be of help to indicate the scarcity, or otherwise, of the example the reader may have under scrutiny.

Engine	number built
Volvo 1800	99
Ford 1500	82
Ford 1650	32
Ford 1600	192
Ford 3-litre V-6	100

From which we can proceed to describing just what is involved in the purchase and running of these slightly unusual but beautifully-styled motor cars.

Bodywork
The distinctive bodywork on the Marcos is made from glass fibre and while this naturally eliminates rusting, there are nevertheless problems and these are mainly concerned with stress cracks. Starting at the front of the car, carefully examine the state of the one piece forward hinging bonnet. The most likely area is where the wing line joins the bonnet proper and also around the engine bulge. Once these cracks have appeared, it is very difficult to get rid of them, I am assured. Filling will suffice for a time, but the gaps do tend to open up again. In addition to the bonnet area, cracks have a habit of appearing around the four corners of the windscreen, another vital check point.

One of the prime areas for investigation are the doors. Make a point of examining the seals as they have a habit of deteriorating with use. The result of this is that water tends to find its way inside the car, being retained by the sound deadening material contained therein.

Also keep an eye open for rippling of the glass fibre, which may indicate that there is trouble ahead. The colour is, incidentally, sprayed on to the glass fibre atop of a grey primer, the tones being white, blue, tangerine red, tartan red, chrome yellow, Bahama yellow, grey and green.

The windscreen on the car was specially made by either Triplex or Tudor, the rear one being plastic. Earlier examples had ventilation slots which do tend to crack over the years.

Chassis
As previously mentioned, the unusual thing about the Marcos chassis is that it is made of wood, no less than 386 pieces going into each chassis. On the Marcos, the chassis forming seat backs, floor, dashboard supports, boot and transmission cover, support for engine frame, rear axle tunnel and wheel arch supports are made of marine quality West African mahogany plywood, Douglas Fir plywood and Sitka spruce, glued together with Aerolite, to make a semi-monocoque base.

In the main, the rather unusual chassis material has lasted well over the years, but there are a number of vital checks to be made. The principal one is directly below the sill. Here the lagging, providing cushioning between the chassis and the body tends to retain water to the detriment of the wood. In addition to this, the plywood tends to rot from the *inside*. The other important check areas is where wood has been drilled to accept metal parts. Over a period of time the bolt holes tend to elongate. At the same time check the condition of the rubber mounting washers as these tend to split and perish. The most likely points are the front sub frame mountings and the rear axle radius arm mountings. These can be clearly seen inside the boot.

Suspension, steering and brakes
Front suspension is basically Triumph Vitesse/GT6, though a modification has been effected which combines the spring and the shock absorber. There is a particularly important check to be made on this unit, which applies whether you are examining a car with the intention of purchasing it, or if you are already running an example. The forward lower wishbone mounting is slightly prone to becoming detached from its sub frame, so don't skimp this check. In addition to this, the suspension suffers from the usual Vitesse/GT6 problem of trunnion wear, the lower being the usual culprit.

The rack and pinion also springs from the same Triumph ancestry, but don't make the mistake of assuming that a Herald unit will fit because it won't! The steering column is a three piece universally jointed affair running in rose joints. One of the snags associated with its positioning is that the column runs *through* the fan belt drive on the V-6 engined models. Therefore the column has to be taken out if a new belt is fitted, though the usual dodge is to wire a spare belt within the arc.

As far as the rear suspension is concerned, I've already mentioned the problem associated with the radius arm mountings. The same applies to those cars fitted with a Panhard Rod. Again the mountings can give trouble. It is probably an appropriate moment to reflect on the various type of rear suspension available. The original Volvo-engined car used a de Dion rear axle, though this particular unit developed an appetite for half shafts and this was replaced with a conventional live rear axle from the Mark II Cortina fitted with a 3·56:1 ratio or a 3·77:1 unit from the Corsair. Naturally when receiving power from Ford four-cylinder engines, the rear end remained trouble free. But with the 3-litre V-6 engine, the crown wheel and pinion is more likely to protest at the unaccustomed revs, so if you're contemplating the purchase of one of these larger capacity cars, keep an ear open for any unfortunate noises from that quarter.

Brakes are discs at the front and drums at the rear. They are Girling parts and are listed in that company's parts list under a "Marcos" heading. And from brakes to wheels. It is particularly important that the wheels on a Marcos are statically and dynamically balanced on and off the car. The rear ones are particularly sensitive to imbalance, resulting in an unpleasant vibration that can be felt throughout the car.

Engine, gearbox and transmission
Fortunately the engines fitted in the Marcos range were reliable units in their own right, though there were a number of modifications made to them, which should be noted. First the Volvo unit. This is a

standard B18 engine, though the exhaust system was made specially for the car. Trouble can be experienced with the rear mounting clamps. The four-cylinder Ford engines present no particular problems (from 1967), but the V-6 (from 1969) was something of a squeeze and was fitted with a small bore exhaust system and used TR6 silencers at the back of the car. This particular engine was the type used in the Ford Zodiac and a desirable modification is to fit the sump from the post-1972 Granada as the bulky part of the sump is situated at the rear of the engine rather than the front, where it was far more vulnerable. Ground clearance problems are an ever present consideration with any Marcos. Another change to remember with this engine is to fit the smaller of two oil filter sizes. Again space is the limiting factor. Some of the V-6 models also suffer from overheating. This can be overcome by fitting a four-core radiator, as a factory oversight resulted in some cars being sent out with the three core variety as used on the V-4-engined Fords.

Gearboxes present no major problems as they are firmly attached to their respective engines, with the exception of the bulky V-6 unit. It suffers from an impossibly low first gear, so that overdrive, in effect, becomes top gear. The electrical connection to the overdrive unit has a habit of becoming detached, while slow engagement is usually caused by a low oil level in the gearbox. It is therefore important to keep a regular check on the level.

Interior

The main problem with the interior of the Marcos is lack of ventilation during the summer months. The problem can be eased by driving with the windows open, but the electrically operated variety only allow two-thirds of the window space to be utilised.

During the winter your enemy is rain! As already mentioned, this tends to enter around the door seals, but also gets in via the side windows, settling on the torsion box carpeting. Water also gets in around the front and rear screens. Visibility is also impaired by the V-6's larger power bulges on the bonnet and for this reason the seat-pans were heightened. As a result even the most hardened Marcos owner isn't quite sure where the end of his bonnet is!

The black interior finish is a fashionable feature, the seats, carpets and dashboard being so finished. The seats themselves are fixed to the bulkhead and are not adjustable. To compensate for this, the pedals carry a six inches adjustment, operated by a wheel mounted below the dashboard.

Another slightly weird feature of the interior becomes apparent when it is necessary to gain access to the windscreen wiper motor. This was entombed at birth, so to speak, and the only way to reach it is to cut out the back of the glove compartment. The box itself is stapled, glued and screwed into place making removal virtually impossible.

How much and spare parts

One of the advantages of a car that uses a number of well-known proprietory parts is that they are still generally available, providing you know what they were fitted to originally! And having said that don't assume that everything will be *exactly* the same. This is just where club membership comes into its own. For if you own a Marcos it's essential to join the Marcos

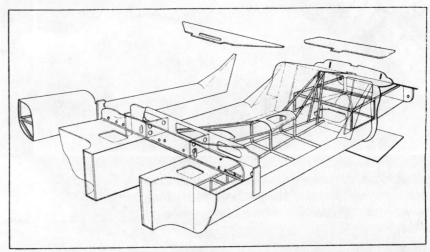

The wooden chassis of the Marcos. It is made of West African Mahogany plywood, Douglas fir plywood and Sitka spruce and contains no less than 386 parts!

Above, left to right, front suspension on the Marcos. The lower forward wishbone mounting should be checked. Centre, under the bonnet of a V6. Note the steering column running through arc of the fan belt. Right, the wooden construction is clearly revealed in the boot.

Left, a 1965/6 Marcos 1800, pictured when new. Below, left, instrumentation is comprehensive and black is used throughout. Right, Marcos owner Richard Walden with his V6 engined car.

Owners Club. They know exactly what came from where and are also a source of glass fibre body parts. The secretary is the aforementioned Colin Feyerabend and his address is 61 Middle Road, Higher Denham, near Uxbridge, Middx.

Parts can also be obtained from Jem Marsh, one of the co-founders of the marque. His address is 153/154 West Wilts Trading Estate, Westbury, Wiltshire (0373 864097). As might be expected, Jem Marsh has all the original moulds and jigs relating to the car's production and he is therefore in a unique position to undertake restoration and refurbishing. This is particularly important if the car in question has

been damaged in an accident when the correct re-alignment of parts has to be undertaken.

Marcos owners are therefore fortunate in having such a vital source of spares and accumulated knowledge at their disposal. And as far as price goes, you can expect to pay around £800 for a running example, though outstanding ones have changed hands for as much as £2,000. And if you really want to see an outstanding collection of Marcos cars then make a note that the Marcos Owners Club are holding their annual rally at Donington Park, Derbyshire, on Sunday June 4. You'll be made very welcome!●

One of the most exciting DIY sports coupés of all time, Jem Marsh's sleek roadcar-cum-racer appears again with modern Ford Mechanicals, even better looks — and performance plus!

MOVE WITH

'Looks like an E-type' is the usual comment when people see the 'big' Marcos — 'big' to distinguish it from its Mini-brother, also originated by Jem Marsh. Not only in its sleek styling, but also in performance did it have similarities to the E-type, when the V6 Marcos first appeared in the late sixties.

In fact, both were raced — and both still race. As late as 1980, Jem was outright winner of the Group 2 Historic Championship — and in 1981 *Roger Eland* was outright winner in a '64 Marcos-Volvo 1800 — beating Lotus 23s, AC Cobras, and the like. And *Mark Hales* has done great things with a '69 V6 3-litre in very recent years.

Good used Marcos cars fetch excellent prices — Ford, Volvo and Triumph-engined models from 10 or 15 years ago, fetching prices from around £2000 to £4500. And the re-introduction of the marque has meant that scarce spares have once again become fairly easy to obtain — not least of which are body mouldings.

It's not a poor man's kit, and anyone wanting to build a kit on the cheap ought to look elsewhere. It is a sophisticated performance car, should be regarded as such, built as such, and may take up to £5000 to complete to the standard of the Marcos motor-show car. And as such it will have, and hold, excellent resale value.

The Jem Marsh philosophy is to ensure that the builder has a good start towards producing a professional-looking job. Thus much of the assembly work is done in the Stage-1 kit. The rust-protected frame, with all suspension fixing points

attached, is bolted to the jig-bonded body/under-tray unit. Bonnet is fitted, as are doors and boot. Front and rear glass is installed and sealed. Special rose-jointed steering linkage supplied, wiring and brake pipes are fitted. Pedal-carriage assembly is supplied, as are pedal surround, battery box, instruments, and moulded grained dashboard.

However, side windows do not come with the *Stage-1 kit*, but with the *Stage 3*. Aluminium frames can be bought separately for £56 each (plus VAT) — as can side-window glass, channels and rubbers. The *Stage-3 kit* also includes electric window motors, filler cap and fittings, boot lock, catches and stay, handbrake cable, plus fuel tank and sender unit.

The *Stage-2 kit* includes numbers of items the builder may care to make or obtain himself — but two are essential to buy, in my opinion. Their Panhard-rod costs £15, and its rose-joint and bushes £6.50 the lot. If you buy the whole kit it will be fitted — and it also includes radius rods and bushes, pedal box and top, front and rear road springs, four adjustable dampers, headlamp covers and fixtures, trimmed seat backs and cushions, and the four bumper sections.

Numbers of other bodywork bits, catches and suchlike, that one might call 'furniture' can be got in *Stage-4*, but can also be obtained from vehicle dismantlers — and the information of what comes from what is included in the *Build Manual*. Sometimes, of course, it is possible to buy such items new from the various original car manufacturers

There are some extra items you'll need — such as an electric (Kenlowe) fan for the forward-mounted Capri radiator — and you discard the original belt-driven unit. A special exhaust for the V6, if you don't want to make your own, is £106 from Marcos — or about £70 for the 1600. The four 5" headlamps come from a Capri with that arrangement, or can be bought from various lamp makers or suppliers.

You can use standard wheels, but the whole image of the car demands something superior. The show car had 195/60-series tyres on 14" sculptured aluminium rims. But Jem advises against super-wide tyres, which are unnecessary and do nothing to improve the already superb handling of this road-car-cum-racer.

In the beginning

Jem seriously suggests you don't bother to use anything but the 3-litre or 1600 Capri as a donor car. Plenty about, and often cheap — but do buy a *driveable* runner, he advises. From that you get the engine, gearbox, back axle, propshaft, radiator, nuts and bolts — and even wheels and tyres if they're OK. You have to get Triumph front parts, including rack and pinion and steering column.

Buying old Cortinas, or fitting Volvo or Triumph engines, usually means yet another donor car, worn parts that must be overhauled, extra costs, and in some cases eventual spares problems, and/or high costs thereof (especially Volvo).

If you want to have a car professionally built, you supply the donor car or its necessary mechanical

CHASSIS

It's constructed of 1½" 16-gauge square-section steel tube. Bonded floor/body attaches with about 50 bolts - the whole assembly forming a rigid stress-bearing structure. Frame can be supplied to take a range of engines.

FRONT UNIT

Suspension basically from big-disc Spitfire, Vitesse, or GT6 - with road-springs available new from Marcos to suit this car. Adjustable shockers also recommended. Biggest rim width 5½"/6" - best tyre size 185/70 on 13" rims.

REAR UNIT

Can't fit leaf springs, so Capri axle located by radius rods and Panhard rod. Marcos sell appropriate coils and adjustable shockers. Capri propshaft is shortened. Standard Capri axle ratio suitable (gives better acceleration).

ENGINE

Car basically designed for 3-litre Capri V6 Mk II from '73/4, or Capri 1600 - with standard manual or automatic gearboxes. Or you can use old Cortina Mk I or II 1600 mechanicals - or later Ford 2.3, 2.8, 2000 - Volvo 1800 or 164.

COCKPIT

Car's driving position adaptable to suit its driver, with pedal-mount adjustable by about 1ft of travel, and steering-column adjustable (by spanner) for length and height. Seat insert can provide higher and closer position.

STOWAGE

Special 11-gallon fuel tank, costing about £25 (part of Stage II kit) fits under rear window. Spare wheel is mounted in the floor, so there is still enough room for reasonable amount of soft luggage. Boot lid held by self-lock stay.

MARCOS

parts, checked and restored if required, and Marcos provide the full kit specification to the builder. The people that he has vetted and recommends are *Specialist Cars, Unit One, Souldern Gate, Souldern, Oxon OX6 9HZ. Tel: Fritwell 292.* Price will depend on what degrees of individual specification you order.

If you are building the car yourself, and you obtain all the various bits to do it, then think in terms of perhaps 100 hours or more to complete the job.

Colour? You'll have to spray the finished car. Due to the complex GRP shape it is difficult to self-colour the glassfibre — and Jem makes a point of saying that pigmented GRP often does not retain its high gloss or original shade. Also, of course, there can be problems once any damage repair has been carried out, as we know only too well.

Then and now

For those who have had knowledge of the original Marcos, needless to say no wood is now used in the construction of the sub-structure. Heating and ventilation is improved, with face-level vents incorporated. Trim used to be black, but is now tan *Dralon* — though *Connolly leather* is optional, and one can, of course, buy Connolly hides from their own factory, and do a complete interior trim in any one of a large number of colours (see *On the Line* for further details).

So far as registration is concerned, you simply use the number of the original donor vehicle, and have the details changed on the registration document — and inform your insurance company, of course. If you want a later registration, then you'll have to buy it in the well-known way, and transfer it. Registering the car as new would introduce problems that I personally would rather not bother knowing about!

What's it like?

I'd like to have driven this latest demonstrator, but time did not allow between completion, and when it left for its stand at the Birmingham Motor Show. It's previous popularity, and racing successes, are fair assurance that its road and track manners leave little to be desired.

A static inspection proved it to be a very practical car — the lifting bonnet making it easy for servicing. By the way, the Rover V8 has been dropped into one or two of these cars — with just room to spare.

Though it is low, access is not difficult — but exiting on to a high pavement may call for some agility, I would guess. It's absolutely superb inside, and I do like the very variable control positions and well-shaped seats — but that bonnet does rather disappear from view — making the judging of distance a bit awkward at first. I would certainly go for that optional sunshine roof — the sliding variety for me.

Would I have one? NOT 'ARF!

Tony Bostock

For full details, and colour brochure, send £1 to Marcos, 153 West Wilts Trading Estate, Westbury, Wiltshire BA13 4JN. Tel: 0373 864097.

The Marcos 3 Litre

Geoff Le Prevost looks at a Do-It-Yourself classic

I thought I knew a bit about cars when I came to *Practical Classics* last year but I soon learned to question even the bit I thought I knew. I had to re-evaluate the makes I had considered "good cars" and those which I had always regarded as "bad cars". There were some surprises and not a little disillusionment. It came as a great pleasure therefore, when given the opportunity to drive a Marcos 3 Litre, to find that it was as much fun as I had always hoped it would be.

I was keen to sample Mr Andrew Graham's Marcos not only because I liked the car as a whole, but because it is fitted with the same Ford three litre V6 engine which is to be found in the Reliant Scimitar GTE which I have been using as an everyday car for a month or so, and I've always wanted to compare them. The Scimitar engine is old and rumbley but I know what it is capable of.

The motor in the Marcos is quieter and fitter but still emitted the characteristic "dub dub dub" of a V-engine. The response was the same, bags of low-down torque and no need to rev over 4,500 because there is nothing there. The gearbox, as with the Scimitar, is somewhat imprecise and although, with some concentrated effort, I could improve on gear change times, it is it not a box which cries out for quick change techniques.

The Marcos as a breed was the creation of engineer Gem Marsh and designer Frank Costin who got together in the late fifties to build a GT car using aircraft technology and materials. The result was a wooden car with an aerodynamic body, topped with what looked like a lean-to greenhouse. Some development work followed and, in 1964, the Marcos GT went into production.

The new car was similar to the protoytpe only in its sleek aerodynamic shape – the design evolution was startling, it was almost like Model T to E-Type overnight and it was hard to credit that one grew from the other. The first Marcos GT was powered by the Volvo 1800 engine which was to be found in the contemporary P1800. Some cars were factory built, many were made from kits.

The car was bodied in glass fibre and, although it had a tubular steel front subframe, it was attached to a monocoque chassis built entirely from marine ply. Now, although that chassis was pretty well rot proof and very strong, it proved difficult, if not impossible, to repair in the event of crash damage.

My use of the E-Type as a development comparison earlier was not accidental, that sleek, low front end, particularly with slim quarter bumpers, looks much inspired by the Jaguar which first appeared in 1961. The rest of the car was very different and that swept-up back was not unlike the rear end of Ferrari 250GT, also of that period. While both of these major designs have passed into history, the Marcos has survived and still has a 'modern' look.

The fastback coupe design lasted the full span of the car's 'first' production life, some eight years, and is virtually unchanged in the car which is once again available new. Underneath the skin it was a different story. The changes were many and varied.

The original rear suspension was an unusual and complex device made up of Triumph 2000 wishbones and springs coupled with a De Dion tube which had a sliding joint and very little to do with the suspension other than holding the wheels upright. On later cars, the live rear axle was located by two lower leading arms and one upper leading arm with the help of a panhard rod.

The Volvo engine was replaced as time went on by a choice of Ford motors – the four cylinder 1,650cc; the two litre V4 and, of course, the three litre V6 which had powered the Zodiac and was, by this time, finding its way into a number of specialist-built cars like the Reliant and the TVR Tuscan, a big rival of the Marcos during the era.

With the suspension improvement came changes to that unpopular wooded chassis which was not only unrepairable but did not meet Federal standards in the lucrative trans-Atlantic market. The new chassis was fabricated from 1½ inch, 16g square section steel tube which attaches to the floor/body shell by 47 bolts. It had to be a well built chassis to replace the wood version which, after all, had proved capable of handling V6 power.

Towards the end of the company's life, the designers turned again to Volvo, this time in the shape of the cumbersome three litre straight six, an engine already type-approved for America and which was to lead Marcos into a big sales drive in the States. The Americans didn't want to know, the sales drive flopped and took the company with it in 1971. In all, just over 1,000 cars were built.

Andrew Graham's car was factory-built in 1970 and acquired, through Gem Marsh, some three years ago. Although the vehicle carries the underbonnet legend that it is a Marcos 1600, checks on chassis numbers indicate fairly conclusively that it was a 3 Litre right from the start.

Before seeing this car for the first time, on a bright but chilly Saturday morning in December, I had known that it would be very low – but this was ridiculous! Motoring journalists are, for some unfathonable reason, quite often very tall. I have always tried hard to top six feet in height but failed. However the Marcos, at 3ft 6½in, makes even the shortest of us look good.

The first problem crops up when you open the tiny door. How do you get in? If you put a cushion under the dining table and then try to sit on it, you will have a fair idea of Marcos

'How do I get down there?' The editor is not particularly tall but towers over the low Marcos.

dimensions. You cannot get into a Marcos *and* be dignified, there is usually something left over, often your right leg.

Having folded myself in, I could then adjust the car to fit my frame. Those racey-looking, laid back seats are fixed. To carry out the adjustments you simply make yourself comfortable in the seat and then turn the large, knurled knob on the dashboard to the right of the steering wheel. This moves the pedals up towards your feet (or away from your knees depending on how they were adjusted to start with). The system might sound a little Heath Robinson, but it works remarkably well.

With the engine fired up and a gear sorted out, problem two looms frighteningly quickly – you can't see out of these cars! The windscreen is raked quite steeply and that long bonnet is topped by the 3 Litre 'power bulge'. The nearside verge disappears altogether as you peer out through a gap no larger than a shoe box.

My panic subsided as I edged the car out into a country road in West Sussex and I discovered that I *could* see where I was going – it is just a case of recognising everything from a different angle. Hand in hand with a low

Possibly the most inspiring view of the Marcos showing the sleek lines and that swept-up tail.

The Marcos 3 Litre

The bonnet hinges forward to provide good access to the V6 engine and the boot lid has a self-locking stay. The 11 gallon fuel tank which sits at the forward end of the boot is a Marcos specification unit and kit builders had to obtain these from the company, not the 'donor' car.

The square section tubular chassis can be clearly seen here. Setting the engine well back in the car gave very good handling characteristics because of the fairly even weight distribution. Marcos were able to squeeze the engine under the low bonnet with only a small 'power bulge', though it is a bit of a squeeze – as well as almost coming out of the bonnet, the engine sits close to the ground. A sump guard is a good idea.

The dashboard of the Marcos is well equipped and the black vinyl was an inexpensive but effective material. Connolly hides can be specified on current cars.

Twin exhausts emit a crisp burble – enough to excite the senses of any motoring enthusiast.

overall height goes a very limited ground clearance. The theory is that is should be around four inches. In practice, with the editor, photographer Chris Graham and photographic equipment on board, it seemed little more than an inch or so and even filling station kerbs have to be negotiated with care.

Out on the open road and the car could be given its head. Driver and passenger are separated by the most enormous transmission tunnel and the gear lever is a mere stub peeking out from the top. Small as that lever is, the travel between gears is quite long. First gear has a very low ratio and is rather fussy. Although I will always select first to move from a standstill, there is more than enough torque available to pull away in second if the car is just creeping forward and I found I could do this quite smoothly.

I had expected a greater sensation of speed, but the car settled at a comfortable 60 on the roads with bends and at an even more comfortable 70 when overdrive (a switch on the side of the gearlever) was selected to cruise the straighter highways. The Marcos steers with racing car precision which makes progress on a bumpy surface exciting, if a little unpredictable. Even on a fairly smooth road I found the car wandering over the undulations. With the driver sitting so far back in a car with a long bonnet, turning in tight spaces was a bit like trying to steer a bus from the back seat!

Controlling this waywardness is something you slip into automatically after a few miles and it is one of the car's very few 'quirks'.

Although the interior is plain black (or sporty black, depending on your outlook), there is nothing to suggest that this is anything other than a 'real' production car. The dashboard, for instance, is far better than that on the Scimitar which has a tendency to crack and pop its instruments out.

I didn't have the chance to drive the car in city traffic but I imagine it would be easy to feel intimidated by a lot of large vehicles towering over the car on all sides. I could also imagine that inching that very long bonnet out into a busy road – or out of a blind exit – would be nerve racking to say the least.

The Marcos, it has to be said, is not much of a practical car. There is about as much boot space as an MGB can boast but there is none of the space behind the seats other than a shallow parcels shelf. To load that shelf would be to lose the already restricted rear view.

Andrew Graham unashamedly keeps his car for weekends and pleasure and this seems like a sensible way to see only the best side of

Squat and purposeful – would you try to overtake it? The rear screen might look quite big, but it is near the horizontal that the view is restricted to little more then a slit. Misted rear windows are a problem with the Marcos, though the current cars have improved heating and ventilation.

the car. I would love one – I think a lesser example would make a good restoration project – but I am not sure I could commute in it.

Although production only just reached four figures (not counting the current 're-vived' version) the cars have lasted well and do come onto the market now and then. It is interesting to note that, in 1970, the 'official' Ford 3 litre engined car (Capri 3 Litre GT) cost £1,291; the Scimitar cost £1,692 and the Marcos a staggering £2,350. It is also of interest to note that the price differential has remained at this level. The Marcos is quite patently a highly desireable motor car. □

The Marcos does show its age in some respects, but it is like driving a civilised, beautifully finished two-seater racing car

Re-emergent Marcos

MIKE McCARTHY takes a look at the resurgence of the Marcos marque.

Let us now praise the low-volume British sports car manufacturer. For a while it looked as if they were a dying breed, almost legislated out of existence by the politicians, not to mention recessions and other below-the-belt blows. But, rather like 'Enery Cooper, some have not only survived, but come up smelling of — well, Brut, I suppose. Their's is still a semi-fragile life, but firms such as Aston Martin, Lotus, Morgan, Reliant and TVR are with us yet, and without them life would be considerably more boring.

Another, of course, is Marcos. The first of the breed appeared back in 1959, and was . . . er, different, to put it mildly. There was a wooden chassis, for heaven's sake, and it looked distinctly odd: both were the work of Frank Costin, an aircraft engineer who never let 'styling' get in the way of aerodynamics. 'The Wooden Wonder', as it was instantly dubbed, was quite a success off and on the track — a certain Jackie Stewart started his competition career in one.

In 1963 a new Marcos was launched, styled by Denis Adams: it was as attractive as its predecessors had been ugly. It wasn't long after that, too, in 1969 that the wooden chassis had to go: it was just too expensive to make, and there had been a market reaction against it. Taking its place was a tubular steel space-frame layout which could take a variety of engines — the 1800cc four cylinder Volvo, 1500, 1600, 2-litre and 3-litre Fords, the 2.5 Triumph and the one of which I have particularly fond memories, the straight six 3-litre Volvo, a much underrated power unit which gave the lightweight Marcos considerable poke.

Alas, the aforementioned regulations and recessions hit Marcos hard, and in the early seventies car production stopped. Jem Marsh, who had started Marcos with Frank Costin (hence, as you probably know, the Mar-cos) stayed with the company throughout its ups and downs, supplying spares, carrying out servicing and even rebuilds and restoration.

He also kept the name of Marcos alive by racing the ex-Jackie Stewart car in historic events with considerable success, including, just a few weeks ago, clinching the Bellini Championship for 1984. He is, to the best of my knowledge, the only Managing Director of a road car company who is active in the sport, which explains why his cars tend to go very rapidly indeed, and handle extraordinarily well.

In the autumn of 1981 Jem was asked why he didn't start producing the Marcos again. He thought about it, and decided to go ahead. Obviously a totally new car was quite out of the question, but why not update the last Marcos to be made? Which is what he did — but with a difference. Apart from various Ford engines, he also offered a version with Rover's splendid 3.5-litre V8, the Mantula. In fact, as long ago as 1965 Marcos had installed an American Buick all-alloy V8 in a car, and, of course, the Buick engine was later bought by Rover, so Jem had some experience to go on.

Naturally, quite a few changes had to be made. The air intake at the front had to be opened up, and a front spoiler added. But the biggest modification came at the rear, where the bodywork was widened by some 4ins, to allow for a wider rear axle. All the restyling was carried out by Denis Adams, retaining the classic Marcos lines: love it or loathe it, you've go to admit it's a head-turner even now, over 20 years after it first appeared.

In order to comply with various build regulations, the Marcos is offered in component form. You have to find your own engine, front suspension (Triumph Vitesse/GT6) and rear axle (Ford Capri), but everything else is available from Marcos in four stages. Kit 1 is basically the chassis/body unit complete with windscreen, wiring harness, instruments and various other components, while stages 2 and 3 are all you need to finish the car off (the list of items for both these stages is rather too long to set out here!). Stage 4 is available to special order, and is basically to customer specification. Prices for the first three stages are £2165, £2914 (which includes 1) and £3785 (which includes 1 and 2) for the Mantula: prices for the Ford-engined variants are somewhat cheaper.

If all this sounds like a lot of hard work, don't be too put off. According to Jem, it's quite easy for someone reasonably competent and mechanically-minded to finish it off, and it shouldn't take too

The rear end has been widened by 4ins to allow for a wider rear axle.

The 'new' Marcos retains the traditional Marcos lines, and is still a head-turner 20 years on.

Enormous grip from those Avons . . .

The Marcos is offered in component form only. You have to find your own engine, front suspension and rear axle, but that is all.

long. Remember, almost everything you need is available from Marcos — and you're saving yourself car tax . . .

There is one hurdle you'll have to overcome first, though, and that is Jem Marsh himself! He tends to look rather closely at potential customers, and has even been known to send back a deposit. He is particularly scathing over the glass-fibre bodied, Beetle-chassised brigade: "The Marcos is *not* a VW special," he says most emphatically. "It's a hand-built car and will need some care and attention." There are no dealers, so when you visit Marcos to place your order just remember that you will be appraised as closely as you will be looking at Marcos's catalogues.

Jem has sold some 40 cars since the rebirth, roughly half of which are Mantulas. There is, incidentally, a three-month waiting list, and each car is only made to order and after a £500 deposit has been paid.

Blast from the past

To see what the Mantula was all about, we borrowed Jem's own car for a morning's drive around the highways and byways of Wiltshire, and came back highly impressed. It's a blast from the past that's as good as some of the

The Rover V8 provides plenty of power whatever the revs. Below: The interior is snug and comfortable, and tailored to fit. Leather seats are an option.

state-of-the-art machinery you can buy today — and better than many.

It is, of course, very low, so entry and exit can at times be a little undignified for portly Technical Editors, but once you're in it's splendidly snug and comfortable. The car has been tailored for Jem, who is tall, to put it mildly, so the seat was too low for me, but then that's the sort of thing that is built to individual requirements. Pedal positioning was no problem: a knob on the dashboard moves the whole pedal assembly back and forth until it's just right for reach. There are not many cars with *that* refinement!

With the exception mentioned, the seating position is excellent. There is the large tunnel to your left, the door to your right to hold you firmly in place, and in front of you a neat, small steering wheel and an adequate array of instruments.

The engine in the car we tried was, believe it or not, a 1970 unit out of an old Rover Coupé! Mind you, it has been refettled, and put together properly by David Isles, complete with Holley carburettor and Offy manifold, so it pushes out a lot of horsepower. Jem hasn't strapped a fifth wheel on the back, but reckons the 0-60mph time is under 6 secs, and top speed approaching 150mph. Whether these claims are accurate or not I cannot say — but the straight-line performance is, without doubt, highly exhilaratng. There is pure power from that V8 whatever the revs, and it sings sweetly and smoothly right up to the red line. With each change of the rather notchy Rover 'box there is that hefty and instantaneous shove in the back that leaves you goggle-eyed and grinning: any

and every short straight has you flooring the throttle just for the hell of it. Along with the performance is roadholding and handling to match. At low speeds — and the V8 is superbly flexible and tractable — the steering feels slightly sticky, the ride jittery (typical, in fact, of a light car on big fat tyres), but the faster you go the better it becomes. In corners the Avon 205/60VR14s hang on as if they're hardly working, giving enormous grip, and then it's just a case of twitching the little steering wheel and you're through with the minimum of fuss, roll or drama.

Of course the Marcos does show its age in some respects. Ground clearance is pretty minimal, there isn't much luggage space, there's nowhere to put your left foot since the tunnel is up against the clutch pedal, and the brakes feel a bit dead at low speed (although they work incredibly well when needed in an emergency), but against that there is the blinding performance, the astonishing roadholding and handling, the ultra-precise steering and the general overall feeling of tautness. It's a bit like driving a civilised, comfortable, beautifully finished two-seater racing car.

One final point: if you want an ashtray it will cost you £150. Jem is a non-smoker . . . ∎

STOP PRESS . . .

Following the success of the Rover-engined Mantula, the model has been uprated to accept the 190bhp Rover Vitesse Injection engine, including a variety of specification improvements such as leather trim and air conditioning. The price is £12,500 plus VAT for the full specification Mantula model. All enquiries to Jem Marsh on (0373) 864097.

"Ruddy journalist" Kevin Blick went to visit Jem Marsh and try out the Mantula, which is basically the classic Marcos with revised bodywork and a Rover V8 engine. Photos by Lipscombe

.born AGAIN MARCOS

Top left: no prizes for guessing the identity of the man posing on the Mantula's bonnet. Above: a massive centre tunnel dominates the leather and walnut interior

JUST like Carnaby Street, Mary Quant, floral ties and love-ins, Marcos is a name from the swinging sixties. The Beatle-cropped hero of some self-consciously pretentious British film of the day might as likely as not call to pick up his mini-skirted Julie Christie clone from her Portobello Road pad in his Marcos.

So when the swinging sixties disappeared in a puff of its own incense smoke and we found ourselves in the sour seventies instead, it seemed almost appropriate that Marcos, just like so many others, should have vanished as fast as they had appeared.

But now it's back – in fact it's been back, quietly, for a couple of years or more – and this year the Marcos name celebrates its 25th anniversary: an achievement few other British specialist car builders from the '60s have managed.

Every enthusiast knows a bit of Marcos history – or thinks he does: that the name links its founders, Jem Marsh and Frank Costin; that the cars had ply-wood bodies; that they used

Volvo engines.

In fact, the plywood bodies and Volvo engines are long gone but Jem Marsh most certainly isn't. Marcos is very much his company and he dominates the scene physically – he's a tall man – as well as by his personality – his gruff, no-nonsense, abrupt manner suggests he doesn't tolerate fools easily. A conversation with him sparks with controversial off-the-cuff remarks about 'pestering telephones', 'useless people', 'ruddy journalists' and other more libellous asides. Put your

reporter's pen and pad down for a moment and he will have picked it up himself, started jotting down dates and facts for you.

But under the prickly exterior is an engaging enthusiast and knowledgeable businessman. He has seen good times and bad since, as a manufacturer of accessories and spares for Austin Sevens, he met Frank Costin in 1959 and put up the money to finance Costin's design for a wooden-chassised car.

The first cars were basically

racers, using Cosworth-Ford 1000cc 'screamers': Jackie Oliver drove one and so did Jackie Stewart – using the same car with which Jem himself has won three classic racing series.

It was at the 1963 Racing Car Show that the familiar Marcos shape first appeared when the Denis Adams designed Marcos 1800 was unveiled; yes, it did have a Volvo engine and a plywood chassis.

In fact the Volvo engine lasted only until '65 when Ford 1500 and later 1600 engines replaced it. Wooden chassis stayed longer – until '69, when time and cost of manufacture dictated a change to a steel spaceframe. By then the Marcos was also being offered with Ford's V6 3-litre and called by many the "poor man's E-Type", with its 130mph performance and spectacular acceleration.

The company was on the crest of a wave; as well as the Marcos, it was also turning out the Mini Marcos kit conversions. Cars were being exported to 16 countries, including the USA.

Then, like so many companies, Marcos took one step too far and introduced the strikingly futuristic Mantis – utterly different looking from its existing model even though it was also styled by Denis Adams. The new model and the move to a new factory that its production had demanded were too much of a financial strain and within a year the company was in the hands of the Official Receiver.

It was bought by Geoffrey Thomas, chairman of the Rob Walker garage group but production was never properly restarted and eventually Jem Marsh bought back all the jigs, moulds and tooling to start a spares, service and restoration business for existing owners. Nearly three years ago, he decided to start building the car again, as well.

"In many ways, things have come full circle and it's just like the late '50s or early '60s all over again. There are a lot of little specialist companies around, all making small numbers of interesting cars," he explained. "But lets get one thing clear; I don't want to see the word k-i-t in your article. The Marcos is a 'component car'. It's professionally engineered and made to a very high standard. I don't want it associated with some of the rubbish that's around."

But, of course, it's a loophole that lets Marcos and its contem-

Left: the Rover V8 is a snug fit in the Mantula's engine bay.

Below: a steel space-frame replaced the plywood chassis in 1969

poraries flourish now as did a similar loophole in the '60s: then it was the absence of purchase tax on self assembly cars, now it is the lack of a need for Type Approval.

"Our car complies with all Construction and Use regulations," explained Jem Marsh. "It would be a sorry day if we ended up like Germany where no-one is allowed to produce a special because of legislation, but I think it is up to the business to monitor its own standards and make sure they are kept up."

These days a Marcos can be anything from the barest kit up to a virtually completed car. "A lot of our customers are young professional people who remember the name. They've got plenty of free time now and they are feeling a bit bored so they buy a Marcos as a project.

"But we do quite a few almost complete cars, too. If you want one of those, you'll have to sit down with me for an hour and go through the detailed specification sheet – we make them up exactly to your personal requirements."

Twenty years on, the Marcos is still a handsome machine. The sweeping curves of its massive bonnet; its distinctly hunched tail are uniquely Marcos, even if there is a trace of E-Type in the dominant proportions of the

bonnet and the perspex covered headlamps. It doesn't have the sleekness of the Jaguar but the classical curves give it a timeless quality like the big cat's and others of that elegant era.

The minimum of necessary changes have disrupted its well known shape since production re-commenced: the rear arches have been widened out by some four inches to take the current, wider track Capri rear axle, while the latest Rover V8 powered Mantula has deeper radiator air intakes and a small front spoiler.

Jem Marsh likes to point out that Marcos were experimenting

Above: the Mantula's curvaceous lines still look good 20 years on

with the Rover engine's predecessor, the Buick V8, back in 1965. The Rover unit drops tidily into an engine bay that can take every Ford motor from 1.5 litre up to 2.8 and 3.0 V6 – only the 2.8 injection V6 doesn't fit and as ample compensation the Motor Show Marcos Mantula will be the first with the 190bhp Vitesse injected V8.

Engine advances apart, the Marcos mechanical specification hasn't altered a great deal over the years. Front suspension and steering are from that special builder's favourite, the Vitesse 2-litre/GT6 – though supplies of the double wishbone suspension are drying up and Marcos will soon have to start fabricating components, as they already do hubs and brake discs. At the rear, the Capri axle is located impressively, using two long radius arms each side that run rearwards from the axle to chassis mounts, together with a Panhard rod. Coil springs and Spax dampers are used all

round. The central section of the glass-fibre body is built up in two parts; the undertray being bolted to the chassis and the top section then bonded onto the undertray. The whole body remains removable from the space-frame.

What you get inside the car depends on what you choose to pay for, but the specification list includes such non-kit-car items as electric windows, air conditioning, leather trim and walnut dashboard.

"The air conditioning is Japanese, I'm afraid. It was the only suitable unit we could get," confessed Jem Marsh. "I like to use British components as far as possible."

The car looks attractive – inside as well as out, with its leather trimmed cockpit. But how will a 20-year-old design perform? Can a car on which, as Jem Marsh admits, "we've just played around with suspension settings" really make the quantum leap necessary to keep up with today's machinery? The remarkable answer seems to be that it can. The Mantula we

drove – Jem's own 9,000-mile-old car – was a carburetted V8, upped to near Vitesse performance with a Crane camshaft and Holly carburettor. But it wasn't the power that made it daunting to drive – it was seeing out past the vast blue rolling ocean of bonnet at the road ahead. Like a Savile Row suit, you get your Marcos made to measure – the seat sits against the back of the cabin and the cushion rests directly on the floor; neither adjust. Instead, you can rack the pedals to and fro via an adjustable pedal box, controlled from a facia dial. But wider adjustments need a spanner and a different cushion: 5ft 10in me had to make do with a jacket under the 6ft 7in seat setting!

That the Mantula is fast comes as no great surprise; just 17½ hundredweight propelled by 185 horsepower ought to be. And it lunges at the skyline with a lovely fruity roar from its V8 exhausts. It's quick to 60mph, probably little more than six seconds, but it's the never ending

charge of acceleration that does impress – at over 100mph the Mantula is still surging, Carl Lewis style, down the road. Jem Marsh speaks of a 150mph + top speed.

But the fact that it goes round corners as well as along straights is more surprising. The road from Marcos' Westbury base past the famous White Horse is a snaking sequence of crests, dips, bends and bumps that would have the live rear axle of a Capri hopping and skipping a jog across its surface. Yet the Marcos rear end never got itself out of control; its rigidly located axle kept the tyres firmly planted on the road, despite the greatest provocation. Add to this remarkably good traction, a sharpness and precision of steering response that feels more like a racing car, and the result is superb cornering ability. There is precious little body roll and in dry conditions the Avon Turbospeed tyres – 195/60HR14 front and 205/60HR14 rear – give all the grip one could ask for.

It feels a thoroughbred, riding poor surfaces with a suppleness that confirms its first class damping and unrestricted wheel movement. Like a thoroughbred, there is a certain nervous quality about it: the sharp steering's sensitivity to small movements has to be appreciated – unless you manage to relax behind the wheel, it can dart about at higher speeds. But it brakes firmly and squarely – the solid discs/rear drums set-up proves reassuringly free from fade, though four-pot calipers and ventilated discs can be fitted. Naturally, it's pretty noisy at speed – you'd better get to like the V8's roar – but it's tolerably free from the squeaks and creaks of many k-i-t cars.

Just two a week is all that the modest little Marcos works presently turns out. Prices start from as little as £1,695 + VAT for a Ford Stage I kit, sorry, set of components (though that leaves a lot for you to find elsewhere to complete the car).

The two-litre ohc Sierra engined car, which will also be new at the Motor Show will cost around £4,700 + VAT built up, while the Mantula 3.5 Injection with a full specification including leather trim and air conditioning will be upwards of £12,500 + VAT.

Some things, like price, do change over 20 years! But if the Marcos is back, perhaps floral ties will make a comeback, too?

Road Impressions:

Marcos Mantula 3.5

IT IS on occasions like this that I am glad that MOTOR SPORT does not always publish road tests. We are careful to call some of our assessments, "Road Impressions". The difference, I suppose, is that a road test should be rigorously quantitative. It should be able to tell you to the nearest cubic inch how much boot space there is or, again, the height of the rear seats. Tests of that sort can be extremely useful but a car like the Marcos Mantula should be approached in a different way.

I have to start by admitting a bias. On first seeing a Dennis Adams styled Marcos nearly 20 years ago, I fell in love with it and the ardour has never cooled. Even had it not been an excellent car under the skin, it would still have been one I'd have considered buying for its beauty. It was clear mine was not an isolated opinion for the Marcos quickly established a reputation as a "bird puller" second only to an E-Type.

Since I was first a student on a grant and then making my way up the ladder of a profession and earning a pittance, I could only admire the Marcos from a distance. Still, I had the consolation that any girl who rode in my Ford Popular was likely to be *sincere*.

Jem Marsh tells me that I fit the typical profile of many of his customers since he revived the car. We desired one a long time ago when it was an impossible dream but now in our middle years, we've made our way, have a saloon to accommodate the

offspring, and wish to indulge ourselves by reviving an old passion. This is why, try as I will, this account can never be completely objective — a mundane conversation with a beautiful woman is alway memorable.

The Mantula, though, is not mundane. The carburettered Rover V8 engine gives a top speed of 135+ mph and accelerates from 0-60 mph in six seconds. It has brakes, handling and roadholding to match. Everything complements the promise of its looks.

The car I drove was Jem Marsh's own and was interesting in that he had built it up in much the same way that many buyers might do. The engine, for example, came from a 1971 3.5 Coupé, the gearbox too was second-hand and the radiator came from a

Rover 3500S. One would never have known, though, without being told.

Entry is surprisingly easy for such a low car (you look *up* at Minis) for the doors are extremely wide. Once seated in the extremely comfortable, supportive, leather seat, the first thing to do is to adjust the pedals for comfort, for the seats are fixed. This is easily done by turning a knob behind the steering wheel. Drivers up to 6 ft 7 in tall can be seated in comfort though short drivers would probably have to have their seats modified.

Marcos offer four engine options, Ford 2.0- and 2.8-litre units and both the carburettered and injected versions of the 3.5-litre Rover V8. The Rover engined cars are known as Marcos Mantulas while the Ford-powered cars, simply "Marcos". Below is the carburettered engine of the Mantula test car.

The main instruments are clearly seen through the small steering wheel (only the main beam indicator light was obscured by my normal driving position). There is a row of (Triumph) rocker switches in the centre of the dash to which one needs some acclimatisation. The test car was fitted with air conditioning which worked extremely well though I would have liked more speed options from the heater fan. With items such as electrically operated windows, the interior exuded an air of luxury not normally found on a car of its performance with a nominal value of only £14,000.

The first impression when driving was a false sense of size. The Mantula is not a large car, but the sensuous sweep of the front wings makes it appear so to the driver and it takes some time before one develops a sense of the car in its space. Similarly, the sharply raked back makes parking a little fraught at first, for the rear is completely invisible.

Rear visibility when driving, however, is excellent thanks to the wide interior mirror and the exterior mirrors which are mounted at eye-level. This is as well for the reclining high-backed seats discourage head turning.

On the road the car is sheer magic. The ride is a perfect compromise between tautness and comfort. The steering is precise and one normally needs only to give little flicks of the wheel yet the turning circle is thirty feet. The over-riding sensation is one of security: the car is stable under all conditions, it feeds information to the driver through its Avon Turbospeed tyres, the brakes (the front discs are ventilated) have not only stopping power but feel, and the roadholding is such that you'd have to be a hooligan to explore its limits on a public road.

The engine adds to this sense of security for the car *contains* the power. Apart from the fact that it will beat almost anything in a traffic lights grand prix, it gives one enormous confidence when overtaking. One of the best memories was driving along a country road in fourth gear (from five)

behind traffic moving at about 45 mph, finding an opportunity to overtake and simply pressing accelerator, allowing the torque of the engine to do the rest. We wafted by the traffic without fuss.

Road noise is minimal though, on the car I drove, wind noise becomes noticeable at 70 mph and was a little excessive by 90 mph.

Like most sports cars, the luggage space is not an outstanding feature but there is space enough to take the luggage for two for a

fortnight's holiday provided you don't insist on taking evening dress.

To explore the limits of the car in safety, Jem arranged a session at Castle Combe circuit. It was wet and slippery but even when I became over ambitious on one corner and my knuckles shone white, yet still it forgave though I deserve to have finished in a tyre wall. She's not only lovely but has impeccable manners as well.

The longer I drove the car, the more relaxed I felt. Most cars reveal themselves in under an hour of driving, some within a few minutes. The Mantula is one of the few that you wish to explore slowly and you feel it will surprise and delight for a long time.

When the time came to hand it back to Jem, I found myself muttering about delivery dates, cost etc against the day I replace my GTI. I'd like to get to know the new two-litre version which should offer an excellent compromise between performance and economy (the Mantula averages about 20/21 mpg) and which would match my everyday requirements very nicely.

The styling may now be 20 years old, but the car still turns heads like few others. It took me two decades from being first smitten by a Marcos to driving one. I was prepared to be disappointed but was not. This is one ravishing beauty with a heart of gold. The passion continues unabated.

— M.L.

The extremely high standard of interior appointment can be seen in this shot. The Marcos manages to combine traditional values of quality with the best of contemporary technology.

Ugly Duckling to Swan

Within five years a nameless 'ugly duckling' was transformed into one of the most widely acclaimed British GTs ever. Jeremy Coulter tells the first part of the Marcos story with help from Jem Marsh, Dennis Adams and the Marcos Owners Club

HUG 400

W HEN Jem Marsh exhibited a 'new' Marcos at the 1982 Birmingham Motor Show, it was something of a shot in the dark as far as he was concerned to see whether there was still any interest in the car. He suspected there was and many people had told him there was. In the end he needn't have worried because by the close of the show he had sold over 2000 brochures relating to the 1983 Marcos and orders had been taken from all round the world. So the Marcos was back after a break of nearly ten years and if Jem Marsh has his way it won't go away again!

The path that led Jem Marsh to the NEC with that sleek and familiar car is a tortuous one that leads right back to 1959 and a tumbledown shed in north Wales, where the expertise of Francis Albert Costin and the ideas and enterprise of Jeremy George Weston Marsh came together to produce a strange little GT, which came to be known as a Marcos only after it was completed — MARsh/COStin. Both men were already well known in the motoring world, Costin as stylist of the Vanwall and various wind-cheating Lotus models, having trained in the aircraft industry, and Marsh as proprietor of a successful tuning business called Speedex Castings & Accessories of Luton. Marsh recalls starting the business with capital of only £44 and agreements from various companies to supply him with parts and service on credit. The money went on paying for an advertisement in *Motor Sport* offering tuning parts for Austin Sevens. The response to this, plus of course the skill of Marsh's salesmanship, was sufficiently good to pave the way to the establishment of a profitable business.

Early steps

Following a chance encounter with Frank Costin in early 1959, Marsh outlined to him at several subsequent meetings his ideas for building "a GT car — something like a Lotus 6 with a top on". There followed the founding of the Monocoque Chassis & Body Co to build such a car based in, of all places, Dolgellau in North Wales. Dolgellau was Costin's wife's home town but there was also the possibility of aid from the Welsh industry board, which was anxious to attract new enterprise to the region.

The firm set up shop in a dark converted stone coachhouse behind Dolgellau's Lion Hotel. Costin started on the new car working alone on a collection of trestle tables and he progressed steadily but towards the end of the year it became clear that extra hands were needed. This led to a three-way correspondence between Costin, Marsh and Dennis Adams with whom Costin had worked previously on the spaceframe Lister racing car. Adams had made it clear that he would like to work with Costin again and so it came about that in December 1959 it was agreed that Adams would join the fledgling Monocoque Chassis & Body Co at a salary of £51 per month, with the job title of foreman. Soon afterwards a third member joined the team, Dennis' brother Peter, who was a skilled carpenter.

Under the agreement that Marsh had made with Costin, Marsh was to supply all the mechanical parts and sundry other items not available in Wales, while Costin and his team were to build the chassis and body units. So it was that Marsh and/or one of his Speedex mechanics regularly made the tedious journey from Luton to Wales in an ancient Ford van that Dennis Adams recalls Costin could drive at such hair-raising speeds that no-one would ride with him in it! Whoever delivered the parts from Luton usually ended up lending a hand in the workshop for a day or weekend and by early 1960 the first prototype was indeed completed and driven to Luton by Costin and Marsh.

The new car bore witness to the fact that in Costin's mind aesthetics certainly took second

Colour page, HUG 400, the latest Marcos demonstrator with a six-cylinder Volvo-powered 3.0-litre in the background and the early 'ugly duckling' raced by Jem Marsh. Above, the first production chassis ready for its journey from Luton to Dolgellau. Below, the prototype complete and ready for test at Silverstone.

place to efficiency. The little GT, by now called Marcos at the suggestion of Costin's father-in-law Idwal Roberts, was by no means the most attractive vehicle ever made, with its Lotus Seven-inspired cycle-wing front and its bent perspex windscreen, reverse-rake rear window and gullwing doors with non-opening windows. Concerning the name Marcos, Jem Marsh now muses that the only thing wrong with it is that he didn't think of it! Xylon, the Greek for wood and even Cosmar were considered but rejected.

Costin drew on his experience of wartime Mosquito aircraft construction when building the Marcos. He considered a spaceframe design but decided against it on the grounds of tooling and production costs and at an early stage opted for a monocoque, not of steel, aluminium or glassfibre, but of wood, marine ply and spruce, bonded with synthetic aerolite glue. The basic design was immensely strong and, as it turned out, long lasting. The structure comprised three torsion boxes running fore and aft along the car and three cross ways. The two side torsion boxes were of triangular section facing downwards while the central box enclosed the propshaft. These three boxes were linked both by the stressed floor and the three transverse boxes. The foremost transverse box was mounted between the front wheels and picked up the front suspension while the middle box formed the cockpit area and the rear one linked to the rear suspension. Perhaps surprisingly, the roof, with its gullwing doors adds minimally to the torsional stiffness of the chassis.

The prototype, registered DFF 529 was fitted with an 1172cc Ford sidevalve engine and slant-mounted gearbox. There was an Austin live axle with parallel locating arms and a Panhard rod. Front suspension with its Costin-fabricated wishbones was from a Triumph Herald and drum brakes were fitted all round. This 8 cwt car was

driven extensively and developed on road and track by Jem Marsh although his racing results have been somewhat overshadowed by the many production Marcos racing successes that followed.

With the basic soundness of the design amply demonstrated, the by now five-strong team moved to slightly better premises in Dolgellau that they themselves had helped convert and there they started to build the first production car. This looked the same as the prototype but had a productionised front subframe to ease assembly and a four-piece windscreen. Anyone who thinks that the terrible word 'productionise' is an Eighties innovation might be amused to learn that in Frank Costin's original letter offering Dennis Adams a job he wrote: "Dear Dennis . . . it is possible in the New Year that I shall be looking for someone to help me *productionise* and improve the vehicle I am building at present."

The first production car was duly completed and collected by Marsh in May 1960. It was fitted with a 997cc three-bearing Ford Anglia engine tuned by Cosworth to produce a remakable 75bhp. Speedwell-tuned BMC engines had been considered for the production cars but Marsh was convinced on the superiority of the relatively new Ford unit. The car was sold to racing driver Bill Moss who drove it in 1.0-litre GT races from June 1960. His results speak for themselves — ten starts and nine wins — the only failure being the first race for which he forgot to change from road-going spark plugs to racing plugs, blowing up the engine as a result.

Predictably the racing fraternity greeted the Marcos GT warmly but the general public were less than impressed with the car's styling, an attitude reinforced by motor racing commentators and the motoring press who started to attach the epithet 'ugly duckling' to the newcomer. Eventually Costin was prevailed upon by Marsh and the Adams brothers to revise the styling somewhat and the second production car left Dolgellau with a rather more attractive fully enveloping front. Bill Moss' car was in fact returned to the works in mid-1960 to have its original nose and cycle wings replaced with the new design.

By November 1960 the Marcos order book was in a healthy state and six cars had been completed. One of these was sold to Barry Filer, a wealthy director of Courtaulds, for the use of Jackie Stewart. Jem Marsh recalls driving this car up to Scotland himself, handing over the keys to Filer and being given an air ticket to fly back to

Ugly Duckling

Luton. Some years later he was able to buy this car back and he races it today in various UK historic championships.

By the time the sixth car had been completed it had become painfully obvious that better premises were essential. With the help of the Welsh industry board a suitable place had been found at the former RAF depot at Llanberis but the negotiations over the terms of the lease dragged on to the extent that as a stop gap, Caernarvonshire County Council arranged for the firm to move to the former dining hall of Brynrefail Grammar School, also in Llanberis. Dennis Adams remembers the pristine polished condition of the school parquet floor which, despite initial efforts to preserve it, was soon sacreligiously covered with glue spills and wood shavings.

Disquiet over the styling of the Marcos GT, still widely known as the ugly duckling despite the revised nose, led Dennis and Peter Adams to attempt some sneaky changes while Costin was away for the day. A discreet ¼in was removed from the height of the roofline to make the car sleeker. "It was hardly noticeable," muses Dennis Adams, "yet as soon as Frank walked back into the workshop he spotted it and blew his top. He made us put it back, naturally." Dennis, once a true disciple of Costin was by now becoming increasingly disenchanted with his mentor's attitude to styling "for its own sake" and his refusal to modify the car any further.

After the completion of the eighth chassis, Dennis decided to leave Wales and he went to Luton to join Jem Marsh. This left Peter Adams to head the production team back in Llanberis. However, by now Costin was becoming increasingly distracted by non-Marcos projects as diverse as power boats and organs. As his interest waned, so the Adams brothers influence grew to the extent that by the end of 1960, the Marcos design had indeed been refined further. Four cars were actually made in the schoolroom but only the last two were built to the revised design.

Dennis Adams refers to the latter pair as the 'Llanberis smoothies' as they had widened chassis with parallel sides which now completely covered the rear wheels as well as the front, so the rear mudguards could be dispensed with. Other features upon which Dennis had been working in Luton included the much narrower screen pillars. The early cars had wide aluminium T-strips supporting the four glass sections. Dennis was convinced that these were unnecessary and that the glass would support itself with only rubber mouldings between the pieces. Costin disagreed, but eventually Adams prevailed and the later cars benefited from the improved visi-

bility with, as it turned out, no ill effects. Also the front lights were fared in and the rear light lenses made flush-fitting while the roof line was lowered and various other changes made to give a generally much more pleasing appearance.

At around the time of Costin's diversification of interests came his growing disagreement with Marsh about the direction in which the Marcos should develop as the latter had clear ideas about refining the car further still and moving away from the racing market. The final break came in early 1961 when Marsh "took a pantechnicon up to Llanberis and simply took everything connected with Marcos back to Speedex in Luton." The job of running the project, which from the start had been entirely in Marsh's name with Costin working on a self-employed basis, was then handed over to the Adams brothers, Peter having joined Dennis in Luton at the time of the evacuation from Llanberis.

Installed in Speedex's Windsor Road, Luton premises, Dennis carried out an interesting design exercise and cut the top off the prototype Marcos, DFF 529 to make the first Marcos 'spyder'. "It looked quite nice and went like hell", remembers Dennis, who wonders where that car is today. "I did it because I disliked the early roofline more than for any other reason," he jokes!

While examples of the by now well-known and widely acclaimed young marque were happily winning races up and down the country and providing their owners with some of the nippiest road transport around, there followed a break in production of a month or so while preparations were made for a move to a former hat factory owned by Speedex at 33 Jubilee Road, in a run-down part of Luton. Having cleared away the accumulated mess of the former occupants who had made parts for the Welsh operation and bodies for Speedex's 750cc racers, Peter and Dennis set about constructing the first of the 'Luton gullwings' on one of two partially finished chassis brought down from Wales. The brothers had previously sat down with Jem Marsh and discussed exactly how they should improve the car. Points they came up with included generally improving the lines, abandoning the unusual

reverse rake rear screen, adding sliding side windows, developing a one-piece windscreen and producing more of the non-stressed body parts in glassfibre.

Dennis duly produced the drawings and Peter began producing the prototype from which the new glassfibre moulds would be taken. Although this work was carried out on a Welsh chassis, Peter had also begun to build a considerably revised chassis which became known as the 'symmetrical' type as identical footwells were provided for the driver and passenger, whereas the first cars had a driver's footwell only. The pattern for the bonnet was produced in aluminium over Peter's wooden formers by Williams and Pritchard of Ealing and delivered to Luton in March 1961. From this pattern and the bucks they had produced themselves for the doors, roof and boot, the brothers assembled the moulds they needed. The changes to the chassis necessitated revision to the engine mounting and suspension pickup points and these Dennis and Peter jointly engineered.

The 'new' and much more attractive Marcos GT shape was first seen on the two 'asymmetrical' Welsh chassis. The very first was sold in April 1961 to racing driver Jack Oliver who subsequently crashed it comprehensively, fortunately with no harm to himself, while the second example, registered 3FNM, was retained by the company and raced at the Le Mans 24-hour race of that year. After running well, driven by Hine and Prior, it retired in the early hours of the Sunday morning with an engine malady, regularly having clocked 129mph on the Mulsanne straight with its 1500cc Ford engine.

Fading fortunes

Both racing enthusiasts and sporting road-drivers took to the new car and sales of the 'Luton gullwings' went well, the car being offered at £830 for a complete kit with either a 105E Anglia engine or a 109E Classic unit. Close ratio gears, disc brakes, aluminium bellhousing and various other go-faster goodies were offered as extras. Contemporary road testers noted how much more civilised the new car was than its predecessors, commenting on the effectiveness of the 'Silent Travel' insulation and the comfort of the cockpit with its glassfibre bucket seats, padded fascia, carpets, parcel shelf, map light, and adjustable steering column.

The healthy demand for the keenly-priced and rapid Marcos GT presented problems of its own by the latter half of 1961 because despite knocking down most of the hat factory's internal walls, there simply wasn't sufficient space in Jubilee Road to house that volume of production and the activities of the ten-strong workforce. This difficult situation led to discussions with the owner of a former Mosquito aircraft producing factory in Sawbridgeworth for the sub-contracting of chassis manufacture. Remember that Costin had drawn upon his aircraft experience when designing the original chassis so the disciplines had much in common. A contract was eventually drawn up for the supply of 25 chassis units from Sawbridgeworth and the future seemed secure.

Unfortunately all was not well with the Speedex side of Jem Marsh's interests as a gradual decline in the popularity of 'special' building and the outclassing of Speedex's formerly competitive cars led to a loss of business and the accumulation of serious debts. The drain that this placed on the reserves of the sister Monocoque Chassis & Body Co proved too much for it and despite the encouraging sales of the new car, the firm closed its doors in January 1961. Clearly its potential had not been fulfilled and equally clearly it could not be allowed to rest for too long.

Sadly disillusioned with the way things had turned out, the Adams brothers retreated to their home village of Great Shelford near Cambridge to

Top, left to right, the original Marcos team of Frank Costin, Dennis Adams and Peter Adams discuss a design point in Dolgellau. Below, one of the later smooth-sided cars, still with the wide screen pillars

Ugly Duckling

concentrate on their own design work. Dennis can't remember exactly how they survived financially at that time although he recalls buying and selling various cars and parting with his much prized special-bodied Vintage Lagonda. He designed and built the body for that car himself in the late Fifties and was considerably amused to see it crop up for sale in the early Seventies as a unique and 'original' coachbuilt example of the marque at the 'bargain' price of 50 times more than he sold it for!

In a corrugated iron shed, light-heartedly known as Stonehill Motors, the Adams brothers concentrated on two interesting design projects. Peter had managed to accumulate sufficient Marcos bits and pieces, including the first 'symmetrical' chassis to start constructing the second Marcos spyder which he considered a logical development of the gullwing theme. The resultant car, assembled with Triumph independent rear suspension, was a good-looking, brisk performer and Jem Marsh, who kept in touch with the brothers at this time and paid them regular visits was suitably impressed.

However, the brothers' main project for 1962 was the construction of a futuristic vehicle codenamed the XP. Ironically, the brothers' lack of formal training in automotive design was probably advantageous as far as the XP was concerned, for an unblinkered outlook led them to adopt unconventional engineering solutions to many problems and explore unusual avenues of design. The XP looks futuristic even by today's standards. The design had three-abreast seating, a rear-mounted engine, sliding doors and central steering to name but a few of the notable features. The car had a smooth underside in Marcos traditions and it is interesting to note that in an appraisal of the design by Larry Bonstein, attached to the Ministry of Aviation, the attitude of the nose and the smooth underside is remarked upon because: 'Sweeping up the underside of the nose as you suggest may actually help in keeping the nose down as the acceleration of the air as it enters what is effectively a half nozzle will reduce its pressure and suck the car down.' Who said the ground effect concept for racing cars was invented in 1978? The drag coefficient of XP was estimated independently as below 0.3Cd and possibly as low as 0.25.

Work on the project continued apace, with the construction of a prototype buck well advanced and the two brothers gradually developing the many special parts needed for the innovative car. Meanwhile it became apparent that Jem Marsh, who had found a job with a Mini tuning parts and conversion centre called LMB Components, was planning to re-start Marcos manufacture as soon as he could. Of the parties with whom he discussed finance for the restarting of production wealthy retired naval commander Greville Cavendish proved the most receptive. It was actually Cavendish who Marsh persuaded the Adams brothers to meet in October 1962. The encounter was fruitful and an agreement was reached whereby Cavendish would pay off the company's debts and finance the re-establishment of the car-making operations. The new company would concentrate on the development and manufacture of the Adams' remarkable XP, plus spyder versions of the gullwing car, as developed by Peter.

Work actually started once more in premises to the rear of Gaston's garage in Kingston. Dennis remembers these decrepit buildings as being little better than the Stonehill Motors sheds, yet he and Peter were happy to be able to concentrate fully on the new cars once again. It was possibly to Gaston's surprise that within weeks of the team moving to Kingston, the enterprise upped sticks and moved again to Greville Cavendish's Freshford Motor Company in Bath. "The place at Freshford was very small," recalls Dennis Adams, "and it was obvious we had to find somewhere else fairly quickly. We seemed to spend ages visiting possible factories until eventually we found one we all liked — the old Enfield motorcycle works in Bradford-on-Avon." There indeed it was that the revitalised Marcos Cars Ltd, with Greville Cavendish as chairman, Jem Marsh as co-director with Dennis and Peter Adams as design and development engineers began its third and most successful phase although, as we shall see next month, it was initially far from plain sailing. ⬢

Continued next month

Below, changing Marcos shapes, with, on the right, and early 'Ugly Duckling' with an Adams Luton Gullwing next to it. A later small door 'breadvan' on the left is where the story continues next month. Right, the Adams brothers' futuristic XP which the revitalised company intended to produce in 1963. This artwork was painted by *T&CC*'s Lionel Burrell in 1962. This drawing of XP did not feature the interesting central steering

Rise and fall

Jeremy Coulter continues the Marcos story with the help of Jem Marsh, Dennis Adams and the Marcos Owners Club

L AST month we saw how Marcos was founded, how the firm grew but eventually succumbed to a financial crisis. Resuscitated with a wealthy backer the firm prepared to set up in new premises.

The Adams brothers took charge of the company's move to Bradford-on-Avon. Anyone who remembers the winter of 1962/3 will not need to be told that this was the worst conceivable time to undertake such an operation. Much time was spent fending off frost bite and digging away the snow drifts that blocked the path to the factory. Nevertheless, late December 1962 saw the newly revitalised Marcos Cars Ltd firmly ensconced in its new premises and ready to start production once more, with a staff of nine including the Adams brothers and directors Greville Cavendish and Jem Marsh.

Jem by now realised that so long as Marcos produced cars that were widely considered as 'racing cars', production could never progress beyond relatively small numbers, no matter how successful and competitive they were. For this reason it was decided to concentrate on making road-going versions of the Marcos spyder which had been devised by Peter Adams at Stonehill Motors during 1962's lull in production. Development of the futuristic XP would, however, continue as a priority. In January, 1963 the spyder was exhibited at London's prestigious Racing Car Show where it received a mixed reception from the customers, who expected Marcos to produce 'real' racing cars. Orders for the spyder did not come flooding in but there was no shortage of work as existing customers kept the team busy with rebuilds, repairs and modification to the many older North Wales and Luton cars. Greville Cavendish's enthusiastic backing obviously gave the firm a sound base for expansion and development for by mid-1963 the staff, most of whom had been recruited locally, numbered 20.

Customers might not have wanted Marcos spyders in 1963 but they were still receptive to the Luton gullwings and several more were made before a hardtop was designed for the spyder as a replacement for the gullwings. This seemed to expand the car's appeal overnight. The story of the design of this hardtop has passed into Marcos folklore and Dennis Adams himself still smiles broadly when recalling the day that he and Peter procured a vast block of polystyrene which they proceeded to sit on top of a completed spyder. Having secured the block to the car, they armed themselves with breadknives and saws and "set about the block until it looked about right". The shape they ended up with looked more than "about right". In fact it made what had been a rather unusual-looking car into a very attractive one. The polystyrene block was treated with glassfibre and filler and moulds were taken for the production of a run of hardtops. Only two cars were sold with the hardtop detachable — others had it bonded into place. The hardtop

Colour page, the Marcos Mantis as tested by *Motor* magazine in 1971 with inset, the Marcos 1800 prototype once owned by *T&CC*'s Lionel Burrell. Above, racing fastback/breadvan showing the 'polystyrene block' hard top. Left, "How much? — You've got to be joking!" Prince Philip with Peter, Jem and Dennis at the racing car show of 1968

Above, Dennis Adams photographed recently with the original Marcos 1800 artwork which he thought was "a bit wrong". Left the prototype at Bradford, showing off its Adams-designed magnesium wheels

resulted in doors that were so small one needed to be a contortionist to get into the car but customers didn't seem to mind and sales of the 'breadvan' as it came to be known, provided a good boost to Marcos' profitability in late 1963.

However, sales of the 'breadvan' were still mainly to racing customers and the mass market was still out of reach. Predictably, development of the XP was going slowly: "We encountered so many problems," remembers Dennis Adams. "We got round them, but slowly, and there was no way we could have started production before late 1964, a year later than we really needed it." It became clear that sales of the 'breadvan' would not hold up at a worthwhile level until then so a 'stop-gap' was needed "pretty damned quickly," to use Jem Marsh's words.

There's nothing like a tight corner to bring out the best of people and when Dennis produced a 'back of envelope' sketch of what he imagined such a 'stop-gap' should look like, everyone at the Bradford-on-Avon factory became very enthusiastic. What Dennis had shown them was the first drawing of what people generally think of as a 'Marcos' today. "I think I can best sum up my car design philosophy as 'meanest, leanest, cleanest, purest' " reflects Dennis Adams today.

"The Marcos 1800 was well on the way to what Peter and I ultimately produced in the self-indulgent Probe series of cars in the early Seventies."

Once the go-ahead had been given for the 'stop-gap', Dennis and Peter set about producing detailed drawings and profiles for the new car and constructing the first chassis. The Costin principles of wooden construction were retained but extended and modified in almost every way. Jem Marsh, who is 6ft 4in tall, recalls that he acted as the prototype driver and "sat in what seemed to be just a pile of wood", while Dennis and Peter measured and arranged various parts of the structure around him. This was then taken to the Hartin brothers in Ealing who made an aluminium buck from which the moulds for the glassfibre body would be taken. Dennis Adams now admits that the body didn't turn out quite as he had imagined: "When the first artwork (see photo) was produced from my drawings by a firm in Bath, I told them they'd got it wrong as some of the perspectives weren't as I thought they should be. However, as soon as I sat in the prototype I found they were right and I'd been wrong" which was rather annoying at the time.

Dennis and Peter would have liked to produce a Marcos engine and complete suspension but

financial constraints or maybe common sense prevailed and a proprietary engine was used. Early examples were, however, produced with an interesting semi-independent rear suspension. On the subject of the engine Dennis says: "I could never quite reconcile myself to the idea of tuning a 1000cc or 1500cc unit up to the eyeballs to produce say 100 or 120bhp when a larger, lightly stressed unit would in my opinion do the job just as well, if not better." So it was that Dennis obtained a wall chart which showed comparative specifications of just about every engine available at the time: "On all counts of weight, power, torque, size, revs and even tuning potential, the boring Volvo 1800 unit came out tops."

The Marcos 1800 was running in prototype form by January of 1964 and it made its first public appearance at the Racing Car Show of that month where its sleek lines and claimed performance caused quite a stir. The car was offered at £1687.10s complete, or £1320 in components.

Marcos for everyman

Here at last was a Marcos that appealed to the non-racing customer although of course they were still raced. Sales went well right from the start, aided by extensive and enthusiastic media coverage along the lines of: "If you think a car this pretty can only come from Italy, you'd be wrong." As with any specialist car there were teething problems. The Adams rear suspension was not a success, as well as being expensive to produce. Rather than modify it to cure problems of wheel wobble and axle half-shaft wear, the firm reverted to a live rear axle, employing a hefty Ford unit. Around fifty independently sprung cars were made although many of these were subsequently fitted with the live axle.

With the workforce expanded to as many as 60 people, production of the 1800 started to nudge five or more cars per week. By mid-1964 the XP project was finally abandoned and the specialised parts and the single prototype were either dispersed, lost or left to gather dust.

With the 1800 established as a winner, the Adams brothers found that their talents were no longer fully employed at Marcos now that XP had been abandoned while from Jem Marsh's point of view, he no longer really needed them. With the aid of Greville Cavendish and his wife, the brothers branched out on their own to form Adams Design. This was nominally an independent styling house but was still connected to Marcos in the sense that most of the design work was routed to the brothers through Marcos, an arrangement with which Dennis in particular was not happy as he felt some interesting projects were not reaching them. By way of compensation for the termination of their direct employment with Marcos, the Adams brothers were given the prototype Marcos 1800. At the time of their leaving they were still being paid the originally agreed sum of £70 per month each, which surely makes the 1800 a fairly cheap design! Peter Adams subsequently fitted the prototype 1800 with an Oldsmobile V8 engine to produce a frighteningly quick car which Dennis recalls would spin its wheels in any gear with the smallest provocation. Minus its V8, this car was later sold by Peter to *T&CC*'s deputy editor, Lionel Burrell who maintained the V-theme and fitted a Ford V4. What became of the car after Lionel parted with it is unknown.

Adams Design set up in premises known as the Old Forge in Bradford-on-Avon. The forge had still been used by the local blacksmith and once settled in, the Adams brothers found that they could profitably occupy their spare design time by keeping up the blacksmith's trade. This wasn't exactly planned says Dennis: "People kept wandering in and asking us to make this or that,

Rise and Fall

until one day Peter and I looked at each other and said why not? Before we knew where we were, we'd become blacksmiths! We designed machines and tools for turning out fancy wrought-iron in a fraction of the usual time and quite soon we had to take on staff!! Various design project were undertaken alongside the blacksmithing, including one for a GT racer for Anglia Cars, a small city car as part of an Anglo-French design project, a Bentley GT for a rich private owner and a BMC-based four-seater GT for a South African company. Ultimately the brothers turned their hands to the Probe series of cars which received such extensive media attention in the early Seventies although only a handful were ever made. One of these cars featured in the successful film *Clockwork Orange*.

Once the Adams brothers had left Marcos, all development work was undertaken by the in-house engineering team headed by Stan Gray. The most significant of the changes that occurred in the latter half of the Seventies was the fitting of engines other than the Volvo 1800. Ford straight-four 1600, 2.0-litre V4, 2.5 and 3.0-litre V6 units, plus Triumph 2.5-litre, and Volvo straight-six 3.0-litre units found their ways at various times into the engine bay.

However, before Dennis and Peter left the company, a new car appeared in whose design they had not been involved. This was the Mini Marcos? "I thought it was as ugly as hell and would never sell", says Dennis, "But that just shows how wrong you can be because they went like hot cakes — we could hardly make enough". The precise origins of the Mini Marcos are a little unclear. Jem Marsh states that the concept was his but certainly at the time of the car's gestation, several similar vehicles were in the throes of production. These included one involving two Marcos employees who had joined the company at the time of the closure of one of Greville Cavendish's other less successful entrepreneurial ventures, Falcon Cars. Wherever the design or inspiration actually came from, the diminutive Mini-powered car, offered in kit form at a modest price, found a ready market. The project was sold in 1976 to Howard Dermott, ultimately to reappear as the respected and extensively re-worked Midas.

Although by 1969 the Adams brothers no longer worked directly for Marcos, the company still made use of their design and prototype buildings skills. Marcos Racing, an offshoot of the main company founded by enthusiastic competitor Jem Marsh, commissioned the pair to design a mid-engined GT racing car, possibly for Le Mans but certainly for international sportscar events. Jem outlined exactly what was required and it was agreed that the team at the Old Forge would produce such a car for £3800. Despite directives as broad as: "The engine bay should be capable of housing anything from a Renault 16 engine to a V8 or even a BRM V16", a car was indeed produced in double-quick time. It was duly delivered to Stan Gray at the main works for final sorting and installation of the Brabham V8 engine for which Jem had paid a hefty £3000 in hard cash! Amusingly, Dennis Adams recalls that the design of the racer, known as Mantis, was somewhat influenced by the fact that it was built in the loft of the Old Forge and subsequently dismantled and passed out through a hole in the floor — the only available entrance or exit. Fortunately this fitted in very nicely with racing 'state of the art' sub-assembly design at the time.

For whatever reason, the new car was put to the test too early at a race at Spa and with its development incomplete, its debut was, hardly surprisingly less than impressive. This coupled with a financial squeeze at Marcos Racing and a severe hounding by an infamous purchase tax inspector (the same one who crippled the Adam's Probe cars several years later) led to the Mantis winging its way abroad.

Although distracted by racing interests, the basic state of Marcos was still healthy in mid-1969. However, a handicap to expanded production was that the chassis were still wooden and construction was a time-consuming business which simply couldn't be speeded up. The course of action seemed clear — the wooden chassis needed to be replaced by one made of steel. Adams Design was once again commissioned to produce a steel chassis which could be made simply, and quickly — but more importantly one that could be put into production without any hiccups. Output was then running at eight to ten cars per week and the loss of even a day's manufacture was serious. The brothers produced the required chassis and at one blow knocked 15 hours from the production time of each car.

By 1970 Greville Cavendish was reducing his involvement with Marcos and soon after he was to emigrate to sunnier climes. However, this interest was still sufficiently strong for himself and Jem Marsh to draw up ideas for a four-seater road car which would borrow the name of the ill-fated Mantis racer. Sketches were forthcoming from the Old Forge and the project was given the go-ahead in early 1970. The original Adams design was considerably modified when it was 'productionised' and the car's attractive lines distorted somewhat. However, the prototype was completed in a remarkable nine months and exhibited at that year's Motor Show. "Colin Chapman's face was a picture when he saw it," said Jem Marsh, "because he'd started work on the new Elite but knew it was years away from fruition and here were we with a car exactly along those lines."

Into production

The Triumph straight-six powered Mantis tentatively entered production in early 1971 but bad times were on the way for Marcos. Greville Cavendish had by then handed over completely to Jem Marsh who, through a blend of over-enthusiasm and poor financial advice, committed the firm to move to a vast new purpose-built factory on West Wilts Trading Estate. The 'move' was planned to take only a weekend to interfere minimally with production, but in the event it was nearer two weeks before production was restarted. Additionally a consignment of 27 cars to the USA had been impounded by the American customs, who refused to believe that any company capable of shipping 27 cars at one time made fewer than 500 vehicles per year and was therefore exempt from emission controls. The cars did not meet emission regulations and they sat at the dock in New York gathering dust.

The loss of two weeks production — some 90/100 cars plus the impounding of the USA consignment dealt a mortal blow to the company at a time it could least cope with it, the financial implications of the new factory being positively punitive. Jem Marsh succeeded in attracting considerable financial support to the ailing company, handing over control in the process, but the situation was beyond recovery. In 1972, following various fruitless attempts to recover his investment, Mr Medlock of Hebron and Medlock, whose engineering company had provided the financial injection, sent in the receivers and the company closed having produced around 500 cars including the Mini Marcos. "Contrary to popular opinion" reflects Jem Marsh, "the Mantis wasn't the downfall of Marcos but a combination of unfortunate circumstances. In 11 months we made 33 Mantis and sold every one while sales of the original car were still going well apart from a badly timed sales crisis. Without that crisis we would have definitely recovered."

The receivers eventually, sold Marcos to a firm of west country asset strippers who disposed of the factory and effects. Jem Marsh meanwhile continued to produce the Mini Marcos and operate a Marcos spares business. During the Seventies he found time to open a garage with a Datsun, Lancia and Suzuki dealership and develop two motorcycle shops. In 1976 he was able to buy back the Marcos name and moulds, which had languished in various hands since 1972. With a considerably modified outlook on the car manufacturing business and very aware of the dangers of over-expansion, Marsh began production again in 1981. The revitalised company now operates on a modest basis making two or three kits per week. With the self-confessed aim of 'doing a Morgan' with what he belives is a timeless design, the 'new' Marcos is being subtly changed and improved with the help of Dennis Adams, who now operates a freelance design consultancy in Bradford-on-Avon. Not least among the changes are a revised nose, a Rover V8 engine installation and even a convertible version for the hungry US market. So the Marcos has survived through thick and thin for almost 25 years and in a world now starved of man-produced sports cars it looks set to live on long still. Jem Marsh and Marcos can be found at 153 West Wilts Trading Estate, Westbury, Wilts. BA13 4JN, telephone 0373 864097.

Right, Jem Marsh today, outside Marcos' Westbury HQ. Below, one of Dennis Adams' early styling sketches for the road-going Mantis which looks rather different in reality. Below right, another Adams sketch for a racing Mantis derivative, much like the later Probes

FRESH AIR FORCE

MARCOS MANTULA

OVER THE years, like most specialist manufacturers, Marcos has suffered the slings and arrows of outraged creditors but, unlike many of them, the company's founder is still in charge. Jem Marsh is happy these days to produce his cars to special order, from the factory in Westbury, Wilts, and the output is now roughly 50 cars per year, most of them convertibles like the one tested here. The latest incarnation of this machine is called the Mantula.

The basic body shape of the Marcos has altered little since it appeared 25 years ago. It no longer looks 'futuristic', but it has stood the test of time. Perhaps the rear wing detracts from its lines, but it is an optional extra. The body is wider and longer than was the original, but you have to look closely to spot the difference.

The chassis hasn't altered much either, since the switch from ash frame to steel in 1969. Neither has the suspension system: double wishbones are used at the front (still Triumph-based) and a live rear axle sprung by concentric coil spring/damper units, and located by four radius rods and a Panhard rod. Some would consider this 'crude', but there is nothing wrong with traditional designs when they are well resolved.

The greatest changes to the Marcos over the years have been under that long, front-hinged bonnet, whose latest occupant is a 3.5-litre Rover Vitesse engine, standard except for the exhaust system, which raises the factory output to 200bhp at 5,280rpm, while peak torque is 220lb ft at 4,000rpm.

Since the Marcos is relatively light (approximately 17.5cwt), the performance brought to it by this V8 is seriously impressive, with a top speed of around 140mph and 0-60mph acceleration in less than 6sec.

The way it performs is splendid, with the wide torque spread permitting rapid driving on twisty roads with fewer gearchanges than in smaller-engined sports cars.

Unlike the TVR, the Marcos leaves most of the roar of its engine hanging in the air, and though there is some gear-

box whine and clonking from the suspension, it is actually rather a refined car in many ways, without too much wind rustle with the hood raised and minimal buffeting with it lowered. Once the complexities of the hood system (a lined Happich system in our test car) are properly mastered, it can be put in place or removed in a reasonably short space of time.

There is much to be said in favour of a properly sorted live rear axle, for it eliminates camber and toe-in alterations induced by throttle opening or road surface. The Marcos's rear end is exceptionally well-located, the chassis admirably rigid and the steering transmits plenty of true 'feel' of what the front wheels are doing.

Up to the point at which power breaks the traction of the rear wheels, the Marcos understeers gently, and the transition into oversteer is progressive, accompanied by minimal body roll. The cornering angle adopted from thereon is largely dependent on throttle opening and who might be watching.

That's all the good news. On the debit side must be listed a fairly stiff ride (occasionally transmitting pronounced jolts

through the shell), steering that is heavy in slow and medium-speed bends, a tendency to move off line a little (not to an alarming extent) on bumpy roads, and poor ground clearance. It's a street racer in the classic tradition, though, and

> **"It's a street racer in the classic tradition, and enthusiasts will be happy to put up with its limitations"**

enthusiasts will be happy to put up with its limitations.

Perhaps the most difficult aspect of the car is that its forward visibility, especially through left-hand bends, is hampered by the three large domes formed by the front wings and bonnet hump.

Also in street-racer tradition is the firmness of required brake pedal pressure. The front brakes are discs but, unusually these days, the rears are drums. However, we found the system powerful, progessive and fade-free; again, greater emphasis should be placed upon what a system does rather than whether it is or is not modern. Operation of the handbrake, mounted beside the high transmission tunnel, is awkward.

Actually, it isn't so much that the tunnel is high, more that the seat is low. The cushion is simply placed on the floorpan, the backrest attached directly to the rear bulkhead. Unlike the majority of modern cars, the Mantula is designed with taller drivers in mind, and there is plenty of legroom and headroom. Shorter drivers can achieve a satisfactory driving position by winding the pedals forward or back with a small wheel mounted on the facia.

The driver is securely located in the car, and the backrest is well shaped, but the cushion is unforgiving on long journeys. The narrow footwell disallows a resting point for the left foot other than behind the clutch pedal, and the relationship between brake and throttle renders heel-and-toe changes awkward.

The main instruments are easier for tall drivers than shorter ones to read, but all will find the illumination of the smaller dials, especially the fuel gauge, insufficient at night.

Many of the smaller, specialist manufacturers, having put together a powerful engine in a competent chassis clothed in attractive bodywork, and having given some thought to aerodynamics, have a problem when it comes to sorting out heating and ventilation systems.

We failed to come to terms with the Mantula's system, in which vents are placed out of sight beneath the facia; it is claimed that these provide adequate footwell heating, and can also provide cooling air instead (though there is no face-level ventilation).

'Value for money' is difficult to assess in this area of the market, but you can, with a relatively low level of mechanical expertise, build a Mantula for well under £10,000. This involves purchasing the "Stage 1" kit for £2,995 (the coupé model is substantially cheaper), and then adding a secondhand Rover engine (or one of several Ford engines), and putting it together yourself. The kits come in two other, more complete forms. Marcos do occasionally sell fully made-up cars, and the price for that is £16,694.